W9-BCN-533

Assessing the Lee Teng-hui Legacy in Taiwan's Politics

TAIWAN IN THE MODERN WORLD
Series Editor
Murray A. Rubinstein

TAIWAN IN THE MODERN WORLD

Assessing the Lee Teng-hui Legacy in Taiwan's Politics

Democratic Consolidation and External Relations

Linda Chao
Shu-Heng Chen
Tun-jen Cheng
John Fuh-sheng Hsieh
Yung-ming Hsu
Julian J. Kuo
Tai-chun Kuo

Cheng-yi Lin
Wen-cheng Lin
Ya-li Lu
Peter R. Moody, Jr.
Ramon H. Myers
Shelley Rigger
Suisheng Zhao

Bruce J. Dickson and Chien-min Chao, Editors

AN EAST GATE BOOK

M.E.Sharpe
Armonk, New York
London, England

An East Gate Book

Library of Congress Cataloging-in-Publication Data

Assessing the Lee Teng-hui legacy in Taiwan's politics: democratic consolidation and
external relations / edited by Bruce J. Dickson and Chien-min Chao.
    p. cm. — (Taiwan in the modern world)
"An East gate book."
Includes bibliographical references and index.
ISBN 0-7656-1063-9 (alk. paper) ; ISBN 0-7656-1064-7 (pbk. : alk. paper)
    1. Lee, Teng-hui. 2. Taiwan—Politics and government—1988-2000. I. Dickson, Bruce,
1958– II. Zhao, Jianmin, 1954– III. Series.

DS799.833.L44 A77 2002
951.24'905'092—dc21

           2002021711

Printed in the United States of America

Contents

List of Tables and Figures

Tables

Figures

Acknowledgments

Taiwan's democratization is arguably one of the most important events in the post-Cold War global order, marking a peaceful and orderly trans-formation of a "quasi-Leninist regime" toward democracy. The transition has not only heralded a new era in the political life for the people of Taiwan, it has also fundamentally changed the social norms as well as the culture and identity of the island country. Consequently, political participation has heated up in a society dichotomized and polarized by newly mobilized ethnic tensions, old institutions were amended or dis-carded, and the awakening of a Taiwanese consciousness driving to-wards nativism have all enlivened the political scene in unprecedented ways. Although various aspects of these issues have been addressed by scholars in Taiwan, the United States, and elsewhere, a comprehensive review of the role played by the most important architect of this "great transition," the former president of the Republic of China Lee Teng-hui, is essential. However, as Lee's influence upon Taiwan's politics contin-ued even after his tenure as president ended in May 2000, the focus of this book is on the twelve years that he served as president of the Repub-lic of China.

The idea to offer a preliminary assessment of Lee's legacy in Taiwan's democratic consolidation and its external relations was originally con-ceived in a conversation that we had in Bruce Dickson's home outside Washington, D.C. in the summer of 1998, when we served as directors of the Sun Yat-sen Graduate Institute for Social Sciences and Humanities at National Chengchi University and the Sigur Center for Asian Studies at the George Washington University, respectively. The result of this con-versation was the decision to have the Sun Yat-sen Institute and the Sigur Center co-host a conference entitled "President's Lee Teng-hui's Legacy: Formation and Implications," which was held on May 12-13, 2000 at the Grand Hotel, Taipei. We would first like to express our appreciations to our colleagues for their support and encouragement throughout the event. Thanks go especially to the two very capable assistants at the Sun Yat-sen Institute — Jeng Huei-jen and Hsu Shih-chen. At the Sigur Center, Deborah Toy and Ikuko Turner handled the travel arrangements and financial arrangements with efficiency and good humor.

A group of outstanding scholars from Taiwan and the United States came to participate in the lively debates of the May 2000 conference. We had the honor not only to have their works included in this book but also the opportunity to come to know them better. We extend special thanks to those who offered invaluable comments during the conference, many of which were incorporated into the papers as they were revised for publication in this book. Although their names are too numerous to be listed here, we are sincerely grateful for their contributions. Gratitude also goes to the many NCCU students for their dedication to the conference and the Sun Yat-sen Institute in general. Without their tireless work and flawless coordination, the conference would not have been possible.

All the chapters in this volume were finalized in fall 2001. Subsequent events (particularly the December 2001 Legislative Yuan elections) have superceded some of the comments sprinkled throughout the book. Rather than trying to chase a moving target, we decided to maintain the focus of the chapters on the legacy of Lee Teng-hui, rather than the continually evolving nature of Taiwanese politics.

Several of the chapters in this volume were previously published as journal articles, and we gratefully acknowledge permission to include them here. The chapters by John Fuh-sheng Hsieh and Shelley Rigger were both published in the December 2001 issue of *China Quarterly*, and an earlier version of Suisheng Zhao's chapter appeared in *Problems of Post-Communism* (March-April 2001).

For their generous financial support which made the conference possible, we wish to thank the National Science Foundation under the ROC government; the ROC Association for Humanities Studies; the Foundation for Humanities; the Cross-Strait Interflow Prospect Foundation; the Strait Exchange Foundation; the Chiang Ching-kuo Foundation for International Scholarly Exchange; and the Institute for National Policy Research. Professor Wu Yien-Tsun at the Sun Yat-sen Institute for Social Sciences and Humanities and Dr. Phillip M. Chen Ming at the Cross-Strait Interflow Prospect Foundation have been most generous in helping with the donation. Dr. Richard L. Edmonds, at that time editor of the *China Quarterly*, provided his considerable support and assistance throughout the conference, and kindly agreed to publish two of the papers, as noted above. Finally, we would like to thank Patty Loo and Angela Piliouras at M.E. Sharpe, who shepherded the book through the review, editing, and publication phases with laudable patience; two anonymous reviewers; and EEI Communications of Alexandria, Virginia, which prepared the index. Like most scholarly endeavors, this has been a collective project from start to finish, and we gratefully acknowledge the many people, named and unnamed, without whom this book would not have been possible.

Chien-min Chao
Taipei, Taiwan

Bruce Dickson
Washington, D.C.

Part I

Introduction

——— 1 ———

Introduction

Assessing the Lee Teng-hui Legacy

Chien-min Chao and Bruce J. Dickson

The Lee Teng-hui Legacy

Assessing the legacy of President Lee Teng-hui is not an easy task. During the twelve years of his presidency (1988–2000), he presented different personas at different times and to different people. At the beginning of his administration, he seemed a relatively weak leader, perhaps only a transitional figure, because he lacked strong support among the other leaders in his party and government; by the time he left office, he was criticized for an authoritarian leadership style. He shattered the myth that democracy is not for Chinese consumption and went on to establish the first democratic regime in Chinese history, but he also damaged the quality of Taiwan's democracy by cooperating with criminal elements and corrupt local leaders in election campaigns. He skillfully explored and maximized the hidden energies that Taiwanese society had accumulated during the course of economic and political development, but he also exploited ethnic divisions for his political purposes, sending ethnic tensions to new and more visible heights, the repercussions of which still ripple through the political system. He transformed the Kuomintang (KMT) from a mainlander-dominated party to one that readily adopted policies and programs popular with the Taiwanese society, but he also weakened his party through personal conflicts, factional struggles, and controversial policy initiatives. After he left office, he was expelled from the KMT. He adopted a more flexible foreign policy and opened negotiations and regular contacts with mainland China, but he also exposed Taiwan to an unprecedented level of danger. He brought Taiwan to the center of attention in the global arena by staging the first direct presidential election and visiting the United States, the first such visit by an incumbent president of his country, but these same actions also brought unwanted attention. On the eve of the first presidential election in March 1996, Beijing staged missile tests and war games off the coast of Taiwan, putting it on the brink of an international conflict. In a later surprise move, he put forth his theory of "state to state relations" in 1999 as a formula to regulate relations between the two sides across the Taiwan Strait, putting the island and its people again at grave risk. For his loyal supporters, he is "Mr. Democracy" and the "father of Taiwan,"[1] but for his critics, he not only betrayed and possibly decimated the KMT party that he had led for twelve years but also split the country and divided the society in the process. It is these distinctly contrasting features that characterize Lee's legacy.

For his admirers in Taiwan, he is a true native son, a person who really understands their minds and speaks to their hearts; a grand reformer who elevated Taiwan to a level of development never matched by any dynasty in the history of China and with a speed that brought acclaim from observers around the world; and a strong nationalist who made "Taiwan first" a stock phrase for politicians of all ideological stripes. Indeed, during those years, he captivated the attention of the people of the country so intensely that he became the focal point of Taiwan, leading the country and the society to whatever goals he envisioned.

A Native Son

Except for only a very brief time before Taiwan was ceded to Japan after the first Sino-Japanese War in 1894, native Taiwanese never had the opportunity to govern their island. As the first Taiwanese president, Lee ushered in a new era in which all resources, political and otherwise, would be redistributed. No one else understood the meaning of that better than Lee himself. He adroitly used the campaign known as "Taiwanization" to consolidate his power by exploiting the ethnic differences and by portraying his opponents as not only conservative but also anti-Taiwanese. In the end, both the state and the society were reshaped.

Lee's predecessor, Chiang Ching-kuo, was also a populist, but one of a very different type. Chiang disliked businessmen and preferred making friends with ordinary people, especially the underprivileged. He enjoyed eating simple meals at roadside stands. He led the kind of thrifty and simple life that was in sharp contrast with that of his father, Chiang Kai-shek, and indeed most national leaders.[2] But Lee exemplified another dimension of the word populism. He spoke the same language as the ordinary people, the southern Fukienese dialect. He understood them and shared their grief, embracing the people and their history. He was caught in the margins of the notorious incident of February 28, 1947, as were so many other native Taiwanese.[3] Having just returned from Japan and newly enrolled at National Taiwan University, he was warned of impending arrests and took refuge in a friend's home until the crackdown subsided. Decades later, after he rose to top positions in the party, he was determined to take on political taboos, particularly concerning the KMT's past conduct. To heal the wounds left from the February 28 incident, he authorized a research report on the events and their aftermath, plus built a memorial to the victims and offered financial payments to their families. These steps to rectify past wrongs, honor those afflicted by the tragedy, and compensate families of the victims won him praise as a local hero, a reputation previously enjoyed only by the opposition Democratic Progressive Party (DPP).

Under Lee's leadership, Taiwan rewrote its history to orient and center around the island itself, shifting away from its past history as a part of China. To him, the political beliefs, values, and orientations that influenced and shaped Taiwan were all too "exotic" and "Chinese," a theme emphasized in Ya-li Lu's chapter. Taiwan needed to bring back a distinctively Taiwanese culture and value system. The beauty of Taiwan's geography, cultural traits, and local history were stressed and the attention given to the history and geography of mainland China were deemphasized. Local language, literature, poetry, theater arts, and the like were all promoted as part of the "Taiwan first" drama. Taiwanese dialect was rediscovered and elevated to a status almost equivalent to that of a national language. Lee's broken Mandarin was not to be laughed at but considered a distinctive trait to be cherished. In sum, Lee strove to make Taiwan a place worthy of examination and admiration on its own merits rather than a minuscule part of a once and future great power by the name of China. This may not have been the same sort of Taiwan independence that many opposition DPP politicians had in mind, but both Lee and the DPP shared the same goal of rediscovering and promoting the importance and beauty of Taiwan at the expense of the traditions and culture associated with China.

At the core of his Taiwanization drive was the redistribution of political resources. After the KMT retreated to Taiwan following its defeat in the Chinese civil war, most influential positions at all levels of the party and government bureaucracies were held by émigrés from the mainland and their offspring. In the early 1970s, Chiang Ching-kuo began the Taiwanization of the party and government in order to draw a new generation of talent into the KMT and to improve the KMT's reputation in society. He had to proceed slowly in this effort so as not to elicit opposition from powerful leaders and incumbent officials. The Taiwanization process accelerated under Lee. By the end of his presidency in 2000, native Taiwanese held the most important positions, including the presidency, vice-presidency, and the premiership, breaking a tradition of ethnic balancing set by his predecessor. He also set about adding Taiwanese officers to the top ranks of the military. The official name of the country, the Republic of China, was not abandoned, but the more fitting "ROC on Taiwan" became a popular substitute.[4] Slogans like "Taiwan first," "stand on Taiwan with eyes on the Chinese mainland and also with a global perspective," and "Asia-Pacific Regional Operation Center" gave people reason to be proud of Taiwan's accomplishments and optimistic about its future possibilities and place in the world. A new sense of identity and destiny was in the making.

A Grand Reformer

Under the leadership first of Chiang Ching-kuo and then Lee Teng-hui, Taiwan accomplished a rare feat matched by few other countries: the peaceful transformation of a Leninist party-state system into a democracy.[5] The transformation of this regime was further complicated by the fact that the national identity and indeed the legitimacy of the Nationalist regime were built on the particular political, ideological, and cultural structure first created by Sun Yat-sen. Any attempt to reform Taiwan's quasi-Leninist system would unavoidably threaten to delegitimate it, resulting in its demise rather than its transformation. When Lee became president following Chiang's death in 1988, the government in Taipei still claimed to represent the whole of China. The political structure and institutions were framed before the Nationalist government's retreat to Taiwan in 1949. But by the time he left the presidency, a substantially revised constitution along with a whole new set of political structures and institutions had been installed.

The Constitution of the Republic of China was originally enacted in

1946, three years before the Nationalist government's defeat by the communists. In order to maintain legitimacy and continue the mandate endowed on him as president of China, Generalissimo Chiang Kai-shek froze the constitution on the eve of his defeat on the mainland. In 1948, the Nationalist government appended to this constitution the "Temporary Provisions Effective during the Period of Communist Rebellion," and these provisions became the basis for the martial law that existed on Taiwan for nearly forty years. Consequently, members of the parliament, including the Legislative Yuan, the National Assembly, and the Control Yuan, were not subject to reelection until new nationwide elections (including all of the mainland) could be held, a condition almost impossible to fulfill considering the odds of recovering the mainland. Although sporadic elections were held to replenish the old institutions and to increase marginally the share of Taiwanese representation in them, the newly elected members were not significant enough to redefine the nature of the three chambers. Most members of these three bodies were essentially "representatives" without constituencies. Lee's first step after his inauguration was to rejuvenate the ten-thousand-year-old parliament (*wannian guohui*). In doing so, he risked betraying the revolutionary cause that his predecessors had inherited from Dr. Sun Yat-sen and alienating the regime's most loyal supporters. In the early 1990s, more than forty years after most incumbents had been elected, new elections were held for the entire memberships of the National Assembly and Legislative Yuan. This dramatic step was hailed as a show of Lee's determination to reform fundamentally Taiwan's political institutions and make their leaders accountable to the people of Taiwan.

With new popularly elected parliamentary bodies in place, Lee proceeded to amend the old constitution, stripping the power of selecting the ROC president away from the National Assembly and giving it directly to the people. With the once powerful National Assembly sidelined, the five-branch government, the gist of the old constitutional order based on Sun Yat-sen's official ideology, *sanmin zhuyi* (the "Three Principles of the People") was shattered. As Lee set about changing the constitution to allow direct popular elections for president, the much debated constitutional issue—whether Taiwan's political structure is a parliamentary system or a presidential system—had finally been resolved in favor of the latter.[6]

After becoming the first popularly elected president in March 1996, Lee was poised to streamline the provincial government. This was another political taboo because this level of government was important to the ROC's claim to be the legitimate government of all of China, not just of Taiwan and the offshore islands of Quemoy (Jinmen), Matsu, and Penghu. However, Lee and other advocates of reform argued that the provincial government was redundant and wasteful, in that it and the national government had jurisdiction over essentially the same territory (the offshore islands are technically part of Fujian Province). At the same time, the elimination of the provincial government had been an important part of the opposition DPP's strategy of asserting Taiwan's independence.

The freezing of the provincial government and the elimination of most of its functions also created a schism within the KMT. One of Lee's motives in this reform was to clip the wings of the incumbent governor, James Soong. Soong had been a young protégé of Chiang Ching-kuo and was instrumental in Lee's original appointment as president over the objections of older mainlanders in the KMT. Over the years, Soong proved himself to be a capable administrator and loyal supporter of Lee. Soong was elected governor of Taiwan in 1994 and developed a strong base of popular support. According to many reports, Lee became jealous of Soong's popularity and growing stature as a political leader, worried that if Soong became the next president he would not be beholden to Lee and might not uphold his policies. This may have been an important calculation in Lee's decision to downsize the provincial government and turn the post of governor from an elected position to an appointed one with little authority. This step not only reduced redundancy and unnecessary expenditures, it also eliminated the post of the man Lee saw as a potential rival. Despite their previous rapport, Lee did not share his plans to reform the provincial government with Soong in advance. Relations between the two men were irreparably damaged. This personal conflict between the two former political allies eventually cost the KMT the presidency in 2000 when Soong chose to run as an independent candidate after being denied the KMT's nomination, as will be explained below.

The reforms that Lee implemented were not limited to structures alone. He intended to create a new culture, too. Liberalization was also a big part of Lee's reform strategy. As part of the Taiwanization process, his reforms unshackled the newspapers and cable television networks from government control and scrutiny. Taiwan's media, in turn, played key supporting roles in the reform process. Phrases like democratization, "down with the 'old crooks,'" and "KMT conservatives resisting Taiwanization" became common in the media and captivated the general public. Lee was able to rely on that popular support to consolidate his power base and uproot the old structures and customs that impeded his reformist goals.

When Lee urged the people of the ROC to "challenge the impossible," his critics took that as evidence of his suppressed desire for Taiwan's independence. In retrospect, the boastful statement might have been meant as a reflection of his bold and ambitious grasp for change. He had broken all political taboos and was uninhibited by past conventions in his drive toward reforming the old system. In that regard, he displayed the traits of a true revolutionary.

A Strong Nationalist

As a nationalist who relished the rigor and vitality that Taiwan embodied, Lee was not content with the pariah status that Taiwan had been awarded by the international community. It was a very important part of his grand strategy that Taiwan break out of its diplomatic isolation and participate more actively in the international community. Lee was well aware that the people of Taiwan desperately needed a diplomatic breakthrough to nurse the wounds inflicted by repeated setbacks in the diplomatic field and to rectify the humiliation felt by this island nation. As the chapter by Chien-min Chao shows, over many years Taiwan steadily lost diplomatic partners and was recognized by none of the major countries in the world, despite its economic and political progress. Lee set about maintaining Taiwan's official diplomatic ties, but also recognized the reality Taiwan faced by advancing a "pragmatic diplomacy," which promoted unofficial exchanges with a wide range of countries. Soon after assuming presidency, he took two "ice-breaking trips" to Southeast Asia that reinforced the impression that Taiwan would indeed be different under his stewardship.[7] The grand finale came in June 1995 when, against all odds, Lee was allowed a visit to his alma mater, Cornell University, the first incumbent ROC president ever to set foot on American soil. As chapters by Kuo, Zhao, and Dickson will show, this trip was a defining moment of Lee's presidency. It all but sealed his status among his followers as one of the greatest leaders in the country's history, but also reinforced his detractors' belief that he could be reckless and needlessly provocative.

On top of restructuring Taiwan's political order and institutions and redefining its international relations, it was also during Lee's tenure that Taiwan emerged as one of the major centers in manufacturing personal computers and products related to the information industry. For the first time Taiwan was able to compete with and even surpass the traditional industrialized countries in the West in some of the most advanced technological fields. This goal has been intensely pursued by China since the Opium War in 1840, and under Lee it was first accomplished by Taiwan, giving the Taiwanese people and their leaders cause for great satisfaction.

Lee's Legacy to Cross-Strait Relations

The most controversial issue during Lee's tenure was undoubtedly his handling of relations with China. After a commendable start, he managed to irritate China to the extent that Beijing wanted nothing to do with him and unleashed a prolonged propaganda campaign to vilify him.[8]

Given the turmoil that marked Lee's last few years as president, it is easy to forget that he did a rather good job of institutionalizing the nearly ungovernable cross-strait relationship during his first term. He constructed bridges to allow the two sides to communicate directly and effectively with each other for the first time since the Kuomintang–Chinese Communist Party negotiations broke down in 1948.[9] Knowing the potential danger of an abrupt change, Lee initially adopted a cautious incremental approach. He first moved to end the belligerence that previously existed between the two sides. He announced the end of the period of suppressing the communist rebellion, revoked the constitution's "Temporary Provisions," and acknowledged that the ROC's reach covered only the territories currently under its control, not the entire mainland. He then constructed the National Unification Guidelines and the National Unification Council to reassure people living on both sides of the Taiwan Strait that he and his government remained committed to eventual reunification despite the sudden shift of policy. As a third step, he created the Mainland Affairs Council and Strait Exchange Foundation (SEF) as instruments to implement his new policy of engagement. And finally, he made history when the heads of the two semi-official organizations for handling cross-strait relations, the SEF and its People's Republic of China counterpart, the Association for Relations Across the Taiwan Strait (ARATS), held a summit meeting in Singapore in 1993.

In the early years of his presidency, cross-strait relations looked promising. Under the framework of "one China with separate interpretations,"[10] political animosity gave way to trade and commerce. But although both China and Taiwan appeared mutually committed to promoting peace and prosperity for the first time in decades, by the end of Lee's presidency that dream seemed to vanish. Any hope for progress in cross-strait relations was destroyed when he declared in 1999 that relations between Taipei and Beijing should be conducted on the basis of state-to-state, or at least "special state-to-state" relations. Whether he was a true proponent of Taiwan independence or simply a canny but unorthodox statesman remained an issue subject to intense debate. What was certain was his unequivocal commitment to the pursuit of an independent Taiwanese identity free from the entanglements of the Beijing regime. Differences in developmental strategies and practices, and, more important, the growing gaps in the political and social systems between China and Taiwan had made his mission of regime building easier.

But things started to change for the worse after his visit to Cornell University in June 1995. As the chapters by Kuo and Zhao describe, Beijing's extremely negative and threatening reaction to his visit culminated in missile tests near the major ports on the northern and southern coasts of Taiwan. Lee's 1999 declaration that cross-strait relations should be conducted on the basis of the "special state-to-state relations" was his final bombshell. Not only did Lee fail to notify Washington and Beijing in advance of his announcement, he consulted with no more than a handful of his top aides.[11] Even the director of the Mainland Affairs Council, Su Chi, Lee's point man on China policy, was not involved in the decision making. Lee's sudden shift of policy seemed to undercut the fundamental understanding that underlay cross-strait relations: the shared commitment to a unified China. Su Chi reinforced this impression when he told reporters that Lee's "special state-to-state" formula would henceforth guide Taiwan's relations with the mainland, not continued adherence to the familiar "one-China" policy. This departure from the past framework led China to cancel a planned visit to Taiwan by Wang Daohan, head of China's semi-official ARATS, and to break off all direct communications between the two sides. Beijing found Lee's latest pronouncement to be unacceptable, suggesting in the clearest terms yet that Lee was not committed to Taiwan's reunification with the mainland but instead to Taiwan's independence. Lee's new formula also failed to receive U.S. support and recognition, which would be necessary if Taiwan were to take a tough stand against China. But as Bruce Dickson's chapter shows, the Clinton administration was tilting slightly away from Taiwan after the storm over Lee's Cornell visit and responded to Lee's pronouncement by restating its commitment to its "one-China" policy. Even many Congressional leaders refused to endorse Lee's "two-state theory." The term "troublemaker" was increasingly used by U.S. media and policy analysts to describe Taiwan's behavior, and Lee's provocations in particular.

The increasingly hostile atmosphere in the Taiwan Strait area inevitably compelled Taiwan to increase its military expenditures. As both sides intensified their efforts for military preparations, a new arms race seemed to be in the making (see the chapter by Wen-cheng Lin and Cheng-yi Lin for details on Taiwan's military modernization). In Lee's final months in office, a new controversy erupted: whether the United States should sell Taiwan Arleigh Burke-class destroyers equipped with the AEGIS air-defense radar system. The AEGIS system is among the most sophisticated in the U.S. arsenal, and would have represented a substantial increase in the technological quality of U.S. arms sales to Taiwan. For this reason, China was vehemently opposed to the sale, but key Congressional leaders were in favor of it. The decision on the sale came after Chen was elected president but before he was inaugurated. He did not make a strong push for the sale, allowing the Clinton administration to postpone a final decision until after a full assessment of Taiwan's defense needs, effectively leaving the decision to the next president. George W. Bush also chose to defer a definitive decision on this sensitive issue in April 2001, but approved the largest package of U.S. arms sales to Taiwan since 1992.

What level of arms the United States would sell to Taiwan, and especially whether to provide the AEGIS technology, was largely a symbolic debate. More important, it demonstrated how discussions on cross-strait issues had shifted toward contentious military issues at the expense of mutually beneficial commercial and economic exchanges, the focus long favored by moderates in Washington, Beijing, and Taipei.[12] The outcome is a less secure environment for Taiwan. As Taiwan builds up its defensive capabilities, China builds up its offensive weapons even faster. Even though Taiwan currently maintains the military advantage, many analysts expect the edge to shift in Beijing's favor in the near future.[13]

The flourishing trade and investment that also marked the Lee years

came despite Lee's best efforts. The rising political and military antagonism with China and the surging flow of money to the mainland put the
government in a difficult position. Lee and other leaders were worried
that this increasing dependency of Taiwan's economy on the mainland
was creating both economic and political risks. He wanted to redirect a
sizable portion of the trade and investment projects of Taiwan's companies to Southeast Asia and Latin America as part of his "pragmatic diplomacy" initiative. After the 1996 missile crisis, Lee designed the "go
slow, be patient" policy to slow down the flight of Taiwanese capital to
the mainland. However, his policy failed to achieve its intended goals as
Taiwanese businessmen invested tens of billions of dollars into the China
market at the other side, making Taiwan one of the leading sources of
foreign investment in China. In a dramatic move, the Chen Shui-bian
administration reversed Lee's conservative "go slow" policy in August
2001 and replaced it with a new "active openness and effective management" policy, lifting the US$50 million cap on individual investment on
the mainland.

Chen's efforts to resume a dialog with China and to expand economic
and trade ties had little immediate impact. China did not reject his initiatives, but it felt that those initiatives did not go far enough. After
seeing Lee Teng-hui unilaterally attempt to modify some of the basic
understandings that guided cross-strait relations, Beijing's leaders insisted that Chen commit to the "one-China" principle as a precondition
for resuming exchanges. Whereas China had seemed willing to let growing economic ties lead to political integration during the early phase of
Lee's presidency, by the end of Lee's administration China had grown
frustrated by what it perceived as his efforts to stall progress toward unification and even to promote an ever more explicit independent status for
Taiwan. By the time Chen Shui-bian assumed the presidency, Beijing reversed the order of importance of cross-strait ties: It insisted that a political commitment—namely, the acceptance of the "one-China"
principle—come before any progress in other aspects of the relationship.

A Mixed Legacy

Lee never ceased to amaze the people of Taiwan. When he was in control, politics in Taiwan always promised to be fun and eventful. In a
way, he was a sort of political magician churning out new tricks all the
time. He was the first native Taiwanese national leader; the first presi-

dent to make overseas visits, including to the United States; the one to bring full democracy to Taiwan by restructuring the old constitutional order and ordering popular elections for the three chambers of the parliament, the mayors of the two metropolises, Taipei and Kaohsiung, the gubernatorial post (before downsizing the provincial government), and, ultimately, the presidency itself.

Lee's accomplishments easily won him admiration from within Taiwan as well as around the world. He was amazingly capable of galvanizing people to follow his cause. He successfully transformed the rigid Leninist party-state structure and brought the KMT party much closer to the people, in part by stealing popular policy programs from the DPP, as noted in Shelley Rigger's chapter. It was Lee and the party he stood for, the KMT, and not the DPP, that realized the goal of bringing democracy to Taiwan. The KMT was finally able to cast away the image of an alien force that came from the mainland and imposed its will over the people of Taiwan.

However, while Lee's strong personality had made him daring enough to break away from past shackles and constraints, it also contributed to some of his political problems. As the chapters by Ya-li Lu and by Ramon Myers, Linda Chao, and Tai-chun Kuo describe, he was criticized for his lack of tact in dealing with his colleagues and rivals and in conducting his often complex political maneuverings, which were often bisected by ethnic differences and the conflicting impulses of modernity and tradition.

Lee had the charisma and ability to deliver to the people of Taiwan the things they could only dream of previously. Unfortunately, in the end, he would be remembered not only for those achievements but also for being a leader who lacked the ability to integrate and collaborate with people who had disparate policy views and political goals. It was under his leadership that the once powerful KMT saw its power and base of support erode after repeated episodes of infighting and purges. As John Fuh-sheng Hsieh's chapter describes, the distribution of votes between the "pan-KMT" and "pan-DPP" (i.e., those parties and the individual candidates and smaller parties that splintered off from them) has remained quite stable over the years. However, as prominent politicians left it to run as independents or form new parties, the KMT had an increasingly difficult time winning elections. The problems intrinsic to the KMT along with the peculiar features of Taiwan's electoral system and the divisive national identity issue have strongly influenced voting behavior and the fluctuations in Taiwan's party system, a point emphasized in the chapters by Hsieh, Rigger, and Tun-jen Cheng and Yung-ming Hsu. As a consequence of Lee Teng-hui's style of leadership, the ethnic cleavage has been so intensified that split identity is a real problem.[14]

It was also under Lee's leadership that all hopes for a healthy and mutually beneficial relationship between the two sides of the Taiwan Strait were dashed, leaving brute force as an increasingly likely means of settling scores. The prospect for a vigilant Formosan nationalism standing up to an assertive Chinese nationalism is no longer inconceivable.[15] Even after Lee left office, it remained unclear whether cross-strait negotiations for better relations could ever be restored. The chapters by Julian Kuo and by Suisheng Zhao agree that Lee left his successor a residue of mistrust on both sides and fears in Beijing of Taiwan's "creeping independence."

Lee was widely applauded for his success in bringing full democracy to Taiwan. But in order to compete with the increasingly popular DPP for votes, Lee was forced to rely on the extensive factional networks that had been nurtured by the KMT for political benefits, especially in mobilizing votes.[16] Consequently, big businessmen and people associated with organized crime syndicates gradually moved into politics and were elected to executive and legislative posts at both the local or national levels. The phrase "old crooks" took on a new meaning. In the past, it referred to members of the National Assembly and Legislative Yuan who had been elected back on the mainland and were not subject to reelection. They enjoyed generous salaries and other benefits but had few responsibilities and were not accountable to the people on Taiwan. They lost their perks when new elections were held for these bodies in 1991 and 1992. Now, however, Taiwan's politics are increasingly influenced by real crooks. This trend of the Lee era gave rise to a new phrase: *heijin zhengzhi*, or black and gold politics, referring to the prevalence of criminals and official corruption among Taiwan's politicians, especially in the KMT. The consolidation of Taiwan's democracy is part of Lee's legacy, but so is the spread of *heijin zhengzhi*.

The democratization that was initiated in the early 1970s, accelerated in the 1980s, and consolidated in the 1990s was essentially a process of indigenization, as more native Taiwanese were recruited to participate in the political process. During the transition of power from the hands of the old-guard mainlanders to the native Taiwanese, it was inevitable that Lee would ruffle some feathers. But because of his tactlessness and uncompromising personality, the resentment felt by experienced officials who were replaced or demoted during Lee's personnel changes created ethnic tensions within the KMT and throughout the political system. These tensions compounded the problems of national identity and political legitimacy. The people of Taiwan rallied faithfully behind Lee when some old-guard KMT leaders tried to block him from being reappointed as president in 1992 and continued to fight his policy and personnel changes in what became known as the battle between mainstream (pro-Lee) and non-mainstream (anti-Lee) forces.[17] However, the public was less forgiving toward Lee when some of the young Turks, especially the faction known as the New KMT Alliance, questioned his haughty style of leadership and demanded more intra-party democracy, only to be kicked out of the party. One immediate result of this split in the KMT was the defeat of the party's candidate in the 1994 mayoral election in Taipei, the first direct election of this post since 1964. The New Party, made up primarily of young mainlanders, many of whom had left the KMT, won many of the votes that would have normally gone to the KMT, giving the election to the DPP candidate, Chen Shui-bian. Chen went on to become a superstar within the DPP and eventually won the presidency in 2000, again in a three-man race.

Although Lee often exploited the Taiwanese-mainlander ethnic conflicts in his political battles, he was unwilling to let other Taiwanese politicians take full advantage of these tensions. In the 1998 mayoral election in Taipei, incumbent Chen Shui-bian drew attention to his opponent Ma Ying-jeou's mainlander background, insinuating that as a mainlander Ma could not fully identify with local issues in Taipei. Although many observers believed Lee did not campaign aggressively on Ma's behalf, he responded to Chen's charges by coining the "New Taiwanese" concept. Lee said it did not matter whether people were Taiwanese or mainlander, and that so long as they were committed to Taiwan's continued progress, they should be seen as part of the new people of Taiwan. This formulation took some of the sting out of Chen's attacks on Ma, and contributed to Ma's eventual victory in the election.

Lee's leadership style caused a more damaging split within the KMT that ultimately led to the KMT's loss of the presidency. Soon after Lee was elected president in 1996, speculation began about whom he would support as his successor. The two main contenders were James Soong and Lien Chan, Lee's vice president. Despite his popularity and experience, Lee would not support Soong's bid to become the KMT's candidate for president in the 2000 election. Instead, Lee supported the uncharismatic and unpopular Lien Chan, who had little to commend his candidacy but was seen as an adherent to Lee's domestic and foreign policy agendas. Lee reportedly hoped to be able to influence Lien from behind the scenes, thereby assuring the continuation of his preferred domestic and foreign policies. Soong then ran as an independent, taking most of the KMT's traditional support with him and narrowly losing the election to Chen Shui-bian. Consequently, the richest political party in the world and the party that he had chaired for twelve years was forced out of power for the first time since Chiang Kai-shek united China in 1927. After the election, Soong formed the People First Party, further diluting the KMT's popular support.

Lee's leadership style left the KMT in disarray. He created divisions in the party that led to the formation of new parties. More important, his high-handed style led to three-way races for Taipei mayor in 1994 and president in 2000, both of which the KMT lost. If it had not been for his divisiveness, these elections would likely have been two-man races, pitting the KMT against the DPP, and most observers believe the KMT would easily have won that kind of election. For instance, Chen Shui-bian lost his reelection bid to the KMT's Ma Ying-jeou in 1998, even though he actually won a slightly larger share of the vote than in his first election. The KMT's losses in these crucial elections and the splintering of Taiwan's party system must be attributed in large part to Lee, and are also a part of his legacy.

Soon after his retirement from office, he found himself temporarily politically isolated, abandoned by his own party, many former aides, and supporters. But his isolation did not last long. He was so dynamic that even after retiring from politics, he reclaimed the spotlight by forming what he claimed to be the most authentic native political party, the Taiwan Solidarity Union (TSU).[18] Lee claimed he wanted the TSU to play a stabilizing role as a broker between the new ruling party, the DPP, and the main opposition parties, the KMT and the People First Party. Sixteen months after he was forced to give up the chairmanship of the KMT that he had held for twelve years in order to shoulder responsibility for the KMT's defeat in the presidential election, the KMT expelled Lee for campaigning for TSU candidates and denouncing his former party. His dismissal marked another milestone in the party's more than one-hundred year history: He became the first president in ROC history ever to be kicked out of his own party.

In sum, Lee was a charismatic and shrewd politician. He understood exactly what the people of Taiwan wanted and was able to deliver it to them. He was innovative and full of energy. He brought to his subjects things so mesmerizing that they thought they were on top. Yet, he was also so resolute, so uncompromising, and so inconsiderate. It was a time of pride and glory when he was in charge. But behind this glory lay treacherous pitfalls that could be hidden from the ordinary people.

Overview

The chapters in this volume examine the various aspects of Lee Teng-hui's legacy in more detail. Following this introduction, Peter R. Moody, Jr., begins with an overview of the process of democratic consolidation in Taiwan. He draws on the debates in the literature on democratization to put Taiwan's progress in comparative perspective. As other authors note, Lee's personal and political conflicts with the other KMT leaders, mostly with mainlander backgrounds, led to frequent complaints that he had a nondemocratic style despite the increasingly democratic nature of the political system as a whole. Moody argues, however, that Lee followed the tradition of strong leaders in Taiwan, a tradition established by his predecessors Chiang Kai-shek and Chiang Ching-kuo. Although Lee is also criticized for the rampant corruption in the electoral process that seemed to intensify during his years as president, Moody notes that corruption has been a common feature of democratization in other countries as well. An important element of democratic consolidation is the creation of a unified national identity. This has been one of the most complicated issues in Taiwan's recent history, both during the authoritarian past and following the democratic breakthrough of the mid-1980s. Moody argues that although the national identity issue can be drawn along ethnic lines, it is perhaps more appropriate to see it primarily as a political and attitudinal issue. More important, he argues that the commitment to democratic procedures, on the part of the voters and especially of the political elites, has partially eclipsed the ethnic or national question, reducing the chances that divisions over national identity alone will destabilize Taiwan's politics. Moody's conceptual analysis provides the appropriate framework for evaluating Lee's contribution to the consolidation of Taiwan's democracy, a task taken up in later chapters.

Lee's Political Leadership

After this overview, the subsequent chapters focus on more specific issues of Lee's legacy. The first is Lee's style of leadership and its impact on Taiwan's political development. Ya-li Lu examines Lee's strategy of divisiveness, which took advantage of the ethnic differences in Taiwan and even within the KMT to advance his political agenda. He courted competition with his opponents in the "non-mainstream" faction within the KMT, most of whom were mainlanders. Relatedly, he cooperated with the DPP on key issues of political and constitutional reform, often to the surprise of his own party. Lu also notes the divided public opinion about Lee, a theme noted earlier in this introduction, and examines the propriety of the claims made by both Lee's proponents and his critics. Finally, Lu looks at an aspect of Lee's leadership style that is often overlooked but that had a big influence on Lee's strategy and policies: his critique of Chinese culture, assertion of Taiwan's distinctiveness, and promotion of Taiwan's model for democratization.

Whereas Lu surveys Lee's legacy with a broad focus, Ramon Myers, Linda Chao, and Tai-chun Kuo concentrate on his last term in office after winning the first-ever popular election for president in 1996. They examine the issues of constitutional reform, cross-strait relations, and political corruption during Lee's final four years as president. They note the striking contrast between his divisive tactics during these years and his consensual style of the 1988–95 period, as well as the example set by Chiang Ching-kuo before him. They reach a conclusion similar to that of Lu: Lee employed undemocratic, authoritarian tactics to revise the political system to his liking, especially by concentrating power in the presidential office even though many of the changes he promoted did not enjoy wide popular support. They argue that his style of leadership also contributed to setbacks in cross-strait relations and the spread of political corruption. This is a strongly worded indictment of Lee's leadership, reflecting the divided opinion on Lee more generally.

Rather than look at the specific economic policies adopted by Lee, Shu-heng Chen takes a careful look at Taiwan's economic performance during his tenure. Using a theory originally developed for international trade, Chen takes the basic insight regarding the primacy of economic laws over the impact of individuals, whether they are political or business leaders. Rather than compare Taiwan's economic performance with other East Asian and newly industrialized countries, as do most analyses, he takes the more narrow approach of testing Taiwan's performance against the expectations of economic theory, and finds that economic trends in Taiwan fit comfortably with standard theories. While some have discussed the impact of democratization on Taiwan's economic growth rates and budget deficits, Chen argues that these changes are typical of advanced economies. This is important to consider, especially insofar as economic woes have been an ongoing political problem for Chen Shui-bian.

Taiwan's Party System and Electoral Behavior

Lee's legacy to Taiwan's politics is perhaps most evident in the changing nature of its party system and voting behavior of its citizens. Several contributors to this volume look at the 2000 presidential election from this vantage point, using historical and comparative perspectives to analyze the results of the election. John Fuh-sheng Hsieh's chapter centers on a counter-intuitive finding: Even though the KMT's absolute share of votes has declined steadily over time, the share of votes going to the "pan-KMT," comprised of KMT candidates, KMT members running as independent candidates, and the New Party, which is made up primarily of former KMT members, has remained steady. He argues that the main factor underlying this stability is ethnic cleavage, in that national identity largely determines party identification. Of secondary but still significant importance is the electoral system, which contributes to party fragmentation for both the KMT and DPP. The main problem facing the KMT, then, lies not in shoring up its popularity but in improving its internal cohesiveness so that it can retain all of its potential votes. Hsieh outlines the strengths and weaknesses of the KMT in order to analyze its electoral results, particularly its loss in the 2000 presidential election.

The flip side of the KMT's defeat was the DPP's remarkable success. Shelley Rigger explains how a variety of factors that had contributed to the DPP's limited successes in past elections had changed in its favor by the time of the 2000 election, leading to Chen's stunning victory. The KMT had enjoyed distinct advantages in the past, based on its tremendous wealth, organizational base, and control over the government bureaucracy and media. In the 2000 election, however, each of these assets were detrimental to the KMT. Its wealth was criticized as contributing to political corruption and the spread of "black and gold politics." The strength of its political machine had been declining in recent elections, and, moreover, was less important in the winner-take-all presidential election than in legislative elections, where the allocation of votes among multiple candidates in the same districts had been a KMT trademark. The deep divisions within the KMT created by Lee's leadership were revealed by James Soong's independent campaign, which drew away most of the KMT's traditional votes and nearly won the election. Chen's ultimate victory was made possible by Lee's insistence that Lien Chan be the KMT's candidate. His refusal to back the more popular Soong led to a three-man race, giving Chen a narrow plurality of the votes. Criticisms of the media's favoritism toward the KMT and the limited independence of the judiciary also weakened support for the KMT during the election. Furthermore, the DPP corrected some of its own internal errors, moderating its stand on the independence issue and concentrating on domestic issues of political reform and social justice. The challenge for Chen and the DPP now is to find some way to improve Taiwan's international context, especially in cross-strait relations, introduce political reforms that will further undermine the KMT's structural advantages, and continue to correct its internal errors to prevent organizational weaknesses and policy differences from threatening its popular support.

It is often noted that the ethnic divide is one of the most salient features of Taiwan's politics. The chapter by Tun-jen Cheng and Yung-ming Hsu shows how this manifests itself in elections for elected executive positions: president, governor (before that position was eliminated), and mayor. According to "Duverger's law," these types of elections should lead to a two-party system, but this has not always been the case in Taiwan. Cheng and Hsu describe how "strategic voting" confounds Duverger's law: Voters may choose to switch their vote from their preferred candidate to the second-best candidate in order to prevent a third candidate from winning. This strategic behavior has been evident in several recent elections, creating opportunities for independents and new parties to compete in elections. Even when they do not win, their presence often helps determine the outcome. Cheng and Hsu argue that strategic voting in Taiwan is based on ethnic politics, a primary legacy of Lee Teng-hui, and not on the structural features of the electoral system, as normally suggested by Duverger's law.

Lee Teng-hui's Impact on Taiwan's External Relations

Lee also left his mark on Taiwan's external relations. Chien-min Chao describes the shift toward "pragmatic diplomacy" under Lee. Rather than competing directly with China for formal diplomatic ties, a fight that Taiwan had been losing since the early 1970s, Taiwan began expanding the range of its informal relations with a host of countries around the world. Foreign investment and trade assumed a more prominent and positive role in Taiwan's foreign policy, but they ultimately served political goals more than economic interests. Chao argues that pragmatic diplomacy was a good strategy with achievable goals, but it was hampered by poor implementation. In particular, it is hard for any leader in Taiwan to conduct a foreign policy without the tacit consent or cooperation of Beijing. In the end, progress in pragmatic diplomacy came at the expense of growing cross-strait relations, leaving an uncertain diplomatic future as part of the Lee legacy.

No part of Taiwan's external relations is more important than its cross-strait relationship with mainland China, and no part of Lee's presidency created more tension or received more attention. Julian J. Kuo claims that Lee lacked a sincere strategy for unification or improved cross-strait relations, and that he was simply trying to buy time. Although Lee repeatedly said he was not an advocate of Taiwan independence, Kuo's assessment of Lee's legacy on cross-strait relations does not give credence to these repeated denials. He contends that Lee's goal was to maintain the undefined "status quo" in the hope that time would reinforce Taiwan's separate status from the mainland. Kuo also faults Lee's economic policy, particularly the effort to discourage trade and investment with China while promoting other markets in Southeast Asia and Latin America. How could the government restrict capital flows at the same time that the economy was experiencing liberalization and globalization? Kuo faults Lee for missing an opportunity to trade expanded economic ties for political concessions from China.

In contrast to Kuo's chapter, Suisheng Zhao looks at the cross-strait relationship from Beijing's perspective. During Lee's presidency, the nature of Beijing's approach to Taiwan underwent a fundamental shift: from competition for diplomatic representation and membership in international organizations to the prevention of possible Taiwan independence. Despite uncertainty about whether Lee favored unification or independence, China was initially hopeful that its peaceful reunification strategy would prove successful. It promoted increased trade and investment, hoping that closer economic ties would lead to political negotiations. This hope proved to be misplaced. Lee repeatedly insisted that Beijing recognize "the reality of divided rule between

Taiwan and the mainland" as a precondition for talks, something that Beijing could not accept. As its peaceful overtures failed, China increasingly turned to coercion, including ongoing military modernization, war games, and threatening rhetoric from government and military sources. These coercive tactics also failed to achieve reunification. In the end, Zhao argues, China was left with few options. Peaceful inducements had not worked, nor had military brinkmanship. Beijing's mounting frustration with Lee carried over into the Chen administration, at which point it adopted a wait-and-see attitude but would not resume talks until Chen unequivocally accepted the "one-China" principle, which Chen was unwilling to do. Lee's legacy to cross-strait relations was an increasingly tense stalemate, with no immediate prospects for significant progress.

The increased militarization of the Taiwan strait is also a prominent part of Lee's legacy. Wen-cheng Lin and Cheng-yi Lin assess Taiwan's security environment in terms of diplomatic, economic, and political matters, and then offer a detailed analysis of Taiwan's military security. They argue that the shifting military balance in China's favor was not the fault of Lee alone. More important, the unwillingness of the United States and other countries to sell the weapons that Taiwan sought to buy led it to develop its own defense industry. Under Lee, Taiwan built up a second generation of armed forces, making it a respectable military power in East Asia, but this buildup neither increased Taiwan's security nor kept up with world standards. Lin and Lin credit Lee with the Taiwanization of the military and improvements in its professionalism, both in terms of depoliticization and improved skill and know-how, but they also point out mixed results. Lee still mobilized military votes for the KMT. Moreover, morale was harmed by political divisions over the unification/independence issue. Military officers and soldiers had been educated to strongly favor unification, raising the specter that some would refuse to fight if they believed the government was pursuing independence. Although Lee promoted closer interaction between the military and society, he was not able to improve the social status of soldiers or stem the "brain drain" of young soldiers out of the military. They conclude that Lee moved Taiwan's military in the right direction, but there is still a long way to go.

Finally, Bruce J. Dickson looks at the Lee legacy on Taiwan's relations with the United States. Lee's efforts at forging a pragmatic diplomacy and breaking out of the diplomatic isolation that had been imposed by Taiwan's own past practices and China's current policies was in large part targeted at the United States, Taiwan's main protector. Even though Taiwan's democratization called into question many of the assumptions that underlie American policy toward both China and Taiwan, policy changed only marginally. Many in the U.S. government and policy community believed its "one-China" policy had maintained peace and prosperity in East Asia. Just as Lee used a strategy of division in domestic politics to pit mainlanders against Taiwanese, Dickson argues that Lee also used a similar strategy to pit the White House against Taiwan's supporters in the Congress. This paid short-term dividends, particularly in getting Lee a visa to visit Cornell in 1995, but had long-term costs. Lee in particular, and Taiwan more generally, gained a reputation for being a troublemaker, jeopardizing not only Taiwan's security but also broader American security interests in the region. Lee highlighted the inherent dangers in the cross-strait relationship and the limited ability of the United States to maintain the status quo, much less influence a final resolution. Lee's actions revealed the growing gap between American policy and Taiwan's reality, but in doing so he also made it clear that a change in either American policy or practice would not necessarily improve Taiwan's security. This dilemma—how to reconcile policy and reality without worsening Taiwan's security environment—is an important part of Lee's legacy to relations with the United States and to future diplomacy in general.

These chapters present an initial assessment of the Lee Teng-hui legacy in both Taiwan's domestic affairs and external relations. It is a mixed legacy, and some of the assessments have an emotional edge to them, which befits a man who stirred up such strong emotions during his twelve years as president. While it is too early to render a final verdict on Lee's legacy, we hope that the chapters in this volume will contribute to a greater understanding of both his accomplishments and shortcomings.

Notes

1. Inspired by Chen Shui-bian's self-proclaimed title of "son of Taiwan," some called Lee "Father of Taiwan." See Wei Wou, "Taiwan's Economic Development and Implications to Mainland China" (in Chinese), paper presented at the Conference on New Global Order and Cross-Strait Relations, Taipei, October 18, 2000.

2. Jay Taylor, *The Generalissimo's Son: Chiang Ching-kuo and the Revolutions in China and Taiwan* (Cambridge: Harvard University Press, 2000).

3. After Taiwan was reverted back to China in October 1945, a military government was installed with General Ch'en I as the first governor-general. But Ch'en's

administration was ineffectual as ineptness and corruption soon became rampant. The withdrawal of the Japanese had devastated the economy. Culturally, the two groups, the newly arrived mainlanders and the native Taiwanese, were highly incompatible. All these paved the way for a huge protest triggered by an incident in which a Taiwanese woman was killed by plainclothes police on February 28, 1947. As a result, thousands of people, Taiwanese and mainlanders, were slaughtered. For quite different interpretations of these events, see George Kerr, *Formosa Betrayed* (Boston: Houghton Mifflin, 1965), and Lai Tse-han, Ramon H. Myers, and Wei Wou, *A Tragic Beginning: The Taiwan Uprising of February 28, 1947* (Stanford: Stanford University Press, 1991).

4. The December 1996 issue of the *China Quarterly* was devoted to Taiwan's developments in the first half of the 1990s, frequently using the term "Republic of China on Taiwan" (ROCOT).

5. For a discussion of the transformation of a Leninist party-state system, see Tun-jen Cheng, "Democratizing the Quasi-Leninist Regime in Taiwan," *World Politics* 42, no. 4 (July 1989): pp. 471–99; Constance Squires Meaney, "Liberalization, Democratization, and the Role of the KMT," in *Political Changes in Taiwan*, ed. Tun-jen Cheng and Stephan Haggard (Boulder, CO: Lynne Rienner, 1992); Bruce J. Dickson, *Democratization in China and Taiwan: The Adaptability of Leninist Parties* (Oxford: Oxford University Press, 1997).

6. Hung-mao Tien and Tun-jen Cheng, "Crafting Democratic Institutions," in *Democratization in Taiwan: Implications for China*, ed. Steve Tsang and Hung-mao Tien (Hong Kong: Hong Kong University Press, 1999), pp. 27–29.

7. For more on Taiwan's pragmatic diplomacy, see Chiao Chiao Hsieh, "Pragmatic Diplomacy: Foreign Policy and External Relations," in *Take-off for Taiwan?* ed. Peter Ferdinand (London: Royal Institute for International Affairs, 1996), pp. 66–106, and Bruce J. Dickson, "The Republic of China on Taiwan's 'Pragmatic Diplomacy,'" in *Taiwan's National Security: Dilemmas and Opportunities*, ed. Alexander C. Tan, Steve Chan, and Calvin Jillson (Aldershot, UK: Ashgate, 2001), pp. 84–103.

8. In addition to calling him separatist, the *Renmin ribao* (People's daily) also condemned him as a sinner in Chinese history. See *Zhonggong nianbao, 1996* (Chinese Communist Party yearbook, 1996) (Taipei: Zhonggong yanjiu zazhishe, 1996), pp. 2–28~2–37.

9. Chien-min Chao, "Liangan huifu huishang de qiji yu zhengjie," (Opportunities and problems of resuming mediations between the two sides of the Taiwan Strait), *Zhengce* (Policy) (Taipei) (March 1998): 15–17; "Liangan shiwuxing tanpan jingyan pingxi" (Some comments on the mediations over technical issues between the two sides of the Taiwan Strait), *Wenti yu yanjiu* (Issues and studies) (Taipei) no. 11 (November 1995): 11–23.

10. This was the essence of the so-called 1992 consensus, under which Beijing and Taipei declared their adherence to a one-China policy but defined the term differently. Once Chen Shui-bian became president, China and Taiwan disagreed over the existence of this past consensus and its present relevance as a basis for resuming cross-strait talks.

11. It was reported that the policy was designed by three of his top aides. See *Zhongguo shibao* (Taipei), May 13, 2001, p. 2.

12. For discussion of the militarization of cross-strait relations, see Kurt M.

Campbell and Derek F. Mitchell, "Crisis in the Taiwan Strait?" *Foreign Affairs* (July/August 2001): 14–25.

13. See, for example, David Shambaugh, "A Matter of Time: Taiwan's Eroding Military Advantage," *Washington Quarterly* 23, no. 2 (2000).

14. See, among others, Chien-min Chao, "Taiwan's Identity Crisis and Cross-Strait Exchanges," *Issues and Studies* (Taipei) 30, no. 4 (April 1994): 1–13.

15. Chien-min Chao, "Taiwan zhuti yishi yu Zhongguodalu minzhuzhuyi de duikang," (Taiwanness vs. China's nationalism), *Zhongguodalu yanjiu* (Mainland China studies) (Taipei) 41, no. 1 (January 1998): 54–71; Francoise Mengin, "State and Identity," in *Democratization in Taiwan*, eds. Tsang and Tien, pp. 123–24.

16. Shelley Rigger, *Politics in Taiwan: Voting for Democracy* (London and New York: Routledge, 1999).

17. To understand the fight between the two factions, see Yun-han Chu and Tse-min Lin, "The Process of Democratic Consolidation in Taiwan: Social Cleavage, Electoral Competition, and the Emerging Party System," in *Taiwan's Electoral Politics and Democratic Transition: Riding the Third Wave*, ed. Hung-mao Tien (Armonk, NY: M.E. Sharpe, 1996), pp. 84–86.

18. Although Lee is not a member of the party, the party sees Lee as its spiritual leader.

——— 2 ———

Some Problems in Taiwan's Democratic Consolidation

Peter R. Moody, Jr.

Chen Shui-bian's election as Taiwan's president is one more milestone in the institutionalization of the island's democracy, representing a peaceful turnover of the party holding power.[1]

Taiwan, an island off China's southeastern coast, was taken from China by Japan in 1895 and made into a colony. In 1945, control over Taiwan reverted to China. Misgovernment of the island by armed forces affiliated with China's then ruling Nationalist Party (Kuomintang: KMT) provoked a rebellion in 1947, which was suppressed with great brutality. This led to or enhanced a sense among many natives of Taiwan that the island should become a sovereign country in its own right, independent of China. After about 1948, as his own position on the Chinese mainland was collapsing under the assault by the communist armed forces, KMT leader Chiang Kai-shek began transferring men and treasure to Taiwan, hoping to make it either a base for a counterattack on the mainland or the site of his last stand, where he would go down fighting. In Chiang's view, his own regime, the Republic of China (ROC), remained the sole legitimate government of all China, with Taiwan a mere province of China—even though the ROC kept actual control over only Taiwan and a handful of smaller islands. The new communist regime on the mainland, the People's Republic of China, agreed there was only one Chinese government and that Taiwan was a province of China, but differed on which was China's legal and legitimate government.

In 1947, the Republic of China, then still in shaky control of the mainland, had adopted a democratic constitutional system. After its retreat from the mainland, the KMT regime enforced progressive and effective social and economic reforms on Taiwan. The democratic features of the constitution were suspended, however, under emergency rule or what some call martial law. Taiwan was governed as a sometimes rather brutal police state. While there were local elections, any organized opposition was suppressed. There were no elections at the "national" level. Thus, the legislature of the ROC consisted of those delegates elected on the mainland in 1947 who chose to follow the government to Taiwan. The "mainlanders," the 15–20 percent of the population of the island who (or whose parents or grandparents) came to the island between 1945 and 1950, had no more political liberty than the native Taiwanese, but presumably more sympathy with the regime's goal of mainland recovery.

By the late 1960s and early 1970s, with generational change setting in among the ruling elite and Taiwan losing international support, especially support from the United States, it became evident that mainland recovery was not going to come anytime soon. Chiang Ching-kuo, who was more and more replacing his aged father as the actual *capo de regime*, concluded that were the regime to survive it would have to sink deeper roots into the island society. He introduced a protracted program of both liberalization and democratization, increasing Taiwanese representation in the organs of power, reintroducing and slowly extending the scope of national elections, and tolerating without legalizing at least semi-organized opposition. At the same time, when faced with real threats, especially those outside the regime's approved institutional channels, he did not scruple to use violence.

Picking up in Chiang's last years, the pace of democratization really accelerated under his successor, Lee Teng-hui, Chiang's last vice president, a Taiwanese technocrat who had never been to the mainland. Chiang ended emergency rule in 1987, and the process of democratization has consisted mainly of following the provisions of the constitution and of amending the constitution according to designated procedure. Since about 1990, all political offices on the island have become directly or indirectly responsible to the Taiwan electorate. The constitution has been amended to allow the direct election of the president by the people of Taiwan (and Quemoy and Matsu), and the second of these elections saw the victory of the opposition leader. At this point, should democracy on Taiwan somehow become undone, it would be an instance of democratic collapse, not failed transition.

Democracy's Discontents

This does not mean that democratic collapse is impossible. Students of democracy have recently shown concern about the "quality" of democracy, as both scholars and the public, recovering from the enthusiasm of the 1980s, again realize that whatever else it is, democracy is a political system like any other, with its own characteristic flaws, and that the political system does not abolish all the wickedness and smallness inherent in the human condition. Some are concerned that democratic forms may merely "delegate" power to elites who hold office by virtue of winning elections, elections that may themselves be flawed in their implementation, without controls on elites between elections.[2] Others worry that the Western coincidence of democracy with liberalism may not prevail in the newer democracies, and that democratically elected regimes may behave as arbitrarily and lawlessly as did their authoritarian predecessors.[3]

For analytic purposes the best conception of democracy is probably the broad, tolerant, "Schumpeterian" one[4] (the concept generally used in the 1980s transition literature): Democracy is a form of selecting persons for political office. Democracy requires free competitive elections to offices exercising, at least in law, decisive influence in the formulation of state policy.[5] The electorate must enjoy at least basic civil liberties: freedom of speech and press, freedom to assemble peaceably. For the system to be stable over time there must be, up to a certain level, a rule of law: to assure that laws passed by the democratic regime will actually take effect, and to assure that whatever group takes control through free elections does not abolish the democratic system without following set constitutional procedures. Law is also required to uphold civil liberties, to enforce popular freedoms, and to prevent political opposition from being treated as a crime. All enfranchised citizens (who must constitute a substantial—but otherwise generally undefined—portion of the population meeting qualifications defined by law) must be free to participate in politics (or, possibly not to participate, as they see fit),[6] whether as voters or candidates running for office.

This concept excludes any "substantive" conception of democracy. That is, it does not require the state to enforce economic equity, gender equality, the assurance of basic subsistence, or any of the other things students have postulated as necessary for democracy to function or as the desired fruits of democracy. Attempts to define democracy in substantive terms are tendentious (not to say ideological), and it is not clear what particular rights and privileges are inherently democratic.[7] Formal rights, to be very high-minded about it, are the basis for argument about what the substance of policy should be; and to divorce form from substance allows both argument and research on the consequences and suitability of the forms, without collapsing the idea of democracy into everything good and desirable.

Taiwan at the turn of the century was certainly democratic in the formal sense—and this makes it worthwhile to inquire into the possible consequences of Taiwan democracy and possible threats to it. This chapter briefly surveys four potential problem areas: the concentration of power in the executive; the issue of corruption; the enduring question of national identity; and the closely related issue of China.

Is Taiwan a Delegative Democracy?

Taiwan continues to be ruled under the Constitution of the Republic of China, adopted on the mainland in 1947 and amended during the 1990s. The constitution allocates governmental and political power according to the theories of Sun Yat-sen—the familiar executive, legislative, and judicial, along with additional powers of examination (for recruitment of the civil service) and control (to check malfeasance in the other branches). On its face the constitution seems to provide for a dual executive, a president, and (to use the most convenient translation) a premier. Beginning students of government are familiar with this form in the example of the French Fifth Republic (although the Chinese had it before the French). This system leaves ambiguous the primary locus of executive power. Whether it rests with the president or the premier depends on the political situation and process, not on constitutional law.

In the past the center of power was with the president—the sole exception being the time between the death of Chiang Kai-shek in 1975 and the formal election of Chiang Ching-kuo in 1978. During this period, the "head of regime" was clearly Premier Chiang Ching-kuo rather than President Yen Chia-kan. As a witticism of the early 1990s had it, Taiwan had a presidential system, as long as the president was named Chiang.[8]

The Chiangs, however, were more nearly bosses than holders of an institutionalized role. Their influence did not derive primarily from their constitutional position—indeed, until almost the end of the Chiang era, many relevant constitutional provisions had been suspended in the state of emergency. The institutional bases of regime power were built upon the KMT organization, the state technocracy, the police and intelligence system, and the military. Each of the reigning Chiangs was a "strongman": each had connections and a following in all of the ruling systems, and so each could coordinate regime policy.[9] Lee Teng-hui was Chiang Ching-kuo's vice president; and when he inherited the presidency he lacked the connections, not to mention the temperament and inclination, to be a strongman in the Chiang style. Nor was anyone else available to act as strongman. The political problems of the early post-Chiang transition were met by a reactivation of constitutional norms and procedures.

Both precedent and ambition encouraged Lee to make the most of the power of the president as well as those of the head of the party. Lee met resistance from many of his former peers inside the KMT. Most, but not all, of these were mainlanders. The opposition to Lee, however, probably had relatively little to do with his being Taiwanese, but quite a bit to do with jealousy on the part of those who, had things turned out otherwise, might easily have occupied his place. This establishment opposition tried to delay Lee's elevation to the party chairmanship and it put together a ticket to run against him in the 1990 presidential election (when the president was still elected by the National Assembly, which was still overwhelmingly elected on the mainland in 1947).

Toward the beginning of his administration, Lee tried to avoid alienating the mainlander establishment (an establishment he himself, provincial origins aside, had been very much a part of). At first he kept Chiang Ching-kuo's premier, Yu Kuo-hua, and then replaced him with Li Huan, another sometime close associate of Chiang Ching-kuo. Li Huan sided with the "antimainstream" opposition in 1990 and was fired—to be replaced by Hau Pei-tsun, the regime's top soldier, who had also sided with the antimainstream: as Anatole France once wrote, loyalty must be rewarded—and so must treason.

Hau was the strongest personality among Lee's premiers. Reformist public opinion tended to mistrust him, but he won support, or at least respect, for his success in curbing crime, which was seen as more of a problem after the end of emergency rule. Lee and Hau were soon seriously at odds with each other, the dispute centering somewhat on policy but also on the form of government, and, on a deeper level, over the identity of the political community embodied by the constitutional system.[10]

Even before Chiang Ching-kuo's death there was speculation that one medium-term solution to the China problem in a democratic Taiwan might be for the president to serve as a ceremonial figure and symbol of a united China, with actual executive power exercised by the premier and cabinet. Indeed, in a democratic Taiwan, it would seem that were the president to continue to be elected indirectly, it would *have* to be a cabinet system. In the early 1990s, President Lee's support began to argue for direct popular election, while Premier Hau argued that the ROC was really a cabinet system, whatever its actual political history. In those days the president appointed the premier, but the premier governed by retaining the confidence of the legislature, not by serving the pleasure of the president. Lee and Hau clashed in areas where the authority of their offices overlapped. Hau had long-standing connections in the military and argued that control over military affairs, including appointments, lay with the premier through the minister of defense. Lee, anxious to break up Hau's network and diversify the high command, asserted control in his capacity as commander-in-chief. On the issue over which the final break came, the outsider's sympathy might be inclined spontaneously to gravitate toward Hau: the cabinet wanted to reform the land taxation system, which was originally designed to protect poor peasants, but by the 1990s functioned more to enhance the wealth of land speculators. The reform would have inconvenienced some wealthy Taiwanese upon whom Lee counted for political funding.

Hau's arguments cited the latest themes in the empirical study of democratic transitions. The respected political scientist Hu Fo asserted: "Chinese and Western scholars with a deep knowledge of constitutions universally agree that a cabinet system is the most democratic and stable of governmental systems, and is also the form most suited for a country such as ours in the midst of political transition."[11]

Hu Fo exaggerates in claiming universal agreement on the superiority of a cabinet system, but he accurately characterizes a consensus emerging in the early 1990s. Where neither the president nor the legislature is responsible to the other (as in the American system), and the president holds real power, there may be no effective checks on that power, and the president becomes an elected dictator. Since there can be only one president at a time, a presidential system is winner-take-all, which leads to a disregard of minority interests.[12] When the legislature and the presidency are controlled by different parties (as was the case in Taiwan following the 2000 election) the result may be gridlock. A president is elected probably on the basis of certain positions on issues (although these may not be the main appeal), and, claiming a mandate from the people, he may try to force his program through over legislative objections. The presidential structure makes the system vulnerable to demagogic outsiders who have no sympathy for constitutional restraints or differing opinions. The attention to the person of the president weakens the role of political parties, the only institutions allowing democratic accountability of the state to society.[13] A presidential system, especially in a new or unstable democracy, can degenerate into what Guillermo O'Donnell calls delegative democracy, with the president being in effect a strongman ruler who owes his legitimacy to his election by the voters.[14]

Lee Teng-hui was no elected dictator, whatever the antimainstream claimed. On the other hand, while the constitutional forms and procedures were the surest ground for Lee's position, he was willing to circumvent them and turn them to his short-term advantage. His opponents particularly objected to Lee's convening of his National Affairs Conferences, extra-legal political gatherings encompassing almost all trends of opinion to discuss political change that could be seen as end-runs around established institutions. The constitutional change to direct popular election of the president tipped the balance of power in the executive branch to the president. Lee considered the premier in effect a sort of administrative aide to the president (as the premiers under the Chiangs had sometimes been). With the defeat of Hau Pei-tsun and the appointment of Lien Chan, Lee was able at last to bring this about. Indeed, for a time, Lee seemed to hope Lien Chan might serve simultaneously as premier and as vice president.

The constitutional changes were all made according to due process, and while Lee may sometimes have behaved in a high-handed, even graceless manner, he did not violate the law or coerce his opponents. It is reasonable to think that a constitutional system that might have been appropriate for China a half century earlier would require change to fit contemporary Taiwan—although the changes did exacerbate the provincial-origin rift on Taiwan and increased the expression of hostility from the mainland. And one might wonder whether there was some lack of good faith in Lee's simultaneous use of, and disregard for, constitutional provisions.

The election of Chen Shui-bian has brought back into question the actual nature of the constitutional system. On assuming office, in his rhetoric Chen acted as if he would and could assume the full powers that had accrued to the president: Even though he won only about a third of the popular vote, and in spite of continued KMT control of the legislature, he was the boss, he would be a real president. In his actions he was more cautious and conciliatory, appointing as his premier the professional soldier (and lifetime KMT member) T'ang Fei. In form this looked like French-style "cohabitation," with the president from one party and the premier from the party of coalition dominant in the legislature. French cohabitation is rarely harmonious, and while Chen and T'ang seemed to get along personally, the system has tension built into it. The Taiwan cohabitation broke down a few months after Chen, fulfilling a DPP election promise, cut off funds for the construction of a new nuclear power plant. T'ang Fei (who was already in poor health anyway) resigned, various KMT legislators uttered threats of impeachment, and in the end Chen restored the funds.[15]

Chen also appointed a premier based on the pattern of Lee Teng-hui's last years: a member of the same party as the president, one without a strong base of his own, one who would be a docile tool of the president. As long as the president's party fails to control the legislature, such a premier will have limited, if any, support in the legislature, and the months following the constitutional crisis saw deadlock and recrimination between the executive and legislative branches. This sort of thing, of course, has its proper place in a system of democratic checks on power. Presidential dictatorship remains, intuitively, highly unlikely, although conditions on Taiwan in the abstract may turn propitious for such an outcome. If the KMT continues to fragment, and if the DPP should follow suit or fail to command a majority in the legislature, control over the political system may center in the president by default, with the legislature unable to provide either effective support for the president or an effective check on his power. Elsewhere, particularly in Latin America, a strong president and a multiparty system have been a recipe for presidential dictatorship;[16] but that does not mean this would be the case on Taiwan, and recent political history might incline one to doubt that it would be.

Be all this as it may, the triumph of presidentialism on Taiwan during the Lee Teng-hui era was, in the short run, no obstacle to the island's democracy. A cabinet system would probably have reinforced the position of those who had been on top during the pre-democratic era. Presidentialism gave Lee the leverage to tame those forces and also hammered home the theme that the political order on Taiwan was responsible to the people on Taiwan and to no one else. The focus on the office of the presidency allowed the top of the system to be captured by the opposition party, thus hammering home the impression of democratic consolidation.

Democracy and Corruption

"Delegative" democracy and other abuses of the democratic process are corruptions of democracy. One of the functions of democracy is to check corruption by holding the rulers responsible to those they rule; but in some ways contemporary democracy may itself encourage corruption. The notoriously high price of electoral politics may breed unsavory alliances between those who aspire to office and those who can provide the cash.

Taiwan's politics are not without corruption, at least if one believes what political figures say about their rivals. The Taiwanese political scene is said to be highly personalistic, with alliances built on webs of family alignments created or solidified through intermarriage.[17] When he served as governor of Taiwan, Lee Teng-hui is said to have cultivated various local political and financial bigshots,[18] and, in the democratic era, he turned for support to various "golden cows," Taiwanese plutocrats able to finance his campaigns. Taiwan elections are notoriously characterized by vote buying, the going rate in 1997 said to have been NT$500[19] (about US$15 in that financially turbulent year). Selling a vote was not a way to get rich: The function of the transaction was less to "buy" a vote than to solidify a connection, cultivate *ganqing*, to return a favor (money) for a favor (a vote). But the payment turns the public act of voting into a private deal.

Corruption is somehow related to democratization, although only in special ways. Vote buying preceded the democratic transition (and probably dates back to Japanese times); but when elections were primarily local and counted for very little, pecuniary corruption was itself largely local and small scale.[20] During the democratic era, candidates for office, including KMT nominees, increasingly had to raise their own funds. In the days of the Chiangs, the Central Organization Department controlled party nominations and campaign funding. In arranging the ticket, the Center would allocate nominations among locally based factions or force a faction now holding a certain office to yield a turn to its rivals. Declining control from the Center over money and nominations forced candidates to shift for themselves and also raised the political stakes at the local levels, as rival factions, some of which have underworld or "black society" connections, are no longer balanced against each other but compete directly, each seeking to eliminate the others. This encourages close connections between politics and money and also enhances the appeal of politics as a path to money.

Some, at least since the articulate Tammany ward heeler George Washington Plunkitt regaled a quick-witted young news reporter with disquisitions on "honest graft,"[21] have argued that corruption may to some degree foster democracy. Chalmers Johnson once suggested that the wheeling and dealing of former Japanese Prime Minister Tanaka Kakuei helped democratize the Japanese system, in that it forced arrogant bureaucrats to deal with elected politicians, not simply to dictate to them.[22] Lucian Pye hypothesized that money politics might accustom the East Asian public to the truth that liberal politics is about the conflict and accommodation of interests, not the manifestation of virtue.[23] On Taiwan the more flamboyant political practices have historically been identified with the more democratic sectors of the polity, these practices disdained as corrupt and superstitious buffoonery by the mainlander establishment.[24]

None of this is very convincing as an apology for corrupt practices. Tanaka's methods may have resulted in a greater number of pork-barrel projects than there would have been otherwise, but evidently they did not enhance popular participation in the making of state policy or expand democratic responsibility. And while East Asian politics often does take a moralistic tone, there is no reason to think that the East Asian public has ever taken politicians' self-serving moral posturing at face value. Conversely, liberal democratic politics, especially America's, are rarely a matter of cold interest calculation without any moral component. Political moralism is often hypocritical, distasteful, and unhelpful, but a virtueless play of interest, with no consideration whatsoever of either the general interest or justice, would be even worse.[25] There is probably no reason to be shocked that democratic politics may be corrupt, but neither is there a reason to celebrate.

Whether or not democracy is a sufficient condition for corruption, it is hardly a necessary one: for, otherwise, nondemocratic regimes would not be corrupt. The current mainland rulers are notorious for their avid devotion to "rent-seeking,"[26] but even in the Maoist era the well-placed were able to translate political position into material gain.[27] Corruption was hardly unknown on Taiwan prior to democratization, and many of the current manifestations of corruption (the alliance of political factions with the underworld, the intertwinement of government and business, and for that matter, the sizable slush fund supposedly at the disposal of candidate James Soong) go back to the Chiang period.

Corruption, or the interrelation of corruption and the style of politics, does, however, make some difference to the quality of democracy. During the phase of rapid economic development (the famous growth with equity), the Taiwan state was autonomous from, and dominant over, local society.[28] The connection between state and business, with the state calling the shots, has been credited with fostering the general economic miracles in East Asia.[29] During the 1997 economic crisis this pattern was reinterpreted as crony capitalism.

Taiwan escaped many of the initial consequences of the 1997 failure. Nonetheless, the relationship between business and politics continues. By and large, Taiwan political relationships are not based on "class," interest, or even opinion,[30] but instead they center on personal connections and rivalries (with vote buying a manifestation of this). Because parties lack both clear principles and strong institutionalized connections with relevant social bases, democracy may not serve as an effective way to keep power holders accountable or to change the system in a direction the majority (or transient, shifting majorities) considers just.

A functioning democracy should, simply by virtue of its functioning, reduce the autonomy of the state, so that the "state" (politicians and officials) becomes more responsive to "society," particularly that part of society that is able and inclined to finance political activity. The politicians may even have an incentive to maintain state-economy connections, so the plutocrats will continue to have a reason to fork over the lucre. There may thus be a systemic connection between Taiwan's democracy and the apparently increasingly unequal distribution of income. The danger is that if ordinary people come to see democracy as an inside game of politicians and plutocrats, they may come to lose an interest in democracy.[31]

Democracy and Community

Taiwan's democratization brought into open political contention the question of the identity of the state and the people. The relationship between national identity and democracy is a complicated one on Taiwan.

Some lines of reasoning hold that democracy requires a consensus on questions of basic political identity: rule by the people implies that there is a *people*, with the identity of that people beyond political contestation.[32] In states with strong divisions along ethnic lines, unadulterated democracy can be seen by minorities as the tyranny of the majority, and in these divided states there may be special procedures to guarantee minority interests.[33] But while the divisions on Taiwan can be presented in ethnic terms, the actual divisions are probably more accurately construed as political and attitudinal; and the commitment to democratic procedures, especially by the establishment, of all things, may have trumped the ethnic or national question. On Taiwan democratization may have gone far toward resolving the question of identity—although there is ample room to doubt that international conditions will allow that resolution to be sustained.

During most of the Chiang era, the Taiwanese were given to understand that they were Chinese. They might have had their own regional peculiarities (mostly to be depreciated, as far as the authorities were concerned), but Taiwan was a province of China. This one-China stance derived from the nationalism of the mainland rulers but also rationalized the perpetuation of the authoritarian system. Between the mainlander newcomers and the Taiwanese there was certainly a division, even an antipathy, reinforced by memories of the events of the spring of 1947, with each group tending to regard the other as crude and lacking in culture. Especially during the first two decades, there was obvious political discrimination against Taiwanese (compensated for, in the mainlander version, by Taiwanese control of the economy)—but no real or sustained attempt to extirpate Taiwanese culture.

Overtly or covertly the identity of the state and even the nation has been the central theme of Taiwan politics since 1949 (or even 1947); but this has normally not implied direct ethnic (or subethnic) confrontation. The *dangwai* (outside the party) movement and the Democratic Progressive Party were almost exclusively Taiwanese in composition, but for decades the KMT itself had been overwhelmingly Taiwanese. The KMT used to try to play off and exacerbate differences among the ethnicities within the Taiwan population, encouraging local factionalism or rivalry between the Hokklo and Hakka natives of the province. Indeed, while some in the DPP might hope to construct a general Taiwanese identity, there may be some shortage of raw material for this. To some degree "Taiwanese" remains a synonym for Hokklo, and James

Soong's 2000 candidacy not only received overwhelming support from mainlanders but also disproportionate support in the Hakka population.

Perhaps paradoxically, in spite of its centrality the identity issue was not really a partisan one between the KMT and DPP, at least not until the KMT's defeat in 2000. At one point the rivalry might have been presented as a conflict of Chinese and Taiwanese nationalisms, but in practice the partisan positions converged.[34] The consensus was also shared by the seriously ailing New Party and its presumptive successor, James Soong's People First Party. The "operational" (as opposed to the declaratory) policy of the KMT regime was hardly ever the recovery of the mainland and almost always the preservation of Taiwan's autonomy. The Beijing authorities may wax nostalgic about the good old days of Chiang Ching-kuo (not to mention Chiang Kai-shek), but in his day they were eloquent with diatribes against his alleged desire, if not for Taiwan independence (*Tai du*), then for an independent Taiwan (*du Tai*), and his pursuit of "Chiang-style" (or "B-style") independence. Even prior to Chiang Ching-kuo's death, the KMT had effectively given up any ambition to reconquer the mainland (proposing instead to "reunify China on the basis of the Three Principles of the People") and had ceased to advocate even in the abstract, the desirability of one China. Rather, the regime sought to convince the Taiwan public that a clear commitment to a unified China and continued KMT control of Taiwan was the best guarantee against a mainland attack and thus the best way to preserve Taiwan's autonomy. The Lee Teng-hui program can be interpreted as a natural extrapolation of that of the Chiangs but without the violence.

The DPP, for its part, had Taiwan independence in its platform, but from its founding had been vague about what this might specifically entail. The pro-independence stance became even more attenuated after the 1996 elections, provoking the formation of the splinter New Nation Association. This did not bespeak a change of heart concerning Chinese nationalism. Rather, it was a recognition that the mainland might indeed be serious about one China, and too open a commitment to independence would cost votes—again, not because the voters were thirsting to transfer sovereignty to Beijing, but because they feared that the unambiguous closing off of that possibility would be asking for a Chinese attack. At the same time, some of the erstwhile more radical DPP activists had toned down their traditional hostility to the Chinese Nationalist heritage. In his 1998 campaign for reelection as Taipei's mayor, Chen

Shui-bian led the voters to believe that he enjoyed the posthumous endorsement of Sun Yat-sen.

Prior to assuming the presidency, Lee Teng-hui had extensive connections among the older generation of mainlander technocrats, but none within the military or security systems and at most a limited foothold in the KMT apparatus. Both ambition and opportunity reinforced principled conviction in directing him in his chosen strategy: to push Taiwanization, to present himself as a Taiwanese who had shared the pain and humiliation of all Taiwanese, and as Moses leading his chosen people out of the land of bondage. This fostering of his own ambitions also served Taiwan democracy—through the full reelection of the legislature and the National Assembly, and, possibly, the institution of direct presidential elections and the 1991 unilateral declaration of peace with the mainland.

A corollary to this strategy, however, was that it alienated many "second generation" mainlanders,[35] particularly those of a reformist bent who had shown the capacity to attract votes. Thus, the very popular Jaw Shaw-kang came to feel so unpopular in the KMT that he became one of the founding members of the ostensibly pro-unification New Party. In his early presidency Lee Teng-hui relied heavily on support and advice from James Soong, who had personally been very close to Chiang Ching-kuo. Lee ultimately turned, however, to the half-mountaineer Lien Chan, the least charismatic of the KMT second generation, as his lieutenant and heir—and in the process, he lost subordinates who, while they certainly might rival him, also had the ability to help him.

It can be argued that marginalizing the second generation mainlanders helped Taiwan's democracy. It prevented the DPP from making mainlander control an issue, even while the substance of Lee's policy remained very much on the trajectory set under the Chiangs.[36] Short-term retrospect suggests that the alienation of James Soong was a mistake for Lee and possibly a problem for democratic consolidation.

The return to the popular election of the mayors of Taipei and Kaohsiung in the early 1990s was another of Lee's democratizing reforms. On its face so was the institution of popular election for the governor of Taiwan: the caution here was that the Taiwan independence movement had long argued for the abolition of the provincial government as something superfluous that served only to maintain the fiction that the national government was the government of all of China. The "freezing" of the provincial government shortly after its redemocratization might indeed be justified in terms of efficiency. But it exacerbated

tensions with the mainland (whose position on that subject was the ob-
verse of that of the Taiwan independence movement). It could also be
interpreted as a power play by Lee Teng-hui to cut back the growing
influence of the mainlander James Soong, who had won the governorship in a landslide. During the 2000 presidential campaign, stronger
KMT vitriol was splashed onto Soong ("that candidate") than onto Chen
Shui-bian. The post-election assertions by KMT stalwarts that Lee Teng-
hui deliberately threw the election to Chen may turn out to be more
literally true than seemed plausible at the time, and they have at least a
poetic validity: Lee's feud with Soong and his promotion of poor Lien
Chan were the conditions for Chen's victory.

Lee's strategy politicized provincial cleavages at a time when the
gap between Taiwanese and mainlanders had been narrowing. In particular, the descendants of the old mainlanders may feel less at home
on Taiwan than is healthy for the political system. The aftermath of
the 2000 elections also raises questions about the future of the party
system—a strong party system being desirable and perhaps even necessary for a functioning democracy. By 2000, the New Party seemed
to have dwindled into irrelevance: and one suspects the same awaits
James Soong's new party. In the recriminations that were bound to
follow defeat, Lien Chan and other KMT stalwarts returned, to some
extent to the stance of Chinese nationalism, calculating, perhaps, that
if the party were to have any future, it would somehow have to expand
its scope into a "greater China," and not limit itself to Taiwan alone.
This provoked Lee Teng-hui, in his retirement, to encourage his erstwhile mainstream followers in the legislature to break with the KMT,
forming a splinter, the Taiwan Solidarity Union (TSU), more in sympathy with an independent Taiwan. Lee, for his pains, was expelled
from the KMT. The short-run aftermath of the DPP victory, then,
seemed to be an exacerbation of the ethnic cleavage combined with a
general muddying of the exact lines of cleavage. Chinese nationalism
(which, one suspects, barring major international changes) will continue to lack much of a market on Taiwan, remaining parceled out
among two minor parties and a probably diminishing KMT. And what
principled cause was there for a voter to choose the TSU over the
DPP? Given Taiwan's historic lack of politicized class or economic
divisions, it may take awhile for lines of cleavage to clarify and assume a stable form. The medium-term Taiwan democracy may be an
amorphous jockeying for power among shifting and ephemeral factional

combinations—as people used to say about the *dangwai* movement, a herd of dragons without a head.

Thunder Across the Bay

This assumes, of course, that there is a medium term. The major obstacle in the way of full consolidation of Taiwan's democracy is the threat of war from China. It is at this point that the American policy of ambiguity lurches toward incoherence. The American Secretary of Defense William Cohen was admirably evenhanded in his spring 2000 Asian tour, exhorting both Taiwan and the mainland to tone down the rhetoric: but, as it happens, all of the Taiwan presidential candidates had been going out of their way for months to avoid being provocative. More to the point on all of this was the analogy made by a reporter at PRC Premier Zhu Rongji's news conference held a few days before the election (an analogy the premier found "very witty" [*hen fengqu*], and to which he really had no response): that China is telling Taiwan, in effect, "Marry me or I shall kill you."[37]

As structured, the situation seems to present a genuinely irresolvable dilemma. Democracy in and of itself implies Taiwan independence, a connection long recognized on the island itself.[38] Democracy means that the government answers to the people it rules. To turn sovereignty over to some other authority not fully under the control of the people of Taiwan would dilute democracy at best, placing restrictions on democratic power.[39] But there seems to be absolutely no space in the international community for a formally independent Taiwan, and any move to create such a space would be grotesquely destabilizing and risky.

The claim of the Taiwan government prior to the 1990s that it represented all of China was based not, despite the impression it gave, on some notion of the KMT's inherent right to rule, but on the principle of *fatong*—legal or constitutional continuity.[40] In 1947 the ROC had established a constitution, and, subsequently, the Communist Party, a rebel bandit organization, took control of certain parts of China by violent and illegal means. This usurpation, however, did not affect the legal status of the ROC as a state.

The communists had no use for the ROC or its constitution, but especially in retrospect developed a secret soft spot for the *fatong* as a vindication of the one-China position. Lee's democratic reforms, however, directly attacked the *fatong*—through the full reelection of the legislature and, especially, the National Assembly,[41] from Taiwan alone; the direct election of the president by the people from the same area; the freezing (abolition) of the provincial government; the 2000 post-election proposal to abolish the National Assembly. Lee Teng-hui's assertion in July 1999 that Taiwan and the mainland had a "special state-to-state" relationship was not completely an innovation, but a logical projection of Taiwan's own 1991 proposals for reunification: that as far as Taiwan was concerned the civil war was over; that the PRC was legitimate in the territory under its control and the ROC legitimate in the territory under its control; that reunification might be possible once the mainland became democratic; that in the meantime the mainland should cease to threaten war and to hinder Taiwan's attempts to acquire international status. This, in turn, was perhaps a further development of the Chiang Ching-kuo proposal to reunify China under the Three Principles of the People.

Taiwan's democratization probably does enhance the sympathy it enjoys in the international community, most relevantly in the United States. But the steps taken in conjunction with democratization also pose risks to the United States, putting America in a position of either provoking China or seeming to condone Chinese pressure against Taiwan. Lee Teng-hui was the constitutionally elected head of a democratic political system, but, in 1994, the United States decided it could not let him get off an airplane on American soil. This indignity led to the issue's politicization within the United States, with Taiwan fueling the politicization. In 1995 Lee was allowed an "informal" visit to the United States, which led to tensions between China and America, and, in 1996, a confrontation that wavered on the brink of war. President Clinton's servile reassurances in 1998 that America "does not support" (he did not quite say it opposes) Taiwan independence and other prospects the Chinese find unpalatable was a reaction to how dangerous things had become. Lee Teng-hui's otherwise seemingly gratuitous pronouncements a year later on state-to-state relations may have been his attempt to stir China into what America would see as unreasonable anger against Taiwan, thus correcting the American attempt to correct its own earlier tilt toward Taiwan.

The American position may vary according to domestic politics, but sympathy for Taiwan is apparently easier for those out of power than it is for those in power. In fact, even during its first few years in power the Clinton administration seemed to be moving toward a de facto "acknowledgment" of an independent Taiwan, culminating in the 1996 crisis: The perception of an actual prospect of war seems to be the main reason for the later change of course. Early in his presidential campaign George W. Bush made statements implying that America would certainly defend Taiwan. On April 25, 2001 (during a period of relatively high tension with China over the detention of the crew of the EP-3 surveillance airplane), President Bush, responding to a question in an interview on ABC's *Good Morning America*, announced that the United States did have an obligation to defend Taiwan if Taiwan were attacked. During the remainder of that day, State Department and other officials issued comments on, and qualifications of, the president's remark, including reiterations of Clinton's one-China position. This reinforced the ambiguity of American policy, even though the ambiguity may give the impression of stemming more from confusion and indecision than from a shrewdly thought-out strategy.[42]

In February of 2000, the Chinese declared they might go to war should Taiwan continue to refuse to negotiate about reunification. This was not really new: The condition had been mentioned as early as 1984. But it had not been stressed in recent times. China declared that its patience might not be infinite probably because it saw it was actually running out of time. The world supports the Chinese position on Taiwan not because it finds that position intrinsically just or reasonable, but because China demands it as a price for good relations.

Taiwan's movement to democracy cannot but provoke China, and this exacerbates international tensions. The sympathy of the "international community" for Taiwan's democracy may be matched by irritation with Taiwan for being the reason for conflict that community would rather avoid. It does not take much imagination to see America eventually pressuring Taiwan to take China up on its offer of "one country, two systems."

Conclusions

This analysis must seem somewhat on the pessimistic side. It should not suggest that there are poor prospects for a stable and enduring democracy on Taiwan: It is merely that the problems are more evident than the prospects.

This chapter has examined potential challenges to Taiwan democracy stemming from the presidential system, corruption, the unsettled nature of the nation or community, and the claims posed by China. While theorists of democratization within the discipline of political science have, in their recent trends, argued that parliamentary systems would be more representative and more stable, on Taiwan, presidentialism has so far not been detrimental to democratic development, and, indeed, the strengthening of the presidential system has actually helped nourish the process of democratization. This does not mean that the constitutional form will never be a problem. Neither Lee Teng-hui nor Chen Shui-bian seem the dictatorial type; but Lee turned the presidency as such into an institution more powerful than the one the Chiangs had occupied and Chen seemed ready to use fully and possibly to expand those presidential powers. The play of politics after the election showed that the relations among the institutions had not been resolved as unequivocally as it seemed in the era of KMT rule, but protracted deadlock or stasis among the institutions might provide temptations for future attempts to reassert presidential power. In particular, should the party system become so chaotic that the legislature is unable to summon up the cohesion to check and balance the president, Taiwan could fall into an elected dictatorship.[43]

A more immediate problem is corruption. Democracy, as noted before, is one check on corruption. But any modern democratic system is likely to provide occasions for corruption, at least as long as elections cost money. The corruption on Taiwan, marked by violence and overt gangster participation in politics, is of a particularly vicious kind.[44] The style of corruption may be traceable to local factionalism rooted deeply in Taiwanese society, going back to the Qing dynasty. It cannot be attributed simply to the KMT, although the manner of KMT rule both before and during democratization reinforced these local patterns. The DPP is likely to be faced with temptations similar to those of the KMT, and one should not be overly sanguine that the new rulers will be able to resist these temptations. Corruption is a sufficient evil in itself, and if it becomes too prevalent there is a risk that the ordinary person may come to identify the democratic system as a form of institutionalized corruption.

Taiwan would seem to challenge the plausible hypothesis that democracy, rule of, by, and for the people, requires first that a "people" be identified. Throughout the 1990s, there was no general consensus on the national identity of the Taiwan state. Democratic development was largely a matter of an already strong state's reactivating and reforming its existing potentially democratic institutions: Taiwan became democratic because the state, independently of any people or nation, began acting in a democratic fashion.

Yet, the question of community is not entirely irrelevant. To oversimplify the categories, "mainlanders" and "Taiwanese" (or Chinese nationalists and Taiwan nationalists) may disagree on the identity of the "nation," but during the 1980s and 1990s both came to define their gravest threat as coming from the communist mainland rather than each other. This convergence may have been a necessary condition for democratization; at least it contributed to the process.[45]

The China question is the key to the future stability of Taiwan's democracy. It is bound up with the question of identity, which, in turn, is bound up with the question of constitutional form. The Taiwan issue may test America's commitment to the expansion of democracy, if that indeed remains a part of U.S. foreign policy. The American position of ambiguity increasingly resembles denial, a refusal to face reality. The structure of the situation means that active support for Taiwan democracy comes at the cost of enmity with China, and it is an open question whether the United States can or even should bear that cost. Whatever the justice of it, Taiwan will probably eventually have to agree to political negotiations with the mainland. At least to save appearances, President Chen may devise a way to accept the one-China preconditions for this negotiation, even if untutored common sense suggests that once this is conceded there is not much left to negotiate. The mainland, however, might also find some way to accept the Taiwan precondition of negotiation on a basis of equality. The discovery of a supposed 1992 "consensus" on "one China," in which each side reserves the right to define for itself what one China means, is certainly a creative subterfuge, but it seems a temporary expedient rather than a lasting solution.[46]

The defeat of the Kuomintang will probably make negotiations on an equal basis more difficult. The Chinese have always been willing (in principle) to negotiate on a party-to-party basis, Chinese Communist Party (CCP) to KMT. It would have been politically impossible for the KMT to agree to this. That aside, a CCP–DPP negotiation to determine Taiwan's fate seems (so to speak) even more impossible. A CCP negotiation with a multiparty delegation (something else the communists have suggested) also seems a nonstarter. Equal negotiations would have to be on something like a state-to-state basis, and that has been ruled out. For the foreseeable future, the survival of Taiwan democracy is bound to the survival of the Taiwan state, while democracy in itself exacerbates the danger to the state.

Notes

1. Samuel P. Huntington, *Political Order in Changing Societies* (New Haven: Yale University Press, 1968).

2. Guillermo O'Donnell, "Delegative Democracy," *Journal of Democracy* 5 (January 1994): 55–59; O'Donnell, "Illusions About Consolidation," *Journal of Democracy* 7 (April 1996): 34–51.

3. Fareed Zakara, "The Rise of Illiberal Democracy," *Foreign Affairs* 76, no. 6 (November/December 1997): 22–43.

4. Joseph Schumpeter, *Capitalism, Socialism, and Democracy* (New York: Harper Collins, 1976).

5. In Japan and perhaps in other parliamentary regimes, the formulation of policy may lie more with the professional civil service than with the elected legislature. Nonetheless, the civil service is formally responsible to the legislature, as is the Cabinet.

6. Australia and some other democracies penalize those who fail to vote, but in practice this merely means that you have to show up at the polls, not that you are forced to choose one of the knaves nominated for office.

7. Many democratic theorists have a dim view of property rights, but others might argue these are considerably more "basic" than free speech. In modern democratic politics, property rights are generally subject to democratic contestation.

8. Michael Stainton, *Taiwanese Lambada: Revising the Constitution of the Republic of China* (Toronto: Joint Center for Asia Pacific Studies, 1993), p. 50.

9. For a lively and probably for the most part reliable analytical commentary on the pre-democratic system toward its end, see Sima Wenwu, *Quanli douchangshang di zhengzhi renwu* (Political figures in the arena of power struggle) (Taipei: Bashi niandai chubanshe, 1986). The regime's drift in the early 1980s, when illness sapped Chiang Ching-kuo's strength, showed the obvious limitations of this system, and this experience was one of the elements accounting for the later smooth transition to democracy.

10. Each man argued his case by means of a sympathetic journalist. Wang Lixing, *Wu Kui: Hau Bocun yü zhengzhi zhi lü* (No regrets: The political journey of Hau Pei-tsun) (Taipei, 1994); Zhou Yüguan, *Li Denghui: 1993* (Lee Teng-hui: 1993) (Taipei: Tianxia wenhua chubanshe, 1994).

11. Wang, *No Regrets*, p. xxi.

12. The case against presidentialism would seem to be strongest in countries with a multiparty system characterized by what Giovanni Sartori (*Parties and Party Systems* [Cambridge, UK: Cambridge University Press, 1976], pp. 145–71) calls polarized pluralism. This is not the case in the United States or, so far, on Taiwan— although Taiwan may be heading in that direction. On the other hand, it would seem that in France presidentialism forced the parties to form a fairly clear cleavage of two tendencies and to moderate the differences between the two tendencies.

13. For an elaboration of these themes, see *The Failure of Presidential Democracy*, Juan J. Linz and Arturo Valenzuela, eds. (Baltimore: Johns Hopkins University Press, 1994); *Parliamentary Versus Presidential Government*, ed. Arend Lijphart (Oxford, UK: Oxford University Press, 1990); Alfred Stepan and Cindy Skach, "Constitutional Frameworks and Democratic Consolidation: Parliamentarianism vs. Presidentialism," *World Politics* 46, no. 1 (October 1993): 1–22.

14. O'Donnell, "Delegative Democracy."

15. The constitutional issue was whether, once the legislature had appropriated funds for a project, the president could withhold those funds without legislative approval. A desire to thwart and embarrass Chen no doubt loomed large among the motives of many legislators, but that in itself does not erase the point of principle.

16. *Presidentialism and Democracy in Latin America*, ed. Scott Mainwaring and Matthew Shugart (Cambridge, UK: Cambridge University Press, 1997).

17. *Xin xinwen* (The journalist), January 6, 1996.

18. *Xin xinwen*, March 1, 1996.

19. *Zili wan bao*, November 28, 1997. J. Bruce Jacobs, *Local Politics in a Rural Chinese Setting: A Study of Mazu Township* (Canberra: Contemporary China Centre, Research School of Pacific Studies, 1980), reports the price in the 1960s at NT$100 (US$2.50, at the time). Both the U.S. dollar and the NT dollar were real money in the 1960s, compared with their value in the 1990s: in real terms, the price of a vote rose by rather less than the five- to six-fold implied by the figures given here.

20. The Tenth Credit scandal of 1984 was, however, perhaps a precursor of things to come. See Gregory W. Noble, *Collective Action in East Asia: How Ruling Parties Shape Industrial Policy* (Ithaca: Cornell University Press, 1998), pp. 86–87.

21. William L. Riordan, *Plunkitt of Tammany Hall: A Series of Very Plain Truths on Very Practical Politics* (Boston: Bedford Books of St. Martin's Press, 1994).

22. Chalmers Johnson, "Tanaka Kakuei, Structural Corruption, and the Advent of Machine Politics in Japan," *Journal of Japanese Studies* 12 (1986): 1–28.

23. Lucian W. Pye, "Money Politics and Transitions to Democracy in East Asia," *Asian Survey* 37, no. 3 (March 1997): 213–28.

24. Arthur Lerman, "National Elite and Local Politicians in Taiwan," *American Political Science Review* 71, no. 4 (December, 1977): 1406–22.

25. Sartori's comment on Anthony Downs's "economic theory" of democracy is germane here: It serves not as an example of how democracy comes about, but "how democracies inevitably deteriorate and end up performing as meanly as they do." Sartori, *Parties and Party Systems*, p. 324. Anthony Downs, *An Economic Theory of Democracy* (New York, 1957).

26. He Qinglian, *Xiandaihua di xianjing: Dangdai Zhongguo di jingji shehui wenti* (Pitfalls of modernization: Social and economic problems of contemporary China) (Peking: Jinri Zhongguo chubanshe, 1998).

27. Liu Bingyan, *People or Monsters and Other Stories and Reportage from China After Mao*, ed. Perry Link (Bloomington: Indiana University Press, 1983).

28. Thomas Gold, *State and Society in the Taiwan Miracle* (Armonk, NY: M.E. Sharpe, 1986).

29. Peter Evans, *Embedded Autonomy: States and Industrial Transformation* (Princeton: Princeton University Press, 1995); Chalmers Johnson, *MITI and the Japanese Miracle: The Growth of Industrial Policy, 1925–1974* (Stanford: Stanford University Press, 1982).

30. Shelley Rigger, *Politics in Taiwan: Voting for Democracy* (New York: Routledge, 1999).

31. This is Peter Duus's analysis of the aborted Japanese democratization of the 1920s. *Party Rivalry and Political Change in Taisho Japan* (Cambridge, MA: Harvard University Press, 1968).

32. Compare Dankwart Rustow, *A World of Nations: Problems of Political Modernization* (Washington, DC: Brookings Institution, 1967). The chapter by Hung-mao Tien and Yun-han Chu in *Contemporary China*, ed. David Shambaugh (Oxford, UK: Oxford University Press, 1998) argues that democracy was fostered by a consensus on national identity and an absence of outside interference. In the aftermath of the 2000 elections, there was less ground for optimism about each of these conditions.

33. Andrew Reynolds, *Electoral Systems and Democratization in Southern Africa* (Oxford, UK: Oxford University Press, 1999); S.N. Eisenstadt, *Paradoxes of Democracy: Fragility, Continuity, and Change* (Baltimore: Johns Hopkins University Press, 1999).

34. Chen Tzu-sung, "Taiwan Consciousness: The Invisible Hand that Rocks the Democratic Cradle," Ph.D. dissertation, University of Notre Dame, 1996.

35. For a journalistic survey of this cohort in earlier and happier days, see Yang Xusheng, ed., *Di er dai jieban ren* (The second generation successors) (Taipei, 1986). The appropriation of *jieban ren* in the sense of successor was a Cultural Revolution-era mainland neologism (the Red Guards were *geming jiebanren*, "revolutionary successors"), and its use on Taiwan as late as 1986 was still slightly provocative or daring.

36. Taiwan politics might come to resemble more those of Japan, particularly Japan after the breakup of the Liberal Democratic Party (LDP). During the late 1980s, in fact, some KMT reformers thought their own party ought to evolve along the lines of the LDP, in retrospect perhaps a not very inspired idea. Like that of the KMT at the turn of the century, the LDP's program amounted to little more than retaining its own power and privilege. One possible difference is that the LDP has at least a tenuous connection with the older Japanese tradition and Japanese patriotism, and Japan does not have ethnic lines of cleavage. In 1993, wracked by corruption and bedeviled by a sluggish national economy, the LDP broke up, the divisions slightly related to political opinion but more the result of personal and factional rivalries. These LDP fragments find it difficult to cohere among themselves. One might also guess (or, to keep within the bounds of political science respectability, hypothesize) that were the LDP rump to be frozen out of power for a considerable period of time, it, too, would tend toward further disintegration. In any case, at the turn of the century, a remnant of the LDP had been able to retain and somewhat hold onto control of the government by means of various highly unprincipled parliamentary alliances. A problem with making too close an analogy between Japan and Taiwan is that Japan's parliamentary system may give the LDP an incentive to cohere, an element that is possibly lacking on Taiwan.

37. *Renmin ribao* (overseas edition), March 16, 2000.

38. The moderate independence advocates argued that all independence really meant was democratization—making the government of Taiwan responsible to the people it governed. The more radical advocates sometimes treated democracy as a means to independence.

39. In a federal system, even a democratic one, there are restrictions on the democratic authority of the local units. In the United States, the federal government, as long as it acts within the scope of its constitutional authority, can impose policies on the people of a state that those people would not impose upon themselves.

40. The term is also at least psychologically related to the old concept of *zhengtong*,

the orthodox succession of dynasties: the judgment of which dynasties were legitimate and had the mandate of heaven and which were mere tyrannies and usurpations of power.

41. Prior to the reforms of the 1990s the National Assembly had no legislative powers and very little political influence. Its functions were to elect the president and to amend the constitution, something which was not done under the Chiangs. It can be considered a kind of permanent constitutional convention, and, as such, was a symbolic carrier of the *fatong*.

42. The early Bush administration, however, did continue on the trajectory of the earlier Clinton administration in extending the amount of respect accorded to Taiwan leaders as regular government officials. Thus, the Bush administration permitted Chen Shui-bian "stopovers" in the United States, and also allowed a quiet visit by ROC foreign minister Tien Hung-mao.

43. In the summer of 2000, President Chen seemed to assert not only that his less than 40 percent of the popular vote constituted a mandate from the people, but that his own election had somehow cancelled out any mandate represented by the legislative election of 1998, which the KMT had won (*China News Digest*, Global News G100–088, July 17, 2000). Later, however, Chen backed away from what he had implied.

44. The corruption of the democratic era, however, is different in kind from the equally ugly systemic corruption of the earlier period, when there was less pecuniary greed, perhaps, but when those in authority or their agents would use extralegal means to intimidate and even murder persons perceived as potential threats to their power, or even persons who, for whatever reason, simply displeased them.

45. Chen, "Taiwan Consciousness."

46. Thus, in 1992 Tang Shubei, then Peking's most visible spokesman on the Taiwan question, said: "Presently, Taiwan and the mainland have different understandings of the substantial connotation of 'one China'; however, both the KMT and the CCP leaders have stated their adherence to the one-China principle. This shows that the two sides have the minimum of a common language" (*Liaowang*, August 3, 1992). This suggests that the disagreement over the meaning of the term was between the two parties, the KMT and the CCP; and in this context it seems less a "consensus" than a way to avoid the issue in order to allow cooperation on less politically sensitive matters.

Part II

Lee Teng-hui's Political Leadership

3

Lee Teng-hui's Role in Taiwan's Democratization

A Preliminary Assessment

Ya-li Lu

Lee Teng-hui's term of office as president of the Republic of China (ROC) expired on May 20, 2000. On that day, he became the honorary chairman of the Institute of Combined Studies of National Policy, a well-funded think tank founded by Liu Tai-ying, the former czar of the vast business empire of the Kuomintang (KMT).[1] On January 14, 1988, Lee succeeded Chiang Ching-kuo as president, retiring after twelve years in office. During this period, he gradually accumulated vast powers and made himself a highly controversial figure.[2] His role in the recent development of Taiwan deserves intensive examination and evaluation, particularly his involvement in the democratization, a role for which he is proud of himself, and for which he has been called "Mr. Democracy."[3]

The object of this chapter is to examine Lee Teng-hui's role in Taiwan's democratization and to evaluate his achievements. Three sets of questions guide this inquiry. First, students of political leadership are usually divided into two groups. Some tend to emphasize the particular leader's ability to shape his environment and to utilize social forces to achieve systemic change. In analyzing democratization, their model assumes that the leader has a clear set of objectives, a well-formulated strategy, and adequate power to effect democratization. In the process, he may have to retreat a little, making some compromises with those who oppose him, but eventually he will achieve virtually all he sets out to achieve.[4] In contrast, others believe that environmental factors and social forces are more important than the will and wisdom of leaders in achieving systemic change. If the necessary environmental factors and social forces do not exist, even a leader with an iron will and superb political skill can accomplish nothing significant. To these students, leadership consists mainly of making correct and timely responses to the environment. There is a grain of truth in both views. A political leader certainly cannot create major systemic change if the environmental factors and social forces that favor such a change do not exist, but a successful leader is not passive, and genuine leadership means that the leader may, at critical moments, use the environmental factors and social forces in a skillful way to achieve his political objectives. One focus of this chapter is to examine Lee Teng-hui's leadership skill in Taiwan's democratization in light of the above observation.

The second question addressed in this chapter is popular opinion in Taiwan regarding Lee Teng-hui. Lee is arguably the most controversial figure in Taiwan's public life.[5] Some revere and worship him as the terminator of the hated KMT party-state and the precursor of an independent Taiwan yet to be created.[6] For these people, Lee's democratization is an unqualified success story, even a "miracle" of Taiwan, and, in the whole process, Lee has almost singlehandedly produced the miracle. In contrast to this version, some hold a diametrically opposite view of Lee's role as a political leader, regarding him as the man responsible for the destruction of the KMT and the troublemaker who unnecessarily provoked the People's Republic of China (PRC) and thus endangered Taiwan's future. For these people, the role that Lee plays in Taiwan's democratization is not only a rather limited one, but, by and large, a negative one. I believe that both of these views are more reflections of the ideological positions of their holders than of objective assessments of Lee's role. In this chapter, I shall examine critically these two versions of Lee's role in order to evaluate Lee's positive contributions and negative impact upon Taiwan's political system.

The third question of this chapter concerns the problem of the legacy of Lee Teng-hui, particularly the lasting impact of his political philosophy. The issue surfaced during the recent election. At the early stage of the campaign, Lee once urged the audience at a public rally to support the KMT candidate Lien Chan because Lien would follow the line of Lee Teng-hui when elected, but a few months later Lee denied that there was such a line. A few days prior to the polling day, Hsu Wen-long, a leading businessman in Kaohsiung and Lee's close friend, declared in a press conference that he endorsed the Democratic Progressive Party (DPP) candidate, Chen Shui-bian, because he believed that only Chen would follow the line of Lee Teng-hui. Whether the endorsement given to Chen by Hsu and some other businessmen and academics who were close friends of Lee at the critical moment of the campaign was decisive for Chen's victory is inconclusive; nevertheless, these events have given rise to a widespread rumor that, despite Lee's vigorous campaign for Lien, he shifted his support to Chen during the final days of the campaign in an attempt to prevent James Soong from winning the election. This rumor, though not substantiated by irrefutable facts, triggered a demonstration in front of the KMT headquarters when the result of the election was announced. The demonstrators, composed of Lien and Soong supporters, demanded Lee's resignation from his position as the KMT chairman. After some hesitation, Lee reluctantly resigned on March 24. To some people, the events mentioned above indicate one thing: namely, that the fight had already started between those who want to preserve the legacy of Lee Teng-hui and those who desire to get rid of it. Now, the two important questions are: Just what is this legacy or the elements that constitute it? And under what conditions can the legacy be preserved?

Lee's Political Leadership

Taiwan embarked on genuine democratization in 1986, when President Chiang Ching-kuo decided to lift both martial law and the ban on formation of political organizations that had been in existence since the early 1950s. Admittedly, Chiang made this momentous decision not out of conviction in the intrinsic superiority of the democratic system, but rather due to a shrewd calculation that in the face of growing discontent with the KMT party-state on the part of the emergent middle class as well as the international isolation of Taiwan after its expulsion from the United Nations in 1972, the decision was necessary to ensure the survival of the regime. Regardless of Chiang's motive, this decision was indeed a democratic breakthrough. Chiang started the process of democratization not only in lifting the martial law regime, but also in appointing a special commission to formulate a six-point program for political reform. In that program, the wholesale retirement of senior legislators on a definite date figured prominently.[7]

Upon the death of Chiang Ching-kuo, Lee Teng-hui became the president of the ROC. At the start of his rule, many people thought he would be a weak leader, or even a passing figure who would fill the power vacuum for a short period of time until the emergence of a strong leader. In retrospect, those holding this view made this mistake not only because they tended to put too much emphasis upon his alleged weaknesses, such as a lack of sufficient experience in high-level politics and administration, a lack of close ties with the mighty KMT party apparatus and the military, and his lackluster performance first as a provincial governor and then as the vice president under Chiang, but also because they ignored his strong points, such as his being a native Taiwanese, his deep understanding of the aspirations and expectations of ordinary Taiwanese and ability to manipulate these intangibles to his advantage, as well as his perseverance in the pursuit of power and political objectives.[8]

From 1988 to 1993, Lee was engaged in a series of power struggles with other KMT leaders, mostly mainlanders.[9] The power struggle involved not only Lee's power and prestige,[10] but also major policy issues. In terms of policy, the dispute between the "mainstream faction," which Lee led, and the "nonmainstream faction" concerned two specific issues: constitutional reform and the proper way to treat the Democratic Progressive Party. The "nonmainstream faction" did not object to constitutional reform in principle, but they believed that such reform should not affect the basic structure of the constitution and should not give the People's Republic of China the impression that Taiwan was to abandon the "one-China principle."

The first major dispute was about the electoral system for the choice of the president. Prior to the recent amendments, the Constitution of the ROC stipulated that the president should be elected by the National Assembly, whose members were elected by citizens mainly for this specific task. The DPP proposed to allow the citizens to directly elect the president. This change was regarded by the DPP as the first step to change the cabinet system of government required by the constitution to the presidential system desired by the DPP both for ideological and practical reasons.[11]

The "nonmainstream faction" proposed a complicated system to counter the DPP, which succeeded in winning the support of the majority for their proposal not only because it appeared to be more "democratic" than the existing system, but also because it was advanced at a time when the National Assembly was discredited for the self-seeking behavior of many of its members. According to the proposal of the "nonmainstream faction," the election of the president would be decided by a special National Assembly similar to the U.S. electoral college, which is elected by the citizens. The members of the National Assembly are required to cast their votes in accordance with the direction of the citizens who choose them. This system, according to the leaders of the "nonmainstream faction" has several advantages: The electoral campaign would be less intense, less unpredictable, and thus would not seriously destabilize the delicate political equilibrium. By including a few symbolic "mainland" representatives in the National Assembly, the PRC would be less alarmed by the separatist tendency in Taiwan that the popular election of the president might imply. Insofar as the new system indicated in this proposal would not essentially affect the people's right to elect the president, the "nonmainstream faction" demanded Lee's acceptance of it as the official proposal of the KMT. Lee did give his consent and the proposal was presented to the National Assembly, which was convened in 1991 for constitutional reform, as the KMT proposal. But a few days before the date scheduled for the enacting of the constitutional amendment, Lee suddenly announced that he was for the DPP proposal. Lee's change of position has been variously interpreted, which need not concern us here.[12] But such a Machiavellian tactic was typical of Lee Teng-hui. The dispute over the change of the method of election of the president was only the first major skirmish between Lee and his political rivals within the KMT. In the protracted warfare over the constitutional reform, Lee repeatedly employed the same strategy and tactics, but he won each battle and the final victory. The "nonmainstream faction" was eventually totally defeated.

Lee's strategy consisted mainly of three main components: first, to rally the support of public opinion and to use it adroitly to his own advantage; second, to forge an alliance between his own supporters in the KMT and the DPP by adopting the program of the DPP wholly or partially; and to use tactics flexibly to pursue fixed goals. I shall elaborate on this strategy after finishing my discussion of the dispute within the KMT over the treatment of the DPP.

The DPP charter contains an article, according to which the main task of the Party is to strive for the establishment of an independent Taiwan. Although the DPP has participated in the elections and taken part in both national and local legislatures since its founding, during the early phase of its existence, it showed in various ways that it did not fully recognize the legitimacy of the ROC.[13] The ideological stance of the DPP became a cause of contention with the KMT. The "nonmainstream" leaders believed that the application of legal sanctions on the DPP when its acts of defiance violated specific laws was not "undemocratic," but Lee Teng-hui ignored his political rivals' demands for law enforcement.[14] Lee's treatment of the DPP was based not only on his concern for social peace (e.g., the avoidance of street demonstrations organized by the DPP, which plagued Chiang Ching-kuo's last years), but also on his previously mentioned strategy.

From 1990 to 2000, Taiwan changed its constitution six times. Except for the most recent change, Lee was the mastermind in the whole process. The constitutional reform had one overriding objective: to augment the power of the president. On each of the occasions when the constitution was to be amended by the National Assembly, Lee was confronted with vehement opposition from his political rivals in the KMT, the intellectual community, and some media people. On each occasion, Lee was able to get what he wanted, though sometimes not immediately. The reason for this is twofold: On the one hand, as the chairman of the KMT, he controlled vast resources and patronage power, which he used to promote his loyal supporters, mostly KMT politicians at the local level, to national posts. The support of these people was the key to his success; on the other hand, his strategy was also an important factor of his success.

I shall select two cases to illustrate the use of the strategy: the enactment of the amendment stipulating direct election of the president by the citizens, and that requiring the downsizing of the provincial administration.

The method of electing president became an issue in 1990, but in the National Assembly meeting of 1991, only constitutional amendments concerned with the abrogation of the so-called Temporary Provisions Effective During the Period of Communist Rebellion, and the change of the formula for allocating of seats in the Legislative Yuan and National Assembly among the provinces and equivalent administrative units were passed. In 1990, Lee Teng-hui convened a National Affairs Conference, whose members included leaders of political parties, leading businessmen, academics, and the like. Nominally, the Conference was the forum where representatives from all walks of life could exchange views with the government, but in reality, this provided the two major parties, the KMT and the DPP, with the opportunity to negotiate and come to some agreements on matters of common concern. This arrangement suited

Lee Teng-hui's purpose not only because it excluded the "nonmainstream faction" (in that most participants were selected by Tsiang Yen-shih and James Soong, who was then one of Lee's most trusted aides, on the side of KMT and some DPP leaders), but because the agreements would appear to enjoy the support of the overwhelming majority of the society. In the Conference, the method of electing the president was duly discussed and the majority of the participants indicated that they supported the direct election method. The proposal for the change was not presented to the National Assembly the next year probably because, at that time, Lee still needed his new Premier Hau Pei-tsun's superb administrative talent in dealing with a host of problems, such as the serious crime situation, and therefore did not want to put their relationship to a severe test; furthermore, the matter was not urgent because there were still six years to go before the expiration of his term.[15] Even in 1990, Lee was aware that when the issue came up, public opinion would be on his side and the support of the DPP was assured. He had probably already made up his mind that when the time was appropriate, he would put the issue on the agenda and reach the conclusion he wanted. But during 1991 and early 1992, he usually told people that he was neutral on the issue, and even gave his consent to the nonmainstream proposal. Then, to the surprise of many, he suddenly announced his support for the DPP proposal (actually his own), when he thought the time was ripe.

This seeming change on Lee's part was followed by a long and bitter power struggle between Lee and Hau. The final decision reached by the National Assembly in 1992 was inconclusive, reflecting a compromise between Lee and Hau. The National Assembly passed a curious amendment, the gist of which was that the previous method of electing the president was abolished, but the new method would not be devised until one year prior to the next presidential election. This "sundown" legislation did not reduce the tension in the relationship between Lee and Hau, but the power struggle took a different turn: The verbal exchanges and debates in the KMT central committee meeting largely disappeared, but verbal assaults on Hau by the DPP legislators and even by some KMT members in the Legislative Yuan became frequent. Newspapers often contained articles and letters by anonymous readers alleging a variety of Hau's misdeeds, including the hatching of a plot to stage a coup against Lee. The power struggle between the two came to an end when Hau resigned after he was openly humiliated by some DPP members in the National Assembly, with the KMT members sitting in their seats showing silent approval. The constitutional amendment was duly enacted in 1994.

A second example of Lee's political strategy concerns the decision to freeze the provincial level of government. Prior to 1994, the governor of Taiwan Province was appointed, but in 1994 direct popular elections for the post were held for the first time. James Soong, the KMT candidate, was elected by a wide margin. Given the gradual erosion of the KMT's local base and the candidate's mainlander background, Soong's victory was largely a personal triumph. Due to his extraordinary diligence at work and his concern for the common people during his two-year service as an appointed governor, he was very popular and well liked. As an elected governor, Soong was regarded by many as the second most powerful man in Taiwan. His power and popularity aroused jealousy and fear. For a couple of years, the media in Taiwan became suddenly interested in the so-called Yeltsin effect. Imaginative people started to speculate on the possibility that the Taiwanese Yeltsin (James Soong) would menace the Taiwanese Gorbachev (Lee).

It was in this context that the KMT decided effectively to eliminate the provincial government. Some experts of administrative science and public administration suddenly discovered that for a small country like Taiwan, it is wasteful to have a three-tier government, and the key to the improvement of Taiwan's competitiveness in the world was to abolish or downsize the provincial government. The DPP was even more interested in abolishing the provincial level. For that party, the abolition of Taiwan Province had a symbolic meaning, namely, that Taiwan's status as a sovereign state could be confirmed in a forceful way by this act.

As both parties were in general agreement on the issue, another conference similar to the national affairs conference was needed, so the National Development Conference was convened in 1996, and the inevitable conclusion was duly reached.[16] In 1997, at the National Assembly meeting, the constitutional amendment stipulating the abolition of the system of popular election of the provincial governor and members of the provincial assembly was passed after an unusually long session of the Assembly.[17] In 1998, James Soong joined the ranks of the unemployed and the provincial assembly was disbanded. Quite a few assemblymen succeeded in filling the added seats in the enlarged Legislative Yuan after new elections were held in late 1998. Others were given sinecures either in the vast business empire of the KMT or in the many foundations set up by the government with public funds. The new governor was appointed by the president, and his power was quite limited, in that many functions of the provincial administration were switched to the center. A provincial Consultative Council was established and its members were appointed by the president. Although the Consultative Council has no specific function, its members receive the same emoluments as do members of the provincial assembly.

Divided Public Opinion Toward Lee Teng-hui

As mentioned previously, Lee Teng-hui's role in Taiwan's democratization has been evaluated very differently by different people in Taiwan. Those who worship him tend to believe that he almost singlehandedly produced the "Taiwan miracle," and whatever he did in the process of Taiwan's democratization must therefore be correct and morally justifiable. His opponents and critics are either politically naive fools or devilish conspirators bent on stealing from the Taiwanese people their right of self-rule in order to perpetuate the mainlanders' monopoly of power. This version of Lee's role usually downgraded Chiang Ching-kuo's contribution, and, in interpreting Chiang's motive, it inevitably asserts that he was motivated mainly by the desire to perpetuate the KMT rule and his own power; while in interpreting Lee, commitment to democratic values and selfless love for the land and people replace any power consideration, particularly the leader's own power and prestige.

Needless to say, this version is hardly objective, and can be easily refuted by historical facts. The important thing is not the version itself, but the large number of people who once held this view. Since Lee's retirement, the number of such people has been decreasing, but a sizable minority still hold it.[18]

A series of public opinion polls conducted by various agencies on Taiwan have tested the general public's approval ratings of political leaders. Lee Teng-hui's scores, as may be expected, have had their ups and downs over his long political career. But the score has never dipped below 60 percent, and has reached as high as slightly over 80 percent during the early years of his rule.[19] A reading of the polls may indicate that Lee was a popular leader who enjoyed the support of his people. This conclusion is generally correct. But a close analysis of the poll findings reveals a different picture.

If we classify the respondents according to their education, then we find that during the early years (roughly 1988–92), education does not make a significant difference in their approval of Lee's performance. Afterward, the polls show Lee enjoyed a much higher approval rating among the less well educated than among the college educated. If we classify them according to their age, then the polls show that Lee was very popular among the senior citizens, quite popular among the middle aged, but far less popular among young people, especially during the final years of his rule. If ethnicity is used as the criterion to classify the respondents, then we find that Lee Teng-hui enjoyed rather high popularity among Taiwanese of Fujian origin, moderately high popularity among Hakka speakers, and rather low popularity among mainlanders. Because Taiwanese of Fujian origin constitute the majority, accounting for slightly over 70 percent of the population, whereas Hakka speakers and mainlanders are almost equal in number, Lee's high popularity was quite natural in the ethnically divided society of Taiwan, where people tend to judge political matters according to their ethnicity.

Most mainlanders have usually held to a different version of Lee's role in Taiwan's democratization, that is, by and large a negative one. While this version does acknowledge that Lee's role during the early years of his rule was positive, it nevertheless maintains that during these years, Lee was simply carrying out his predecessor's plan. Once Lee was out of the shadow of Chiang Ching-kuo and had begun to implement his own ideas of democratization, his role became a negative one, because, on the one hand, the series of constitutional reforms produced an unsound system of government, and, on the other, his style of governance lowered the ethical standard of public service. This version, like the positive one mentioned above, is not objective, and cannot be fully substantiated by empirical data.

The fact that two diametrically opposed versions of Lee's role in Taiwan's democratization exist and are held by two different ethnic groups is indicative of the ethnic division of the society and Lee's controversial leadership. Lee Teng-hui is a national hero to many Taiwanese not only because he was the terminator of the KMT system, which is hated as much for being an "outsiders" regime as it is for being oppressive, but also because he had the guts to defy the mighty Chinese bullies. The venerated Taiwanese patriot is naturally infallible and beyond criticism. To many mainlanders, Lee's cardinal sin was his alleged disloyalty to Chiang Ching-kuo, who wanted him not only to democratize the political system but also to safeguard the integrity of the ROC. In spite of the fact that Lee asserted more than 100 times that he is not in favor of Taiwan independence, most mainlanders did not believe him. Additionally, many mainlanders thought that Lee had been trying to marginalize them politically by blocking politicians of mainlander origin from reaching top positions in the power pyramid.

It seems to me that these two popular versions of Lee Teng-hui's role in Taiwan's democratization are both one-sided and biased. A more objective and balanced view is needed. In my opinion, Lee did play a positive role in Taiwan's democratization during the early stage of his rule. His major contributions were as follows:

1. the termination of the old system, including the forced retirement of all members of the national legislative bodies elected on the mainland in 1946, and the abolition of the Temporary Provisions;
2. the extension of civil rights and liberties including the full restoration of rights for political dissidents and former political prisoners, the abolition of black lists that were used to ban designated political dissidents residing in foreign countries from entering Taiwan, and the revision of unnecessarily restrictive statutes, such as Article 10 of the Criminal Code, which imposed heavy penalties on those allegedly committing acts of "sedition," a term that was rather loosely defined;
3. the extension of the scope of political participation in the sense that certain appointed offices were changed into elected ones, such as governorship of Taiwan and mayoralty of the two municipalities, Taipei and Kaohsiung. The changed method of presidential election is also an improvement; and
4. the improvement of the relationship between the KMT and the DPP. Although Lee Teng-hui's policy toward the opposition was very controversial and may not have been appropriate on various grounds during the last stage of his rule, during the early years, it may have had a positive impact on Taiwan's democratization, because it made the party's alienated intellectuals and former political prisoners identify more with the system, strengthened the moderate elements in the party and reduced the influence of extremists, and induced the party to emphasize parliamentary methods of influence as opposed to street demonstrations.

After 1996, Lee's role in Taiwan's democratization became far less positive and some of his actions may have produced a rather negative impact. The foremost of these was constitutional reform. The series of constitutional reforms produced a system of government that most constitutional scholars in Taiwan consider either as unworkable in the long run,[20] or as granting the president too much power without making him accountable to the legislature.[21] The defects of the system of government established on the basis of the revised constitution have been fully revealed since Lee left office. A major defect is that the constitution gives the president the power to appoint the premier without the consent of the Legislative Yuan. President Chen Shui-bian, relying on this exclusive power, not only refused the demand of the KMT, the majority party in the Legislative Yuan, to form a coalition government, but also declined to consult the KMT leadership in the formation of the cabinet. This constitutionally legitimate exercise of power cost the administration dearly, due to the KMT-dominated Legislative Yuan's refusal to cooperate with the government. Another defect is that the constitution sets up a system with two chief executives without a clear demarcation of their power. The president receives his mandate from the people and has the exclusive power to appoint the premier, and thus legitimately considers himself the principal decision maker, yet he is not accountable to the Legislative Yuan, whereas the premier is the leader of the executive branch of the government and is accountable to the Legislative Yuan. In such a system, the policy differences between the president and the premier cannot be ironed out smoothly; and the premier, who is responsible for the implementation of policies, usually has a very difficult time when the policies of the president are not acceptable to the Legislative Yuan. The resignation of Tang Fei, the first premier of President Chen, after his open disagreement with the president concerning the issue of the termination of the construction of the fourth nuclear power plant illustrates vividly the premier's vulnerable position.[22]

The KMT and the administration under Lee Teng-hui have often been criticized for their deep involvement in the so-called black and gold politics.[23] Most KMT candidates for national legislative offices must spend a large amount of money to get elected. Once elected, with few exceptions, the KMT legislators usually become defenders either of their own business interests or those of their wealthy patrons. The unscrupulous ones even use their positions to extort special favors from government officials. At the local level, the quality of the KMT legislators is even worse. According to a former Minister of Justice, 40 percent of the legislators in the twenty-one county legislatures in the mid-1990s were either members of organized criminal gangs or associated with such elements. Although such a deplorable situation was not Lee Teng-hui's own doing, he worsened the situation in two ways: First, in his power struggle with his political rivals, he usually requested the support of the local politicians and tolerated their wrongdoings in return for their support; and second, among his close friends, there were many leading businessmen who usually used their connections with high-ranking government officials to obtain favors such as huge loans from public banks. "Crony capitalism" in Taiwan is certainly not on the same scale as that in Marcos's Philippines, but it has a negative impact on the professional ethics of government officials and thus makes them more susceptible to the pressure of legislators.

A related problem that tarnished Lee Teng-hui's reputation was widespread official corruption in his administration. The Yin Ching-fen case serves as an illustration.[24] Captain Yin Ching-fen, an officer in the ROC navy, was in charge of the procurement of military equipment. Seven years ago, he was murdered under mysterious circumstances. Investigation of the case led nowhere, and the case was eventually shelved after the arrest and imprisonment of a few middle-ranking officers. But many people suspected that high-ranking officers were involved. It seems that Yin, an honest man with personal integrity, was murdered because he attempted to reveal the misdeeds of his colleagues. After Chen Shuibian assumed office, public opinion demanded that the case be reopened for a genuine investigation; and the vigorous investigation in France of the corrupt practices of some high-ranking French officials in the sale of the Lafayette frigates to Taiwan added pressure on the new government. Although some people sounded the alarm that the thorough investigation of the case might "shake the foundation of the state," the new government was forced to take action. President Chen appointed a special task force under the supervision of the prosecutor-general. The investigation is still under way, but the results obtained so far seem to confirm the worst fears of the public. Not only was the procurement of the Lafayette frigates tainted with corruption, but corrupt practices occurred in nearly all arms deals from foreign sellers. It is estimated that the amount of money used for bribery and illegal commissions totaled more than US$200 million during Lee's twelve-year rule. So far, three admirals and several captains (some retired and some still in service) have been indicted for various offenses, although no one has been charged with the murder of Captain Yin.

During the twelve years of Lee Teng-hui's rule, the ethnic problem became quite serious. The mainlanders' resentment toward the regime and sense of alienation from the system increased, and the extremists among them even advocated that the best way to end the plight of the mainlander minority was to seek quick unification with China.

Many mainlanders dislike Lee for several reasons. First, they fear that Lee deliberately tried to marginalize them politically by torpedoing the careers of political leaders of mainlander origin, such as Hau Pei-tsun and James Soong. Second, they believe that Lee was a supporter of Taiwan independence, despite the fact that he asserted more than 100 times that he was not. Third, they believe that Lee admired Japanese culture and was contemptuous of Chinese culture. In this connection, they were especially upset by Lee's remarks, as reported in the media, to some Japanese visitors that Japan should resist China's demand for an apology for the Nanjing massacre, and for his invitation and warm reception of the right-wing Japanese politician Shintaro Ishihara, whose anti-Chinese views are well known.

As for the overall performance of Lee Teng-hui during his twelve-year rule, the people in Taiwan have rated it as moderately acceptable. A survey conducted by a public opinion survey firm, released on May 7, 2000, asked more than 1,000 respondents to evaluate Lee's performance on four items: democratic reform, maintenance of Taiwan's sovereignty, management of cross-strait relations, and handling of the issues of official corruption and money politics. Respondents were asked to score each item on a scale of zero to 100. Lee received an average score of 68 for his overall performance, 73 for his democratic reform, 71 for his maintenance of Taiwan's sovereignty, and 63 for his management of cross-strait relations, but only 48 for his handling of corruption.[25]

In conclusion, it seems correct to say that Lee's contributions to Taiwan's democratization are substantial and of enduring value, but some of his commissions and omissions have been detrimental to the consolidation of Taiwan's democracy. These negative results will continue to affect the situation unless repair work is quickly adopted.

Lee Teng-hui's Political Philosophy

Lee Teng-hui is much concerned with his legacy. On many occasions, he has expounded in some detail the global significance of Taiwan's democratization and his own role in it. Once, when interviewed by a Japanese journalist, he compared himself to Moses leading his people out of slavery under the tutelage of foreigners and waiting for his Joshua to guide them to the Promised Land.[26]

But what exactly is that legacy? Will this legacy survive to enrich and inspire future generations? We have mentioned Lee's contributions to, and negative impact on, Taiwan's democratization, so we shall refrain from any further discussion on that part of Lee's legacy. As far as busy political leaders go, Lee is a prolific writer on Taiwan's democratization and socioeconomic reforms. This final section will discuss his legacy in the area of ideas.[27]

Lee's major political writings include two books entitled, *Managing the Great Taiwan* (1995) and *The Claims Made by Taiwan* (1999). The first book was designed as his electoral program in his bid for the presidency in 1996 and is therefore of temporary interest. Here we shall devote our attention mainly to the second book and some of his short pieces of writing.

Lee Teng-hui believes that traditional Chinese culture is the product of a "feudal and authoritarian" society and has nothing worthy to offer to the modern world. He acknowledges that criticisms of that culture by Hu Shih, Lu Xun, and others are valid, but he regrets that all these leading intellectuals of modern China have succeeded only in identifying the problems of the Chinese, for example, a misplaced and totally unjustifiable sense of pride in their nation, and inflexibility in thoughts and actions, but have offered no solutions to them.

Lee asserts categorically that democratic values are developed in the West; therefore, the views of some Asian leaders, such as Lee Kuan Yew of Singapore, that an Asian model of democracy should be used to guide political development in Asia are criticized by Lee as nonsensical and designed to justify their own brand of authoritarian rule.

In Lee's view, Taiwan, in its evolution and development, has been fortunate in freeing itself from the pernicious influence of Chinese culture. Although the Taiwanese are mainly descendants of immigrants from China who settled on the island in different waves over the past several centuries, they have carved out their own distinct identity as a consequence of their exposure to foreign influences and their separation from the mainland. Lee Teng-hui does not declare, as do many other Taiwanese politicians and intellectuals, that Taiwanese are not Chinese. On the contrary, he states that, by blood and some other factors, Taiwanese and mainland Chinese are closely related. But he does insinuate the possibility and even the desirability of the evolution of Taiwan inhabitants into a new cultural entity.

Concerning Taiwan's democratization, Lee attributes its success to a variety of factors, such as the character of the Taiwanese people, the leadership, and so on.[28] To him, the meaning of democracy for Taiwan is not only that people should exercise their full right of political participation, but also that no outsider regime should be allowed to govern in Taiwan. The term "outsider regime" is not very clear. It may mean the Beijing regime or the KMT regime prior to 1988. The significance of Taiwan's democratization, according to Lee Teng-hui, is twofold: In the first place, the democratic system in Taiwan is the first of such systems ever established by ethnic Chinese during its 5,000 years of evolution, and thus Taiwan inhabitants may well be proud of it; and in the second place, this system may serve as the model for mainland China to emulate. During the early years of his rule, Lee stated that once the PRC became democratic, then the two sides across the Taiwan Strait could negotiate for unification. He also said that Taiwan should offer its model for the mainland to emulate and should assist the mainland in this effort.

But during his final years as president, he was less interested in the prospects of democratization on the mainland. Instead, he was more concerned with the mainland's threat to Taiwan's security interests. In his *The Claims Made by Taiwan*, he echoed a long-standing idea of the Japanese political right that China should be carved up into seven parts. He asserted that he made this suggestion not to harm China, but to help China, because in coming decades, the overcentralized China could well be ungovernable, and, from the viewpoint of management, a drastic decentralized scheme will be necessary. Lee Teng-hui believes that to deter China, Taiwan should do two things: First, it should form a kind of defense alliance with the United States and Japan (this concern was the subject of two long chapters in his book); and second, it should solve the ethnic problem in Taiwan. To do so, he advocates the idea of "new Taiwanese." He seems to think that assimilation is the best solution, and, in the Taiwan context, this means getting the mainlanders in Taiwan to fully identify with Taiwan. To achieve this objective, Lee believes that the content of school curriculum should emphasize Taiwan more and China less; Taiwanese dialect should be learned by all school children, just as Mandarin, and the history and geography of Taiwan should be intensively studied by students.

Conclusion

The present writer believes that whether Lee Teng-hui's legacy will survive and be honored by posterity will be decided not only by the intrinsic value of this legacy but also by the destiny of Taiwan. We shall say nothing more about the value of this legacy because we believe that readers are the best judges. As for the latter point, we think that if Taiwan maintains its separate identity, whether in perpetuating the status quo or in forming a new independent state, Lee's status will be high and his legacy will have a wide niche in Taiwan's history. But if Taiwan ever becomes part of China, whether democratic or not, Lee will not be honored and his legacy will not be treasured by the Chinese.[29]

Notes

1. The Institute is well known for its lobbying activities in Washington, D.C. With the assistance of the public relations firm, Cassidy and Associates, it succeeded in persuading the U.S. Congress to pressure the Clinton administration to permit Lee Teng-hui to visit the United States in 1995, which triggered a period of tension between the United States and mainland China.

2. See Chou Yang-shan, "The Helmsman of Taiwan's Populist Authoritarian System: An Assessment of the Ten Year Rule of Lee Teng-hui," in *Lee Teng-hui's Ten-Year Rule*, ed. Chou Yang-shan (in Chinese) (Taipei: Fengyun luntan chubanshe, 1998), pp.15–22 for a perceptive though slightly biased account of the process.

3. *Newsweek* (March 26, 1996) honored him with this title in 1996, after the popular election for president was held in Taiwan.

4. See Jean Blondel, *World Leaders* (London and Beverly Hills: Sage, 1980).

5. In Taiwan, the term "the emotional syndrome of Lee Teng-hui" has been coined to depict the phenomenon in which people of different backgrounds usually hold diametrically opposed views of Lee. These views are usually based on intense feelings of love and hatred, not reason. The existence of the syndrome is not exclusively caused by the nature of Lee's rule, but reflects the life situation of Taiwan and the different groups in this society.

6. See Antonio Chiang "Let History Be the Judge," *Time* (March 27, 2000). Antonio Chiang is a well-known journalist in Taiwan. His admiration of Lee Teng-hui is typical of some Taiwanese intellectuals.

7. For the role of Chiang, see Steve Tsang, "Chiang Ching-kuo, the Nature of the Kuomintang and the Democratic Breakthrough in Taiwan," paper presented at the International Conference on the Transformation of an Authoritarian Regime: Taiwan in the Post-Martial Law Era, Taiwan, Academia Sinica, April 1–3, 1999.

8. For a detailed analysis of Lee's early years of rule, see Lin Chia-lung, *Path to Democracy: Taiwan in Comparative Perspective*, Ph.D. dissertation, Yale University (1998), especially ch. 9.

9. The first round of the power struggles was about the choice of the KMT chairmanship. Some KMT leaders wanted to select Mme. Chiang Kai-shek to this

KMT post, but their wish was frustrated eventually. The second round was about Lee's choice of his vice president; on that occasion, Chiang Wei-kuo, Chiang Ching-kuo's younger brother, became the main rival of Lee Teng-hui. These two rounds of power struggles have nothing to do with issues, and the people, including many mainlanders, did not support Lee's rivals. The third round of the power struggles was between Lee and Hau. This event caused the ethnic split to occur. In 1993, many KMT politicians of mainlander background left the party to form the New Party.

10. At the start of his rule, Lee was a weak leader, but even then, he was doing his best to protect his position. In public ceremonies and daily routines, he insisted that people should show the same degree of deference to him as they did to Chiang. As an example of his general attitude, in the KMT conference in 1990 to confirm his candidacy for the presidency, he insisted that delegates should confirm his candidacy by ovation (the traditional way) instead of by voting (the new method demanded by some delegates).

11. The DPP believed that direct election of the president by the people of Taiwan was the best way to show that Taiwan is a sovereign state, and may effectively refute the Chinese claim that Taiwan is part of China. Additionally, the DPP believed that it would be much easier for the Party to become the governing party in a presidential system.

12. Lee's sudden change did embarrass some of his staunch supporters and defenders in the KMT. As Lee used the change of public opinion as his excuse, one of his aides told the public that public opinion flows like running water.

13. For example, the DPP legislators and other elected officers usually refused to take the oath upon assuming office, because the oath bears the name "the Republic of China."

14. During the final stage of Chiang Ching-kuo's rule and the early years of Lee Teng-hui's presidency, the DPP usually deliberately violated specific laws and regulations as a way to challenge the legitimacy of these laws and regulations.

15. Lee was elected by the National Assembly for a six-year term in 1990.

16. As a participant in both of these conferences, the present writer believes that they were only prearranged shows. The National Development Conference had an agenda filled with items concerning cross-strait relations, party system, subcounty level election, and so forth, but aside from the issue of downsizing the provincial administration, all other items were placed on the agenda for propaganda.

17. In that session, assemblymen closely related to Soong did their best to frustrate Lee's wishes. Because Lee was not sure that he could secure enough votes to win, he had to rely on both " the carrot and the stick." According to the media, pro–Soong assemblymen were put under strong pressure to change their minds, including having their phones tapped and their tax returns audited.

18. Lee's tolerance of corruption and warm friendship with local politicians and business tycoons of tarnished reputation as well as his luxurious lifestyle cost him some potential admirers among intellectuals. His refusal to change the policy that said "go slow, be patient" and his rejection of the "three links" with the mainland cost him the support of many businessmen. Now his loyal admirers and supporters are mainly senior citizens of the rural communities in the southern part of Taiwan.

19. Chiang Ching-kuo remains the most well-liked leader in Taiwan. According to several polls, Chiang Ching-kuo was popular among almost all people, regardless of education, age, or ethnic affiliation. See *Lianhe bao*, May 20,1998.

20. The present system is, according to its designers, a "dual-executive" system (similar to the semi-presidential system of France) in which the president and the premier share power. Because only the premier is accountable to the Legislative Yuan, the president may make decisions without being accountable to anyone. It is probably for this reason that one scholar calls it the system designed to allow the president "to fish in troubled waters."

21. The constitution grants the president power to appoint grand justices members of the Examination Yuan with the consent of the politically unsophisticated Assembly (this may change now). He may appoint the premier without the consent of the legislature. In addition, the constitution stipulates the establishment of the National Security Council and the National Security Bureau under the president to assist the president in safeguarding national security. This hybrid system combining elements of the French, British, and American systems is unworkable in the long run and, furthermore, it creates a super-president, according to many constitutional scholars in Taiwan.

22. The new premier assumed office in October 2000. He is a DPP member, and, as such, the policy differences between the president and the premier may be minimized, but he was nevertheless even less likely to get full legislative support.

23. Lai La-kuan, a New Party legislator, has amassed a large quantity of data on this problem. See his "An Examination of the Abuse of Power of the Judiciary and the Problem of Black-Gold Politics" in *Lee Teng-hui's Ten-Year Rule*, ed. Chou Yang-shan, pp. 108–28.

24. My narration of the case is based on my reading of extensive coverage in *Lianhe bao* in early September 2000, when the investigation was being actively pursued. After this period, the investigation seems to have slowed down, particularly after President Chen announced that the possible involvement in the investigation of the military and political figures should be separated.

25. The survey was conducted by the San Shui Public Opinion Survey Firm, from May 2 to May 4, 2000, and 1,020 adults (over the age of twenty) responded. See *Lianhe bao*, May 8, 2000, p. 4.

26. The interview was probably given in late April or early May of 1994. The Japanese journalist's report was published in *Asahi shimbun* on May 6,1994. A transcript of the conversation between Lee and the Japanese visitor was published in the *Independence Evening Tribune* (April 28, 29, and 30, 1994). In this interview, Lee says that "the term 'China' is ambiguous"; "Taiwan must belong to the Taiwanese"; "All the regimes that ruled Taiwan before mine are outsider regimes"; and "Even the KMT regime is an outsider regime. When I recall the February 28 incident in which many Taiwanese were massacred, the 'exodus' is the inevitable conclusion." This interview fundamentally changed the basic attitude of mainland China toward Lee and Taiwan.

27. According to the Chinese tradition, a man may seek immortality through virtue, deed, and word. The first category includes religious leaders and saints, the second political or military leaders, and the third philosophers, scientists, and scholars. Lee is often proud of himself for his scholarship and ideas.

28. In his book, he rated the character of the Taiwanese very highly, particularly in comparison with the Chinese. Concerning leadership, he stated that leaders in a democracy should not make their policies solely to please the people or to win the next election but on the basis of long-term national interests.

29. Lee will not be honored by the Chinese in a unified China mainly because he will most probably be regarded by most Chinese as a man who does not support the cause of Chinese nationalism and is contemptuous of Chinese culture. This view might be a biased one, but due to the successful propaganda of Beijing to denigrate Lee, it will persist.

4

Consolidating Democracy in the Republic of China on Taiwan, 1996–2000

Ramon H. Myers, Linda Chao, and Tai-chun Kuo

The March 1996 election gave Lee Teng-hui and his running mate, Lien Chan, 54 percent of the votes in a three-way race, affirming the popularity of Lee with voters and the hopes they had placed in the first elected president in Chinese history.

Four years later, Lien Chan, the Kuomintang (KMT) presidential nominee, suffered a crushing defeat, receiving only 23 percent of the popular vote. The people had finally rejected the KMT's fifty-five-year rule in Taiwan, and, more important, the governing style of President Lee. So galling to KMT members was their defeat that a majority of party cadres and members turned on their chairman, President Lee, demanding he give up the party chairmanship, which he reluctantly did on Friday, March 24, 2000.

As vice president under President Chiang Ching-kuo, Lee Teng-hui had learned how to manage the reins of government. After President Chiang died on January 13, 1988, Lee consolidated the reins of power, first assuming the role of the KMT chairmanship and then removing those in the party and government who opposed his policies. To promote Taiwan's democracy, he:

- Legitimated the Democratic Progressive Party (DPP) as an opposition party
- Established an election process for a new National Assembly and Parliament (Legislative Yuan)

- Reformed the ROC Constitution to establish rules for directly electing a president and vice president, and
- Initiated a government apology to the victims of the February 28, 1947, tragedy and compensated them.

Lee's political changes brought native Taiwanese politicians into the KMT leadership, bringing a new generation of political leaders to power.

When President Lee was inaugurated as the first elected president on May 20, 1996, a majority of citizens supported him, even after the People's Liberation Army held war games across the Taiwan Strait to intimidate Taiwan's people and influence their votes. Voted for by more than half of the electorate and in charge of the powerful, wealthy ruling party, President Lee was now positioned to deepen democratic behavior by consolidating Taiwan's democracy. Did he accomplish that?

Political scientist Larry Diamond reminds us that, for democracy to be consolidated, "electoral democracy must become deeper and more liberal."[1] That is to say, government must be accountable for its performance, law abiding, decentralized, and responsive to the demands of society. Exemplary leadership articulates goals that broadly reflect the people's interests. By building a broad consensus for his goals, the democratically elected leader can implement policies that lead, promote democratic behavior, and consolidate democracy.

After being elected in 1996, President Lee failed to build such a consensus. Instead, he used autocratic means to initiate his policies, thus aggravating the other political parties, particularly the New Party, and dividing his party, the Kuomintang. These developments helped fragment Taiwan's polity after Lee's party lost the March 2000 election, making it impossible for President Chen Shui-bian's administration, which did not control the parliament, to govern by coalition politics.

Second, he consolidated power in the Office of the President and managed state and foreign policies without consulting his ministers and experts. As a consequence, relations between Taiwan and mainland China soured during the Lee administration, making President Chen Shui-bian's task of managing cross-strait relations more difficult.

Third, President Lee's reform of the constitution did not have broad support. His strong-arm methods consolidated the power of the executive branch, weakened government accountability, and left Taiwan's politicians unprepared to govern through coalition politics.

Moreover, President Lee did little to stamp out "money politics" or reform the police system to contain rising crime, thus ignoring the people's demands for "clean" government. (Former President Chiang Ching-kuo had used the Office of the President to limit these poisonous developments in Taiwan's political life.)

These examples, documented below, reveal a pattern of hubris, flawed presidential judgment, and irresponsible political behavior. They illustrate an important lesson: The leaders of young democracies must set a good example of democratic leadership if political life is to be democratized.

The National Development Conference

President Lee achieved one political triumph when he held the National Affairs Conference in June–July 1990.[2] To engineer the conference, Lee sent his brilliant KMT political "middleman," Y.S. Tsiang, to encourage key Democratic Progressive Party leaders to participate in a conference that would review and discuss the major challenges confronting the Republic of China (ROC). Tsiang met publicly with top DPP leader Huang Hsin-chie and included DPP leaders on a committee to design the conference. Despite the suspicions of many KMT members that it was a waste of time, the conference removed some of the chill between the parties, in effect, legitimating the DPP in political life. President Lee achieved this breakthrough by relying on skillful political middlemen and allowing different views to be discussed. By creating an atmosphere of tolerance and bringing the best politicians together to support reform, President Lee greatly advanced Taiwan's democratization.

Six years later, in his May 20, 1996, inaugural speech, President Lee stated that he intended to hold another national affairs conference—the National Development Conference—and to that end he instructed the Office of the President to begin to plan for it. The preparatory committee held meetings, including those of the three leading parties—the New Party, KMT, and DPP—with political leaders and elites throughout Taiwan and developed an agenda for the National Development Conference, which met December 23–28, 1996.

At a high-level KMT meeting on December 16, participants were informed that Taiwan should become an "improved, mixed polity." President Lee wanted the premier to be appointed without the approval of the Legislative Yuan (although it could veto the premier's selection by a two-thirds no-confidence vote) and to be able to dissolve the Legislative Yuan.[3] More important, the group agreed to abolish Taiwan's provincial government.[4] After agreeing to this new reform agenda, the KMT quickly sought and obtained DPP support before the National Development Conference began. When the New Party learned of this meeting, to which it had not been invited, its members were outraged. The day before the conference ended, the New Party walked out in protest.

The KMT and DPP, however, agreed on the above-mentioned political reforms: the president could appoint a premier without Legislative Yuan approval and under certain conditions dissolve that body. The premier could ask the president to dissolve the Legislative Yuan, and the Legislative Yuan could pass a no-confidence vote and thus replace the premier. (The issue of freezing the provincial government and assembly elections was to be further studied by the National Assembly.)

What began as broad consensus-style politics now became a bitter political struggle. Governor Soong learned through the press that the provincial government was to be downsized, souring an important personal political relationship in the Kuomintang and marking the beginning of a growing split in the party.[5] Soong suspected that the president wanted to marginalize him; his comments to the media revealed that a power struggle was under way. Some in the KMT were also unhappy that their party had agreed with the DPP to abolish the provincial government. Many criticized the president for his authoritarian behavior.

On July 16, 1997, an intense struggle took place in the National Assembly over the proposal to eliminate the Taiwan provincial government.[6] The president and members of his government organized a strong lobbying effort to support the measure; the head of the Executive Yuan telephoned assembly opponents urging them to approve the measure. Rumors circulated that opponents of the measure had been threatened with government tax audits.[7] Assemblyman Yang Rongming complained that officials had pressured his father to persuade him to support the measure and burst into tears when he revealed that his daughter-in-law had called him, cursing and threatening that "you will never see our family again if you do not vote correctly."[8] In response to these public charges of coercion and "dirty tricks," James Soong denounced the government's "white terror," a term that described government repression in the early years of martial law.[9]

The strong-armed methods President Lee used in the National Development Conference and the National Assembly had not been in evidence during his presidency of 1988–1995. In those years the president had allowed consensus to crystallize, encouraging open discussions and different points of view.

In 1996–97, however, President Lee used his office to abolish the provincial administration and concentrate power in the presidency by limiting parliament's confirmation of his premier. Many politicians and elites resented the president's coercive methods. According to one public opinion survey, most issues agreed on at the National Development Conference were not supported by scholars of political science, public administration, economics, and law.[10] Even the long-standing discipline within the KMT began to erode as signs of a pending party split became evident. During this critical democratic transition, elite and popular resentment, cynicism, and frustration were growing.

The Management of Cross–Taiwan-Strait Relations

In 1979 the People's Republic of China (PRC) proposed to the ROC a "one country, two systems" arrangement. The ROC regime, however, never countered with a federation formula of its own; thus we will never know if Chiang Ching-kuo's administration would have offered a different federation formula. But in the 1980s, both sides did begin to bargain and reach agreements.

For example, in 1981 the PRC had established stations in its southeast provinces to provide refuge for PRC and ROC fishing boats and their crews.[11] In March 1981 the regimes agreed on a formula that would enable both governments to send athletes to the Olympics. In 1985 both regimes agreed to a formula by which the PRC was able to enter the Asian Development Bank without the removal of the ROC. In May 1986, when an ROC China Airlines plane was hijacked to the PRC, both sides were able to negotiate a resolution in Hong Kong. (The plane eventually was returned to Taipei.) Finally, in 1987 the ROC government allowed retired ROC military personnel to visit the mainland to see their relatives and also allowed retired PRC military personnel to visit their relatives in Taiwan. Meanwhile, trade and investment in mainland China by Taiwanese business firms increased by leaps and bounds. These developments not only culminated in a détente, reached at Singapore in April 1993, but initiated discussions within the ROC government about how to react to the PRC federation formula.

The unforeseen death of President Chiang Ching-kuo in 1988, however, gave President Lee the opportunity to manage cross–Taiwan Strait relations. Would he follow the path of his predecessor or manage them very differently?[12]

President Lee began by establishing a National Unification Council (NUC) on September 21, 1990, which he personally chaired. In early 1991 the NUC agreed to a three-stage blueprint for China's unification, which, instead of countering the PRC's 1979 federation offer, set forth conditions that the PRC had to adopt before serious political discussions of the sovereignty issue could take place. First, the PRC had to renounce the use of force before direct contacts through shipping, telecommunications, and air transport could take place. Then the Chinese Communist Party had to democratize mainland China, establish a capitalist market economy, and make China prosperous. These conditions seemed reasonable in early 1991 because the two societies were so very different. Predictably, the PRC ignored these conditions but continued to make overtures to the ROC regime. Some progress had been achieved by 1994, but in the summer, fall, and spring of 1995–96, the PRC conducted a series of war games, hoping to convince Taiwan's people not to vote for Lee Teng-hui. Taiwan's voters were not persuaded and went ahead and elected Lee Teng-hui and Lien Chan.

In his May 10, 1996, inauguration speech, President Lee blamed the PRC for not recognizing the ROC as a separate nation-state and for orchestrating a campaign to damage his reputation.[13] He also scolded Beijing's leaders for conducting war games but promised a dialogue with them, rejected the road of Taiwan independence, and called for both sides "to terminate the state of hostility between them, which will then make a crucial contribution to the historic task of unification." He expressed his desire to "meet with the top leadership of the Chinese Communists for a direct exchange of views in order to open up a new era of communication and cooperation between the two sides." In effect, President Lee launched a peace offensive of his own.

In August 1996, at a high-level meeting in the Office of the President, President Lee stated that "the ROC's policy must be rooted in Taiwan, and, in order to take off, there must be a sense of 'go slow, be patient'" (*jieji yongren*) so that "the ROC can gradually, unswervingly achieve China's unification."[14] President Lee publicly introduced this new policy in September 1996, and the government began monitoring business investments and disallowing those that exceeded US$50 million. Although many Taiwan business tycoons complained, the Lee administration remained firm.

The Lee administration's new China policy tried to limit the flow of Taiwan investments to mainland China, avoided negotiating with Beijing, and tried to expand diplomatic ties with other nations as well as seeking entry into the United Nations every year. But Lee's policy was not based on consultations within and outside the government. Although the president had persuaded the three major political parties at the December 1996 National Development Conference to agree that the ROC was already an independent state and that negotiations with the PRC should be conducted according to the principles of Taipei's two previous white papers and the NUC guidelines, his policies of restricting Taiwan business investment in the mainland and spending huge sums of money to expand diplomatic ties and enter the United Nations were not based on a consensus within government and elite circles.

Although both Chinese regimes continued to communicate through their nonstate agencies, which had been established at the 1993 Singapore détente, no forward momentum took place. Moreover, the ROC initiated no commonwealth or federation proposal. The second round of Wang-Koo talks took place in October 1998, but it did not produce any results except that both sides agreed to continue to meet. Beijing's leaders patiently waited for Taiwan to discuss their "one country, two systems" formula, but the Lee administration's preconditions made it impossible to have serious political discussions.

Then on July 9, 1999, President Lee informed Deutsche Welle radio in Germany that constitutional reform in Taiwan had created a new "state-to-state relationship" between the two sides, "neither one of a legitimate government to a renegade group nor between a central government and a local government."[15] President Lee's statement angered Beijing, and cross-Strait relations worsened.

President Lee followed up his July 9 broadside to Beijing with an article in *Foreign Affairs* in late 1999 arguing that Taiwan now had a new national identity.[16] He referred to the people of the ROC as "new Taiwanese" and accused Beijing of "regard[ing] Taiwan as a renegade province," a cliché never uttered in Beijing but instead coined by American journalists. President Lee also said that, for Taiwan to negotiate with mainland China, Beijing had to overcome Taiwan's people's fear of the PRC regime; it must renounce the use of force to solve the "Taiwan Strait issue" (not the divided China problem that originated in the Chinese civil war); and, finally, Beijing must initiate a democratic transition before the ROC regime would consider reunification. Again the

Executive Yuan, Legislative Yuan, and National Assembly were not consulted about the president's China policy.[17]

After President Lee's July 9, 1999, declaration that Taiwan would deal with the PRC only on a state-to-state basis instead of a negotiated basis, Beijing took no provocative action. Beijing's leaders, hoping a new president would be willing to negotiate, decided to wait for the election. Yet Beijing's leaders made it clear they were not going to wait another decade, as the PRC's second white paper, issued on February 20, 2000, made very clear.

By avoiding political talks with Beijing's leaders, President Lee had placed the Taiwan people in great peril. Without consulting his administration experts, he managed Taiwan's China policy without telling Taiwan's people of the high risks involved. President Chen Shui-bian was left with the task of coping with a PRC leadership that has grown increasingly distrustful and frustrated.

Political Corruption

The March 18, 2000, elections showed that elections mattered and that the people of Taiwan had generally complied with the election rules. Taiwan had already experienced a half-century of elections, which were held roughly every three years and in which councils and leaders were elected from the village level to the provincial government.[18] Electing central government leaders on a small quota basis began in 1968, whereas the National Assembly still elected the nation's leaders every six years. Not until September 21, 1991, did Taiwan's citizens finally elect a new National Assembly; on March 21, 1996, they finally elected a president and vice president.

But in Taiwan's local elections, local factions influenced election outcomes and the behavior of elected politicians. Those local factions, based on lineage or other forms of power, originated from local elites and their supporters, who bonded together according to their local cultural custom, beliefs, and strong family-friendship ties. Once elected, local leaders dispensed political and economic favors to their constituents, especially the factions. In this gift-giving Chinese society, favors received are reciprocated by favors given. Local factions established boundaries and tried to place their supporters in village councils as well as in the leadership and council positions held at the township, city, and county and district levels to return favors for the groups they represented. But to do that, factions first had to mobilize support for their candidates through gifts, typically money or commodities. As prosperity increased, first under Japanese colonial rule and later under the KMT-led government, local factional representatives became heads of granaries, irrigation societies, credit associations, and so forth as well as members of political councils. Factional representatives thus supported their own through laws and approving expenditures for improving education, building roads, bridges, irrigation projects, and so on.[19]

As Taiwan's wealth rapidly increased in the 1980s and 1990s, a construction boom rippled across the island. Construction companies contributed large sums to local council members and members of the Legislative Yuan, who, in turn, approved public-works projects. Having inside information about the bidding for such projects, these elected politicians could repay their business patrons by passing it on and receive additional fees. Financial trust companies also bribed Legislative Yuan members.

Using business proceeds to obtain political favors accelerated in the 1980s, especially after President Chiang Ching-kuo's death in January 1988. Under President Chiang, the state government and provincial bureaucracy did not tolerate political corruption, quickly punishing any parties involved in such behavior. His officials were reluctant to associate with leading businesspeople. But by the mid-1990s, laxness in government had become pervasive. President Lee's burgeoning friendships with leading business tycoons set a new standard for political personal relations throughout the island.

As elections broadened after 1990, the scale of vote buying increased, as did the price for bribing voters. Many KMT members believed they had to engage in vote buying with local political factions to win elections. Furthermore, the Lee administration was lax in disciplining its candidates who had reportedly engaged in corrupt election behavior. The public perception that KMT corruption had worsened was pervasive in the March 2000 presidential election.

As political corruption increased, so did the incidence of violent crimes such as rape, murder, and kidnapping. Criminal elements were able to organize their activities in Taiwan's densely populated cities. The new Mafia-type organizations were called *heidao* (those engaging in illegal and deviant behavior), and they used their illegal income to bribe politicians, thus giving rise to the term *heijin*, or "black gold." Therefore, it was no surprise to many when, in 1995, Minister of the Interior Wu Pohsiung published a list of elected district leaders and city councils showing that, of the 858 in office, 233 had been charged with engaging in illegal activities.[20] Of that sample, some 300, or 34 percent, had been involved in law-breaking activities. Many also charged that criminal elements had infiltrated the city councils and the Legislative Yuan.

By 1998 some companies were beginning to relocate to the mainland because of threats by *heidao* elements.[21] Because *heidao* elements had fixed bidding prices, companies also found it difficult to bid for land. On March 9, 1998, the minister of justice, Liao Chenghao, stated that "the *heidao* are so entwined in politics that such activity is rare to see in the world; this development can ultimately shake the foundations of our country."[22] Minister Liao urged people not to vote for any politician who might have connections with the *heidao* but conceded that his office was having difficulty bringing indictments against the *heidao* because they could bribe judges and officials.[23]

The *heidao* also tried to influence elections by printing "black letter" cards (*heihan*) about candidates they opposed in order to smear their reputations.[24] The *heidao* also bribed and threatened city wardens (*lizhang*) and small city wardens (*bangjiao*). In the past six years, according to one report, there were 780 cases of criminal activity involving 8,000 people, of whom 800 were actually prosecuted and brought to justice.[25] (Of those prosecuted, only 250 were convicted and fined and/or imprisoned.)

Furthermore, some *heidao* offered bribes to win seats in the Legislative Yuan. These *heidao* legislators used every conceivable means to influence the Legislative Yuan's Judicial Committee's policies regarding police affairs. They also manipulated their way onto the Financial and Monetary Committee. These developments, referred to as "black and gold politics," added to the growing resentment of the Lee administration.

It was the random killings in late 1996 and early 1997, however, which may or may not have been linked to *heidao*, that finally spurred the public to action.[26] First, the magistrate of the Taoyuan District, Liu Bangyu, was mysteriously murdered. The DPP's Director of the Women's Affairs Department, was raped and murdered in Kaohsiung City. Finally, the daughter of the actress Bai Baibing, Bai Xiaoyan, was raped and murdered. In the first two cases, the police were unable to find any suspects.

Thus, on May 4, 1997, a huge throng of people paraded in Taipei protesting the government's failure to provide law and order. Many carried banners demanding "the freedom of being free of fear."[27] The press denounced the president and his administration for being unable to provide security. On May 18, another rally was held in front of the Office of the President, during which a laser was used to imprint on the spire of the Office of the President the Chinese characters *ren cuo*, "admit your mistakes."[28] Five hundred social groups were represented in this rally, as well as the five top political parties. On May 24, in another great rally, throngs stood and sat along the grand boulevard leading up to the Office of the President; many lit candles and stayed the night.[29]

President Lee responded by publicly apologizing to the nation, promising that he and his administration would take steps to rectify the situation. Newspaper polls showed that the approval ratings for President Lee, which had stood around 75 percent after his election, had declined to 50 percent and that Vice President Lien Chan's rating had dropped to 30 percent.[30] On May 9 the government's minister of justice, Ma Ying-jeou, even resigned, giving this reason:

> After serving in government for sixteen years, I regret that the political atmosphere has so changed before reforms could take place. The use of power for personal gain and the competition for achieving only to conceal mistakes have only produced political resistance to reform. Our people have accumulated so much resentment, and so many major problems have now emerged in our nation. For these reasons the people have taken to the streets to demonstrate. As a member of this Cabinet, I only can feel pain and helplessness. For these reasons, I am resigning.[31]

Meanwhile, newspaper editorials continually criticized the president and his administration.

Reforming the Constitution

Between March 1991 and July 1997 the National Assembly revised the 1947 constitution four times. In the spring of 1991, the National Assembly agreed that it would be elected only by the people of Taiwan and members of the overseas Chinese community. In March–April 1992, the new National Assembly codified the new election rules. In 1994 the National Assembly agreed on direct elections of a president (four-year term) and vice president, who would serve no more than two terms. Finally, in May–July 1997 the members of the National Assembly agreed to abolish the Taiwan provincial governor and government, strengthening the power of the president and weakening the powers of the Legislative Yuan.

The National Assembly meeting held May 5–July 19, 1997, was especially significant because it strengthened the presidency at the expense of parliament and other branches of government. The KMT, under Lee Teng-hui, and the DPP, under Hsu Hsin-liang, combined to push to eliminate the Taiwan Provincial Government and give the president broad new powers. Were these rule changes good for Taiwan's democracy? Many elites strongly criticized the changes. By abolishing the Provincial Government, however, the Lee administration argued that the ROC was already an independent state. Eliminating some checks and balances in the old constitution enhanced the power of the Office of the President, as seen in the following examples.

First, the National Assembly's reforms reduced the power of the Control Yuan. The 1947 constitution enabled the Control Yuan to approve or disapprove the nomination of fifteen Grand Justices.[32] The new rules (set forth in Articles 5 and 6) allowed the president to nominate and appoint these officials subject *only* to the approval of the National Assembly. As long as the president had a majority in the National Assembly, he could select those officials he, not the Control Yuan, wanted. The new Article 7, which abolished old Articles 91 and 93, empowered the president to nominate and appoint, subject to the consent of the National Assembly, the twenty-nine members of the Control Yuan.[33] The president thus reduced the number of Control Yuan officials, limited their terms of service, and, more important, dominated the nomination.

Second, the 1947 constitution had created a cabinet-centered government in which the president nominated a premier who in turn was confirmed or rejected by the Legislative Yuan. The new Articles 2 and 3, approved by the spring 1997 National Assembly, created a president-centered government.[34] Article 2 gave the president broad powers to issue emergency orders, checked only by the Legislative Yuan's power to ratify or reject those presidential decrees within a ten-day period. Again, if the president's party held a majority in the Legislative Yuan, his power was enhanced. But if not, gridlock ensued and the executive branch could govern through coalitions in parliament. More important, Article 2 gave the president the power to dissolve the Legislative Yuan if that body gave him a no-confidence vote,[35] followed by a sixty-day period in which to hold an election for a new Legislative Yuan.

Article 3, which was heatedly debated in 1997 by the National Assembly and barely passed, called for the president to appoint the premier or president of the Executive Yuan without approval or rejection by the Legislative Yuan, as allowed by Article 55 of the 1947 constitution.[36] This new rule enabled the president to appoint anybody he wanted, even a subordinate. The 1947 constitution had been designed to divide power between the cabinet and the president to check the power of the executive branch. Prompted by President Lee, the National Assembly enhanced the president's power. It also deprived the Legislative Yuan of the power to exercise budget control over the Judicial Yuan by mandating that the Judicial Yuan's budget be independent of the Legislative Yuan. The National Assembly argued over the wording of Article 9, which, in effect, abolished the elections for a provincial governor and assembly by designating the appointment of nine persons, one to serve as provincial governor to manage the provincial administration, which, in turn, was greatly reduced in personnel.[37] The premier of the Executive Yuan would nominate the nine people, and the president would appoint them, meaning that there was no longer any independent provincial budget or government to manage the affairs of Taiwan. This downsized provincial government had to answer to the Executive Yuan regarding its administration of Taiwan's counties.

As the political struggle wound down in favor of endorsing the Lee administration's blueprint for constitutional reform, public opinion polls showed that the citizens were confused and alarmed. One poll revealed that 48 percent of the people believed that their demands were not being respected by the National Assembly.[38] Another showed only 27 percent agreeing with abolishing the elections for the provincial governor and assembly, with 52 percent disagreeing.

Many constitutional experts and the press pointed out that the constitutional reform was, in fact, a "constitutional destruction" that "not only changed the polity but also converted the nation's structure."[39] Current rules did not stipulate that an election must have a majority of voters, greater than 50 percent, to elect a president and vice president. Thus a well-organized minority might impose its will on a silent majority.[40] If Taiwan's democracy is to function effectively, the nation's leaders must be elected by a popular vote of more than 50 percent of the electorate. Although many scholars warned of the dire consequences for Taiwan's democracy,[41] the Lee administration had made no effort to design a plurality rule-based national election system.

Former KMT heavyweights Liang Surong and Hau Pei-tsun also criticized the 1997 constitutional reforms.[42] As mainlanders, they defended the 1947 constitution, pointing out that the new rules for governance now strengthened the Office of the President in undesirable ways. Was the constitutional revision good for Taiwan's democracy? The 1947 constitution had been designed to check and balance the power between the five agencies, or *yuan*, of the ROC government. The Lee administration's revisions had removed most of those checks and balances of the old government structure and concentrated power in the Office of the President. Moreover, these reforms had not strengthened the judiciary.

One final incident deserves mention. In late 1999, the National Assembly was convened by President Lee to discuss extending the terms of members of the National Assembly and the Legislative Yuan in order to have simultaneous elections for those bodies in 2002. Despite considerable public outrage, the National Assembly passed the proposal by the necessary three-fourths vote. A rumor then surfaced that the speaker of the National Assembly, Su Nancheng, had approached members of the assembly about extending the term of the president, but that was never confirmed. Even so, Taiwan's voters had elected the National Assembly and Legislative Yuan members to a term of only four years. Now that body had extended its term for an additional two years. Oddly, the president did not criticize this undemocratic action.[43] (In spring 2000 the Grand Justices overturned the National Assembly's decision to extend its term and that of the Legislative Yuan.)

Conclusion

Instead of governing by consensus, as he had done between 1988 and 1995, Taiwan's first directly elected president imposed his power through questionable means that were criticized by much of the media and many elite. President Lee ignored the irregular practices of the National Assembly in the spring of 1997. The tapping of telephones[44] and the heavy-handed pressure used by some outsiders on members of the National Assembly were unacceptable practices and should have been vigorously condemned by the Office of the President but never were.

President Lee managed Taiwan's foreign and China policies on his own, rarely consulting his critics and ignoring the advice of many experts. In fact, neither the National Security Council nor any other government agencies were consulted about President Lee's decision on

July 9, 1999, that his administration intended to engage in special state-to-state relations with the PRC regime.[45]

President Lee had roughly a decade in which to build domestic support for a Taiwan commonwealth formula that would challenge the PRC's 1979 federation formula. But he never did so. Moreover, President Lee eventually rejected the KMT's historical mission to reunify Taiwan with mainland China through political negotiations. In his final four-year term, President Lee never challenged the PRC regime to negotiate a commonwealth framework whereby Taiwan and mainland China would share equally the sovereignty of China and cooperate to reduce the arms race across the Taiwan Strait, expand direct contacts between the two sides, and allow Taiwan to participate in the United Nations and other international organizations. President Lee could have become the great peacemaker in the Asia-Pacific region, had he championed cooperation with mainland China. By repeatedly confronting Beijing's leaders and redefining Taiwan's relations to mainland China as a sovereign state outside the orbit of the Chinese civilization, President Lee not only put Taiwan at risk but threatened the peace and security of the Asia-Pacific region.

The spread of Mafia-style political activities and corruption also worsened during the Lee presidency, and the Lee administration took few actions to deal with these dangerous developments. Neither did President Lee's government begin to reform the nation's police administration or support the Ministry of Justice in prosecuting criminals and Mafia-type politicians.

Lee did initiate six constitutional amendments in his twelve-year rule. The early amendments expanded the electoral process, an achievement owing much to the president's consensus-style politics. But after 1996 he reverted to undemocratic means to reform the constitution his way.

Can a leader of a young democracy use undemocratic means to consolidate democracy without poisoning the political process? We know of no successful example. If a democratically elected president does not build consensus based on democratic practices and uses coercion to force political change, what kind of moral behavior can be expected from the other politicians, the elite, and ordinary people?

If such a leader's policies bear fruit and satisfy the majority, he will have successfully advanced democracy. But if that leader uses autocratic behavior to advance democracy, the likely consequence will be political turmoil, gridlock between parliament and the executive branch, and the retrogression of democracy. Moreover, autocratic actions will more likely inspire others to use the same means. Under these circumstances, democracy erodes and the rule of law disintegrates. The political developments in President Chen Shui-bian's administration will confirm whether President Lee's political legacy will continue.

Notes

1. Larry Diamond, *Developing Democracy: Toward Consolidation* (Baltimore: Johns Hopkins University Press, 1999), p. 75.

2. For an account of that key political event, see Linda Chao and Ramon H. Myers, *The First Chinese Democracy: Political Life in the Republic of China on Taiwan* (Baltimore: Johns Hopkins University Press, 1998), ch. 9.

3. See Linda Chao, Ramon H. Myers, and James A. Robinson, "Promoting Effective Democracy, Chinese Style: Taiwan's National Development Conference," *Asian Survey* 37, no. 7 (July 1997): 671–72.

4. Ibid., p. 674, Table 1.

5. "Guomin liangdang dazhen yajing fandong sheng leisa xianchang" (The KMT and DPP used their combined power to overcome those who opposed and wept), *Xin xinwen* (The journalist), no. 541 (July 20–26, 1997), p. 21. This authoritative political weekly argued that President Lee wanted to eliminate Governor James Soong because he now feared Soong's power base and could no longer support his policies.

6. Ibid. The account that follows is based on this editorial.

7. "The Improper Artifice of Constitutional Revision Will Cause Endless Sequels," *Yazhou zhoukan*, July 21–27, 1997, p. 6.

8. Ibid.

9. Ibid. It was reported that Governor Soong became so furious after learning about the revelations at the spring 1997 meeting of the National Assembly that he destroyed glass furniture in his office.

10. See, for example, Joong-huh Huang and Chilik Yu, "Evaluation of the National Development Conference by the Intellectuals: Results from a Professional Survey," *Public Opinion Research Quarterly* (April 1997): 87–116.

11. Hsin-hsing Wu, *Bridging the Strait: Taiwan, China, and the Prospects for Reunification* (Hong Kong: Oxford University Press, 1994), p. 176. The examples cited in the same paragraph come from this excellent source.

12. See the Hoover Institution Essay in Public Policy by Linda Chao and Ramon H. Myers, *The Divided China Problem: An Essay in Conflict Avoidance and Resolution* (Stanford, CA: Hoover Institution Press, 2000).

13. See "Inaugural Address: Lee Teng-hui, President, Republic of China, May 20, 1996," mimeo issued by the ROC Government Information Office, p. 4. The quotes in this paragraph are from this address.

14. Chen Zujian, *Maishang liangan tanpan* (Toward détente between mainland China and Taiwan) (Hong Kong: Taiping yang shiji chubanshe, 1998), p. 411.

15. Mainland Affairs Council, *Taipei Speaks Up: Special State-to-State Relationship: Republic of China's Policy Documents* (Taipei: Executive Yuan, Republic of China, 1999), pp. 1–2.

16. Lee Teng-hui, "Understanding Taiwan: Bridging the Perception Gap," *Foreign Affairs* (November/December 1999): 9–14.

17. For a discussion of President Lee's arbirtrary decision-making style, see Yang Kai-huang, "Cong 'yansu koti' dao 'jieji yongren' lun Li Denghui congtong liangan jiaoliu zheng ce" (From "solemn issues" to "go slow, be patient" in Lee Teng-hui's policy on the two sides of the Taiwan Strait) (Taipei: Feng-yun lun-tan, 1998), pp. 227–50.

18. For a discussion of how these local elections began and evolved during the martial law years, see Linda Chao and Ramon H. Myers, "How Elections Promoted Democracy in Taiwan under Martial Law," in "Elections and Democracy in Greater China," ed. Larry Diamond and Ramon H. Myers, a special issue of *China Quarterly*, June 2000.

19. For an account of how elections for Provincial Assembly members resonated in political preference for local representatives, see Ramon H. Myers, "The Devolution of Power, Democracy, and Economic Development in the Republic of China on Taiwan: The Taiwan Provincial Assembly, 1949–65," in *The Political Economy of Taiwan's Development into the 21st Century: Essays in Memory of John C.H. Fei*, ed. Gustav Ranis, Sheng-cheng Hu, and Yun-peng Chu (London: Edward Elgar, 1999), vol. 2, pp. 311–34.

20. For a discussion of the *heidao* and the Zhanghan episode as a turning point in their rapid rise to power, see Li Hua, *Di sanzhi yanjing kan Taiwan* (The third eye watches Taiwan) (Beijing: Zhongguo shehui chubanshe, 1997), p. 454.

21. Ibid., pp. 454–55.

22. Li Wenbang, ed. *Chuanpo houzhuan* (To break through the dense barricade) (Taichung: Wenxue jie chubanshe, 1999), pp. 66–67.

23. Ibid. See also the editorial in *Xin xinwen* no. 505 (November 1996): 30, which stated that Liao Zhenghao wanted to eliminate those black elements (*heidao*), but he had to deal with a younger generation of politicians, many of whom were suspected of being involved with *heidao* to get kickbacks from construction magnates. Such younger politicians included the son of Lin Yanggang, the son of Chen Chuanhuan, and Zhuang Hendai, a police officer.

24. Ibid., pp. 234–35.

25. Ibid., p. 235.

26. For a discussion of these three murders, see *Lianhe bao*, May 1, 1972, p. 2 editorial (*shelun*). See also *Lianhe bao*, May 4, 1997, p. 1 lead article. Other major daily newspapers described this violence and government response in similar ways.

27. *Zhongguo shibao*, May 4, 1997, pp. 1, 3. See also *Lianhe bao*, May 4, 1997, p. 1, which states that some 20,000 to 30,000 people paraded in Taipei to signal their discontent to President Lee.

28. *Zhongguo shibao*, May 18, 1997, p. 1; May 19, 1997, p. 1.

29. *Zhongguo shibao*, May 24, 1997, p. 1.

30. *Lianhe bao*, May 18, 1997, p. 2.

31. *Lianhe bao*, May 9, 1997, p. 2.

32. See Government Information Office, Republic of China, *Republic of China Yearbook, 1999* (Taipei: Government Information Office, 1999), p. 693.

33. Ibid., p. 694.

34. Ibid., pp. 691–92.

35. Ibid., p. 691.

36. Ibid., p. 692.

37. Ibid., p. 694.

38. *Lianhe bao*, July 19, 1997, p. 1.

39. *Zhongguo shibao*, July 18, 1997, p. 2.

40. *Lianhe bao*, July 22, 1997, p. 2.

41. *Lianhe bao*, July 25, 1997, p. 2.

42. See the editorial in *Lianhe bao*, March 13, 2000, p. 2.

43. "National Assembly's Scandals—Shame of the Century," *Xin xinwen*, no. 653 (September 9–15, 1999): 10–12.

44. For a report that the telephones of sixty-seven legislators of the Legislative Yuan had been tapped, see "67 ming liwei dianhua bei chuanmian jianting!" (Sixty-seven legislators' telephones were bugged!), *Xin xinwen*, no. 535 (June 8–14, 1997): 58–61.

45. This observation is based on interviews undertaken in Taipei, November 1999.

5

Taiwan's Macroeconomic Performance in the 1990s

An Overview

Shu-Heng Chen

This chapter reviews the macroeconomic time series in Taiwan during the 1990s, and reflects on the Taiwan macroeconomy under the leadership of President Lee Teng-hui. There are two reasons to do so. The obvious one is that President Lee handed over his political power, and, therefore, it is time for such a review. But, the review is also interesting in its own right because of the personal charisma of the outgoing president. Contrary to what politicians want to believe, charisma plays an infinitesimal role in a country's economy, at least in the eyes of economists. As UCLA economics professor Edward Leamer asserted in his book on international trade:

> The resulting image of the workings of the economy is admittedly *cold* and *mechanical*. Neither Henry Ford nor Vladimir Lenin plays a role. Nor does Thomas Edison, Karl Marx, Adam Smith, Queen Victoria, Christ, or Mohammed. . . . What distinguishes countries from one another is only their *natural resources*, *work forces*, and *savings rates*. But this mechanical explanation seems surprisingly complete, and the anomalies not explained by this limited list of resources do not elicit a feeling that Ford, Lenin, Edison, Marx, . . . have much impact on the structure of international trade. (Leamer 1984: xvi-xvii; italics added)

While this quotation is borrowed from a book on trade theory, Leamer's assertion holds for other fields of economics as well. For example, can charisma contribute to a big push in an economy's real GDP?

No. By the Solow growth model, given a growth rate of knowledge and human and physical capital, the potential GDP growth rate is already determined (Solow 1956). Will charisma make the domestic capital market more attractive? No. By Barro's convergence hypothesis, other things being equal, poor countries and areas are in a better position to attract foreign capital than are their rich counterparts, due to their high marginal efficiency of capital (Barro and Sala-i-Martin 1992). Will charisma invigorate the labor market? No. The long-term unemployment rate (or the natural rate of unemployment) is directly affected by institutional arrangements, such as efficiency wage setting (Katz 1986), unemployment insurance (Woodbury and Spiegelman 1987), minimum wages (Brown 1988), and union wage premiums (Summers, 1986). Will charisma help reduce the twin deficits (surplus)? No. According to intertemporal optimizing behavior, these two deficits will have a long-run equilibrium at zero.[1] So, what is charisma worth? Probably nothing as far as the economy is concerned. That is simply a generalization of what Leamer observed. For orthodox economists, the operation of an economy follows certain natural laws, just as a physical or biological system does. The force of these laws is so powerful that it leaves one little room for maneuver.

President Lee has been widely regarded as a very influential, if not the most influential, figure in Taiwan. Therefore, by tracing a set of basic macroeconomic time series over the past decade, one can test the charisma-irrelevant hypothesis and determine whether we can actually identify President Lee's footprints in the process. Nine macroeconomic time series are considered in this chapter. They are the real GDP growth rate, the unemployment rate, the wage growth rate, the savings rate, the inflation rate, the stock return, the GDP share of government expenditures, the budget deficit, and the trade deficit. These nine series cover the three markets in a macroeconomy, namely, the product, labor, and financial markets. The methodology adopted here is very simple. For each time series, we ask whether a trend had already started before President Lee took office. If so, did this trend continue, or was it reversed, under the Lee administration? And what were the major forces contributing to the continuation or the reversal of the trend? Are these forces "natural" so that the economic consequences are inevitable, or are they "artificial," the work of human intervention?

By adopting the above-described research methodology, we do not directly address the consequence of a specific economic policy or a specific set of economic policies that may "define" Lee's economic regime, such as his expanding social welfare program. We implicitly assume that if a policy has a nontrivial impact, then one should actually observe its "force" on one or more series of macroeconomic measures. This research methodology, which distinguishes itself from the conventional approach (Lindsey 1990; Figgie and Swanson 1995), provides a convenient start for this line of research by carefully selecting a set of macroeconomic measures.

Economic Growth

One of the most important measures of economic growth is the real GDP growth rate. The time series behavior of this measure has been extensively studied by economists over the past two decades. One stylized fact about this series that has been identified in advanced economies is that economic growth has a tendency to slow down and get steady; in other words, developed countries tend to experience lower growth rates but less fluctuating economies (Schmidt 1999).

With this background knowledge, we can easily account for the growth experience of the past decade and its relation to previous decades. Figure 5.1 is a time series plot of the real GDP growth rate in Taiwan from the first quarter of 1962 to the second quarter of 1999. To see whether the stylized fact mentioned above fits what we have experienced, let us take a look at Table 5.1, which gives the basic statistics of the growth rate over different time horizons. The growth rate over the entire sample period is 8.56 with a fluctuation measured by the standard deviation 3.56. A further examination of the statistics over different subsamples reveals a steady decline in real GDP growth rate from 10.26 in the 1970s to 8.15 in the 1980s, and down to 6.14 in the 1990s. On the other hand, the fluctuation also falls from 4.92 in the 1970s to a mere 1.13 in the 1990s. As a result, the growth experience under the Lee administration shows nothing that is inconsistent with the stylized fact observed in other advanced economies.

Unemployment Rate

Real GDP measures the aggregate economic activities of the product market, while the unemployment rate measures the aggregate economic activities of the labor market. Given capital and technology, real GDP

Figure 5.1   **Time Series Plot of the Real GDP Growth Rate: 1961/Q1–1999/Q2**

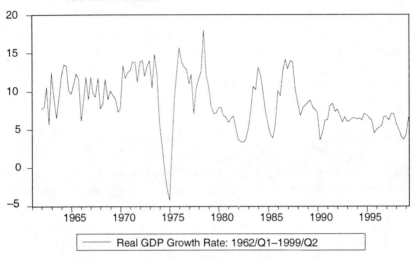

Real GDP Growth Rate: 1962/Q1–1999/Q2

Table 5.1

Real GDP Growth Rate in Taiwan: 1962/Q1–1999/Q2

Periods	Mean	SD
1962/Q1–1999/Q2	8.56	3.56
1962/Q1–1969/Q4	9.82	2.05
1970/Q1–1979/Q4	10.26	4.92
1980/Q1–1989/Q4	8.15	3.08
1990/Q1–1999/Q2	6.14	1.13

(an output) can be considered a function of employment (an input). Figure 5.2 displays the time series data of the unemployment rate from January 1978 to September 1999. Over this sample period, the monthly unemployment rates range from 0.86 to 4.10 with an average of 1.98. For the first half of the Lee administration, the time series of the unemployment rate is similar to that of the preceding years, and the average unemployment rate is only 1.54, much lower than the historical average (Table 5.2). Nonetheless, the second half of the Lee administration experienced a transition to an economy with a higher unemployment rate. The average unemployment rate is 2.63.

From Figure 5.2, we can see that the unemployment rate quickly reached a plateau in 1996 and has stayed there ever since. This development is not beyond our anticipation given a series of policy reforms

Figure 5.2 **Time Series Plot of the Unemployment Rate:
January 1978–September 1999**

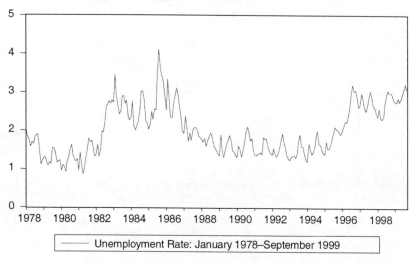

Unemployment Rate: January 1978–September 1999

Table 5.2

Unemployment Rate in Taiwan: January 1978–September 1999

Periods	Mean	Maximum	Minimum
January 1978–September 1999	1.98	4.10	0.86
January 1990–June1995	1.54	2.09	1.20
July 1995–September 1999	2.63	3.21	1.90

related to the labor market, including the import of unskilled workers, the imposition of the pension plan, and the unemployment insurance system. Another contributing factor is the recent social movement, which helps to strengthen labor unions and to increase their power in wage negotiations. This trend may continue, and, if so, what we are experiencing is a transition to a higher natural unemployment rate.

Wages

Another important statistic related to the labor market concerns wages. Figure 5.3 depicts the time series of the average monthly wage of nonagriculture employees and its annual growth rate. A typical employee in the nonagriculture sector can now earn about NT$33,000 to NT$35,000

Figure 5.3 **Time Series Plot of Wages: January 1981–August 1999**

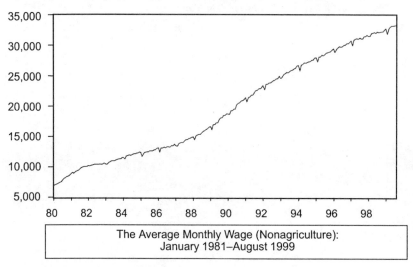

The Average Monthly Wage (Nonagriculture):
January 1981–August 1999

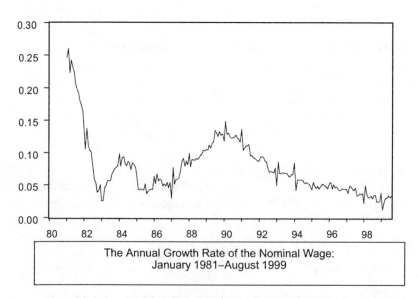

The Annual Growth Rate of the Nominal Wage:
January 1981–August 1999

per month, which is roughly about US$1,100 to US$1,200. In terms of
the annual growth rate (the lower part of Figure 5.3), after a steady growth
in the late 1980s, the upward path of the wage growth rate was inter-
rupted in the early 1990s. Since then wage growth has slowed down
significantly and has not yet picked up. The slowdown in nominal wage

Figure 5.4 **Time Series Plot of the Savings Rate: 1961/Q1–1999/Q2**

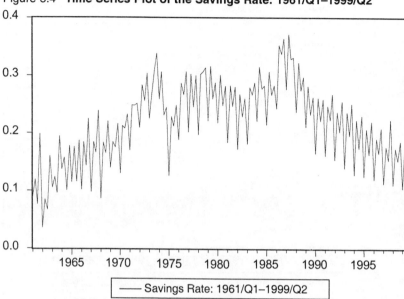

Savings Rate: 1961/Q1–1999/Q2

growth, to some extent, reveals one of the most pressing problems facing the Taiwan economy, that is, the slowdown in labor productivity.

Savings Rate

One of the key sources for economic growth is capital formation, which is in turn determined by the savings rate. Taiwan used to be famous for its high savings rate. Figure 5.4 exhibits the time series of the savings rate from the first quarter of 1961 to the second quarter of 1999. In this figure, Taiwan started with a low 3 percent, but gradually moved to 10 percent, 20 percent, and, in the late 1980s, reached its highest level, 37 percent. However, the 1990s witnessed a reversal of the trend and the savings rate went down steadily to 20 percent, about the same level as that in the 1970s. It is very likely that the savings rate has not hit rock bottom and may drop further in the coming years.

This down-trend development may be partially attributed to the expanding social welfare programs, such as national health insurance, national annuity, and senior citizens' allowance, and support for the disadvantaged. Under these extensive social welfare programs, the livelihood of a household, which used to be a person's own responsibility, is

Figure 5.5 **Time Series Plot of the Inflation Rate: January 1962–October 1999**

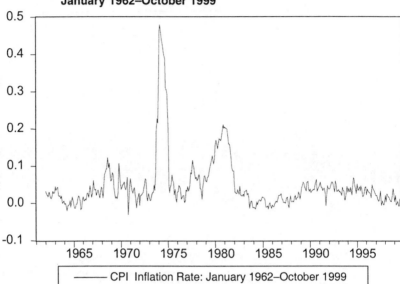

now taken care of by society on a gigantic scale. As a result, the incentive to save has become weaker.

Financial Stability: Inflation Rate

One measure of financial stability concerns the inflation rate. Figure 5.5 is the time series plot of the inflation rate from January 1962 to October 1999. At the beginning of the 1980s, drastic economic, social, and political changes took place, creating a long-term macroeconomic imbalance. Rising oil prices caused consumer prices to rise by 16.3 percent in 1981, followed by a period of near zero inflation in the mid-1980s. From the 1990s onward, inflation has been fluctuating around the 3 percent mark and hence the control of inflation was not the mainstay of economic policy during the Lee administration, in contrast to the experience of the Western world. Rather, policy under the Lee administration focused more on achieving balanced economic and social development.

The revolution in the financial and monetary sectors of Taiwan began in the early 1980s, and the Lee administration continued to pursue this trend. New types of financial assets and liabilities emerged and new markets were created, as a result of the liberalization of the banking

Figure 5.6   **Time Series Plot of Stock Price Returns:
January 6, 1971–September 20, 1999**

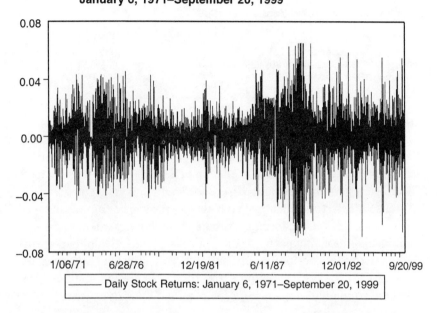

Daily Stock Returns: January 6, 1971–September 20, 1999

sector in the wake of increased competition in keeping with the monetarist's creed.

Financial Stability: TAIEX

The second half of the Lee administration seemed to experience an increasingly tense relation with mainland China. The resultant persistent pressure from the military threats imposed by the People's Liberation Army, such as carrying out large-scale drills and launching missiles by assuming Taiwan as the target, created significant uneasiness for investors. One may anticipate that the stock market would suffer a greater fluctuation than before. Figure 5.6 is the time series plot of the stock price return from January 6, 1971 to September 20, 1999. For this entire period, we compare the volatility of the stock return among four different subperiods. First, we compare the volatility of the decade before the Lee administration with that of the decade after the Lee administration. The result is shown in Table 5.3.

From Table 5.3, it is clear that volatility in the 1990s is almost 50 percent higher than that in the 1980s. This excessive volatility was not unanticipated given the financial deregulation set in motion in the early 1990s,

Table 5.3

Volatility: January 1978–September 1999

Periods	Volatility
January 4, 1980–December 28, 1989	0.013
January 4, 1990–September 20, 1999	0.019
January 4, 1990–December 31, 1994	0.023
January 2, 1995–September 20, 1999	0.015

when the domestic stock market was first opened to foreign investors, and banks were allowed to have a larger share in stock investment. But, if we divide the 1990s, it is somewhat surprising to see that volatility in the second half of the 1990s is in effect much lower than in the first half. Therefore, this initial evidence does not lend support to the assertion that tense cross-strait relations have an adverse impact on the stability of the stock market. According to economic theory, particularly in the spirit of the rational expectations hypothesis, if the Taiwan market (including domestic and foreign investors) is well adjusted to the military threat of the People's Liberation Army, then intimidating gestures from mainland China will not work for the communist regime.

Role of Government

How important a role did the Lee administration play in economic activities? One measure frequently used to address this question is the percentage of government expenditure in GDP. Figure 5.7 exhibits the time series plot of the percentage of government expenditure in GDP from the first quarter of 1961 to the second quarter of 1999. This figure shows a discernible downward trend. Back in the early 1960s, this ratio started at 30–35 percent and gradually slipped down to 15 percent very recently.

This trend also corresponds well to our general impression of the Taiwan economy, which now draws heavily on the market economy and private enterprise. There are several other movements espoused by the Lee administration to solidify this trend, including the transfer of ownership of state-owned businesses to the private sector, and the adoption of the BOT (build-operate-transfer) model in improving the country's infrastructure.

Budget Deficit

Although the Lee administration inherited a market-oriented economy from the Chiang administration, the buildup of a high-deficit economy

Figure 5.7 **Time Series Plot of the Percentage of Government Expenditure in GDP: 1961/Q1–1999/Q2**

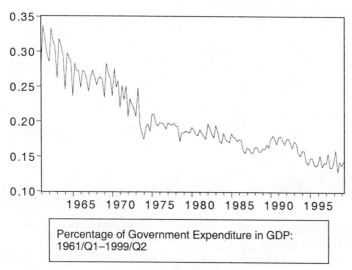

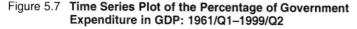

Percentage of Government Expenditure in GDP: 1961/Q1–1999/Q2

during the past decade placed the economy in a budgetary conundrum for which it had little experience. Figure 5.8 plots the time series of the budget deficit from 1967 to 1998. It is amazing for an economy to change from one with an era of zero deficit to one with an annual deficit of more than NT$400 billion. There are several factors to account for this dramatic change. Some are healthy, for example, the expanding programs on social welfare, culture, and education. But, some are not, for example, the corruption of the government. In fact, during the second half of his service, President Lee was questioned several times on his ability to discipline the ruling Kuomintang (KMT) party, and to keep it away from further corruption. However, his failure to meet public demand for a government of high integrity eventually contributed to the defeat of the KMT in the recent presidential election.

Trade Surplus

The experience of Taiwan's economic development, to some extent, provides the empirical counterpart for the theoretical proposition that trade is an engine of economic development. Figure 5.9 shows the time series of percentage of trade volume, that is, the sum of exports and imports, in GDP from the first quarter in 1961 to the second quarter in 1999. This

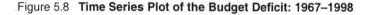

Figure 5.8   **Time Series Plot of the Budget Deficit: 1967–1998**

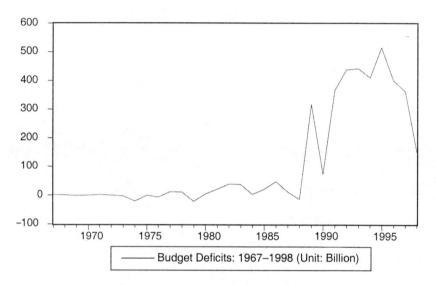

statistic, also known as the trade ratio, is a measure of a country's economic openness. The figure clearly indicates the increasing reliance of Taiwan on integration into the world economy. The ratio was between 20 percent and 30 percent in 1960, but had already increased to 90–100 percent by the second half of the Lee administration. In other words, the sum of the exports and imports has become as large as the whole GDP.

Another equally important factor is the trade deficit, or the deficit (surplus) ratio. Figure 5.9 displays the time series of the surplus ratio during the same period. From this figure, we can see that before the Lee administration, the deficit ratio had an upward trend. It started with trade deficits in the early 1960s, and then the trade balances gradually improved. In the early 1980s, Taiwan became a country with trade surpluses. Moreover, the surplus ratio continued to grow, and, by the end of 1986, it had increased to 18 percent. This persistent and growing trade surplus created an increasing demand for trade balance negotiations. One of the important achievements of the Lee administration was the successful management of the trade imbalance issue, exemplified by a series of policy reforms in opening domestic capital and commodity markets. As a result, the trade surplus ratio underwent a radical decline during the first half of the 1990s. Nowadays, the trade surplus ratio is, at best, only 5 percent.

Figure 5.9   **Time Series Plot of the Trade Ratio and the Trade Deficit (Surplus) Ratio: 1961/Q1–1999/Q2**

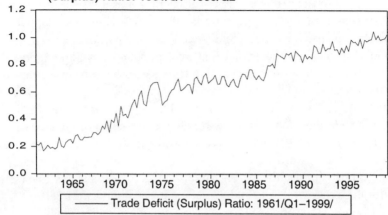

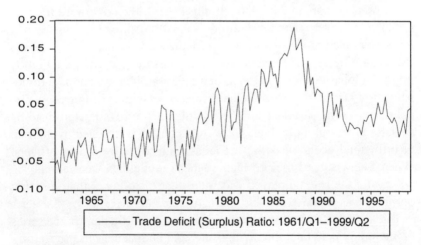

Conclusions

As was mentioned at the beginning of the chapter, the purpose of this study is to offer an initial reflection on the essence of the Lee adminis-tration from an economic viewpoint. In terms of methodology, our evalu-ation is based on a list of some basic but important economic measures. There are alternative measures, of course. For instance, one may follow the case-study style, which details a selection of the important policies and reforms carried out by the Lee administration and examines their possible consequences. No doubt this type of research deserves aca-demic attention, but, if the policies or reforms indeed have a significant impact, then one should be able to recognize it in the time series examined in this chapter. Otherwise, the effect may be only temporary and may disappear as time goes on. Therefore, the review of macroeconomic time series done here provides a bird's-eye view of what we have experienced and delineates significant data that we cannot and should not ignore.

A total of nine macroeconomic time series have been examined in this study. A simple time series plot indicates two types of behavior in these series: one follows the trend, and the other reverses the trend. For the former, the economic growth rate and the share of government expenditures in GDP follow the downward trend, while the trade ratio follows the upward trend. For the latter, the unemployment rate, the wage growth rate, the savings rate, and the trade surplus reverse the upward trend, while the budget deficit starts an upward trend.

One may interpret the former as the pursuit of policy goals started by Lee's predecessors in the 1980s. In this regard, the downward trend in the share of government expenditures in GDP manifests the pursuit of a market-oriented economy and respect for the market mechanism, whereas the upward trend in the trade ratio symbolizes the pursuit of integration into the global economy. In fact, deregulation, liberalization, and globalization can be regarded as the primary guidelines of our economic policies over the past decade. These guidelines were not determined by a single powerful individual, but were a consensus reached by a group of influential economists, businessmen, and top government officers. When Lee assumed the presidency, these guidelines were already in place, and the role he played was more that of follower than initiator. Surprising as it may seem, his charisma finds no place in these series.

But the cases differ for the reverse trends. In particular, for the series of unemployment rate, the savings rate, and budget deficits, Lee's footprints are clearly visible. The economic facets represented by the three series deteriorated either over the entire course or in the second half of Lee Teng-hui's administration. While one can have different and unrelated explanations for different series, there is a major and common cause for the deterioration, namely, increased social welfare expenditures.

To show how rapidly social welfare expenditures expanded during the Lee administration, Figure 5.10 plots the percentage of social welfare expenditures in total expenditures over the past two decades. From 1982 to 1987, the last few years of Chiang Ching-kuo's administration, this figure was quite stable at around 15 percent, but it gradually moved upward during the Lee administration. In particular, from 1993 to 1997,

Figure 5.10 **The Percentage of Social Welfare Expenditures in Total Expenditures: 1976–2000**

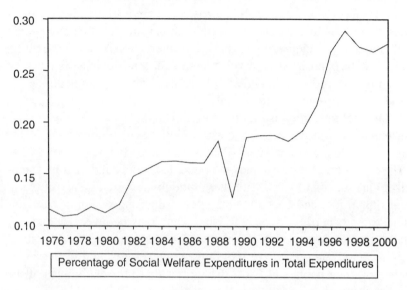

Percentage of Social Welfare Expenditures in Total Expenditures

the ratio increased for five consecutive years, reaching an all-time high of 29 percent (amounting to NT$550 billion). Increased social welfare expenditures clearly have a direct impact on budget deficits.

The effects of social welfare on the savings rate and the unemployment rate have been carefully analyzed in economics. For example, expansionary welfare programs that provide insurance against very low levels of consumption (health insurance, senior citizens' allowance, etc.) can discourage saving (Hubbard et al. 1994), and welfare programs that provide generous unemployment benefits can lead to a higher natural rate of unemployment (Burda 1988). More empirical studies will be required to determine the extent to which these theories account for the declining savings rate and the rising unemployment rate in Taiwan. But it is not absurd to argue that the expanded social welfare programs tended to leave people with the expectation of a less risky or more secure future. With these expectations, their saving and job-searching behavior changed in the direction suggested by economic theories.

The expanded social welfare programs were mainly attributable to the transition to a welfare state triggered by the regime switch, and Lee's legacy to the economy lies here. It is not entirely clear what drove Lee to embrace the idea of welfare states, but it certainly has something to do with elections. The idea of a welfare state was originally proposed and promoted by the Democratic Progressive Party (DPP), the largest opposition party at the time. To increase the chance of winning the election, the KMT, under Lee's leadership, stood on the same side as the DPP regarding social welfare issues. The interaction between the ruling party and the opposition then evolved into a cut-throat competition, which ended in rash promises mainly to please the voters. As a result, the expenditures for social welfare escalated.

Many political scientists argue that Lee should be credited with bringing economic prosperity to this country. While there is some truth in this argument, the road to prosperity had been opened before he took office. Policy guidelines toward a market-oriented economy and a team of technical bureaucrats to work with these guidelines were already in place. Lee's main job, and hence his major contribution, was simply to continue the prosperity. Contrary to what many may believe, Lee's legacy to the economy lies in his efforts to make this country a welfare state. His strategic use of welfare programs, however, resulted in the emergence of huge debts and fiscal difficulties that pursued Taiwan at the turn of the century.

Note

The author is grateful to Mei-lie Chu and Tun-jen Cheng for their thoughtful comments given at the International Conference on President Lee Teng-hui's Legacy: Formation and Implications. The author also thanks Bruce Dickson for constructive suggestions on the paper after the conference, and Chien-min Chao for encouragement to initiate this research.

1. For empirical evidence on these long-term balances, the interested reader is referred to Burda and Wyplosz (1993: 51–52, 59).

References

Barro, R., and X. Sala-i-Martin. 1992. "Convergence." *Journal of Political Economy* 100 (April): 223–251.

Brown, C. 1988. "Minimum Wage Laws: Are They Overrated?" *Journal of Economic Perspectives* 2: 133–146.

Burda, M. 1988. "Wait Unemployment in Europe," *Economic Policy* 7: 391–426.

Burda, M., and C. Wyplosz. 1993. *Macroeconomics: A European Text.* Oxford: Oxford University Press.

Figgie, H.E., Jr., and G. Swanson. 1992. *Bankruptcy 1995: The Coming Collapse of America and How to Stop It.* Boston: Little, Brown.

Hubbard, R.G., J. Skinner, and S.P. Zeldes. 1994. "The Importance of Precautionary

Motives in Explaining Individual and Aggregate Saving." *Carnegie-Rochester Conference Series on Public Policy* 40 (June): 59–125.

Katz, L. 1986. "Efficiency Wage Theories: A Partial Evaluation." *NBER Macroeconomic Annual* 1: 235–76.

Leamer, E.E. 1984. *Sources of International Comparative Advantage: Theory and Evidence.* Cambridge, MA: MIT Press.

Lindsey, L. 1990. *The Growth Experiment: How the New Tax Policy Is Transforming the U.S. Economy.* New York: Basic Books.

Schmidt, W. 1999. "Is the Business Cycle Dead?" *Canadian Shareowner* 12, no. 6: 4.

Solow, R. 1956. "A Contribution to the Theory of Economic Growth." *Quarterly Journal of Economics* 70, no. 1: 65–94.

Summers, L. 1986. "Why Is the Unemployment Rate So Very High Near Full Employment?" *Brookings Papers on Economic Activity* 2: 339–83.

Woodbury, S.A., and R.G. Spiegelman. 1987. "Bonuses to Workers and Employers to Reduce Unemployment: Randomized Trials in Illinois." *American Economic Review* 77: 513–30.

Part III

Taiwan's Party System and Electoral Behavior

— 6 —

Whither the Kuomintang?

John Fuh-sheng Hsieh

On March 18, 2000, 82.69 percent of eligible voters went to the polls to elect the new president of the Republic of China (ROC) on Taiwan. It was embarrassing to the ruling Kuomintang (Nationalist Party, KMT) that its candidate Lien Chan, the incumbent vice president, was not only defeated by the Democratic Progressive Party's (DPP) Chen Shui-bian, but also lagged far behind the KMT-turned-independent James Soong (see Table 6.1). This marks the first time that the KMT was defeated in a major national election in Taiwan over the years.[1]

Of course, the loss in the presidential election does not mean that the KMT will no longer play a significant role in Taiwanese politics. In fact, it still controls a majority, albeit a shaky majority, of seats in the Legislative Yuan (parliament), rendering it an important political force to be reckoned with. In particular, given Taiwan's constitutional form of government, which is theoretically closer to the parliamentary system,[2] the KMT will surely continue to exert a great deal of influence on Taiwan's politics.

Nevertheless, the fact is that the KMT candidate was defeated badly in the presidential election. Right after the election, President Lee Teng-hui stepped down from the KMT chairmanship amid the protest of some traditional KMT supporters demanding that Lee be held responsible for Lien's defeat, or more accurately, for Chen's victory. Lien succeeded Lee as acting chairman, and later chairman, of the party.

A slightly different version of this chapter was published in the *China Quarterly*, no. 168 (December 2001): 909–22. The editors gratefully acknowledge *China Quarterly*'s permission to reprint the article in this volume. The author would like to thank Bruce Dickson, Chien-min Chao, Kuo-hsiung Lee, Shelley Rigger, and the anonymous reviewers for their helpful comments and suggestions.

Table 6.1

Results of the 2000 Presidential Election

Candidate	Party	Votes	Percent
Chen Shui-bian	Democratic Progressive Party	4,977,697	39.30
James Soong	Independent	4,664,972	36.84
Lien Chan	Kuomintang	2,925,513	23.10
Hsu Hsin-liang	Independent	79,429	0.63
Li Ao	New Party	16,782	0.13

Source: Republic of China Central Election Commission.

At any rate, the KMT seems to be seriously demoralized. Furthermore, the independent presidential candidate, James Soong, following his impressive performance in the election, decided to form the People First Party (PFP), which, as can be expected, would probably attract many traditional KMT voters, and thus further erode support for the KMT. Thus, an interesting question arises: Will the KMT remain a formidable force in Taiwanese politics in the foreseeable future? This is the question that will be dealt with in this chapter.

Party Alignment in Taiwan

Let us first take a look at Taiwan's party configuration. Generally speaking, Taiwan's party structure has been, in a sense, very much stabilized in the past decade or so. If we examine the Legislative Yuan elections since 1989, it can be seen that the relative strength between the pan-KMT camp, which includes the KMT, the New Party (NP), the Democratic Alliance (DA), and others, and the pan-DPP camp, which consists of the DPP, the Taiwan Independence Party (TAIP), the New Nation Association (NNA), and others, has remained quite stable.

In the 1989 Legislative Yuan election, for instance, the KMT captured 60.22 percent of the vote according to the Central Election Commission (CEC) data. This figure included any candidate, nominated or not, who claimed to be a KMT member. In 1992, the CEC changed the rule regarding the candidates' party affiliations: Only those who were nominated by the party could be recorded as its candidates.[3] Thus, although the official CEC data show that the KMT received 53.02 percent of the vote in 1992, if, in order to be comparable to the 1989 figure, we also include those KMT candidates who ran as independents but later rejoined the party, the KMT actually won 60.5 percent of the vote, a bit more than it did in 1989. In the Legislative Yuan election held three years later, the New Party that had split from the KMT in 1993 entered the race. By combining the votes received by the KMT and NP, the pan-KMT camp garnered 59.01 percent of the vote, not very different from the KMT vote in the two previous elections. In 1998, putting together the vote obtained by the KMT, NP, and DA, which included many former KMT and NP members, the pan-KMT force received 57.23 percent of the total vote. As these figures show, the electoral strength of the pan-KMT camp exhibits a high degree of stability over the years.

On the part of the DPP, it received 28.26 percent of the vote in 1989, and increased to 31.03 percent in 1992. It performed best in 1995 by capturing 33.17 percent of the vote. In 1998, its vote dropped to 29.56 percent, but by adding the vote received by the TAIP and the NNA, the pan-DPP vote still reached 32.58 percent, similar to what the DPP got three years earlier. Thus, the pan-DPP camp's strength has been stabilized as well.

An important feature of the Legislative Yuan election is that an overwhelming majority of the seats are elected by the single nontransferable vote (SNTV) under which a voter casts only one vote in a district electing more than one candidate. Such a system displays a certain degree of proportionality with respect to the match between each party's vote share and seat share.[4] As a result, a small party or even an independent *qua* the smallest party is often able to gain a foothold.

In Taiwan, the SNTV is the major electoral system used for the election of legislators at all levels of government, including the members of the Legislative Yuan. However, for the election of executive offices, such as president, provincial governor, county magistrates, city mayors, and so on, the method is the single-member district first-past-the-post system, which is very different from the SNTV in terms of its impact on party competition. Normally, only the two major parties are able to compete in these elections.[5] Thus, the DPP, one of the two major parties, often did better in such elections, particularly at the county/city level or higher, in terms of vote shares. In the elections of county magistrates and city mayors in 1993 and 1997, the gubernatorial and Taipei and Kaohsiung City mayoral elections in 1994, and Taipei and Kaohsiung City mayoral elections in 1998, for instance, the DPP was able to capture around 40 percent of the vote. In this sense, Chen Shui-bian's 39.3 percent in the 2000 presidential election was normal for the DPP.[6] In such elections, there had been greater fluctuation for the KMT candidates, but if we include those candidates who were KMT-turned-independents, the fluctuation was not that great. Accordingly, even in elections for executive offices, there is, again, a certain degree of stability between the pan-KMT and pan-DPP camps.

The major factor contributing to such stability is the underlying cleavage in the society that determines the party configuration in Taiwan. In this respect, Taiwan is very different from most of the Western democracies where the dominant cleavages underpinning the party structure are often class and religion, plus occasionally subcultural and rural-urban divisions.[7] In the past several decades, a new politics issue, environmentalism, has also become an important cleavage in molding the party systems in many Western countries.[8]

However, the situation in Taiwan is quite different. Most of these cleavages are not so salient in affecting party configuration. A series of studies conducted by John Fuh-sheng Hsieh and Emerson M.S. Niou finds that among various issues, political issues rather than socioeconomic ones, more often than not, determine popular support for political parties. The national identity issue, referring to people's attitude toward the political association between Taiwan and mainland China, is particularly important in this context (see Table 6.2).[9] In this regard, Taiwanese society can be categorized as a divided society—mildly divided as compared to, say, Northern Ireland.

These studies are based upon surveys conducted by Opinion Research Taiwan and by the Election Study Center of National Chengchi University.[10] The respondents were asked to choose a position between 0 for the immediate declaration of independence for Taiwan and 10 for negotiation with mainland China on unification without further delay. (They were also asked about the positions of the various political parties on such an issue.) To simplify the matter, I regroup the respondents into five categories: extreme independence supporters (0 or 1), moderate independence supporters (2 to 4), status quo supporters (5), moderate unification supporters (6 to 8), and extreme unification supporters (9 or 10). As can be seen in Table 6.3, prior to the 1999 survey, there was a clear trend toward the status quo, neither independence nor unification. On the one hand, the number of independence supporters had gradually increased, and, on the other hand, the number of unification supporters had decreased drastically, with more and

Table 6.2

Ethnicity and the National Identity Issue

Ethnicity	Extreme independence supporters	Moderate independence supporters	Status quo supporters	Moderate unification supporters	Extreme unification supporters	Total
Taiwanese (Hakka)	5.0 (3.6%)	14.0 (10.1%)	70.0 (50.7%)	30.0 (21.7%)	19.0 (13.8%)	138.0 (99.9%)
Taiwanese (Minnan)	57.0 (7.6%)	130.0 (17.4%)	351.0 (47.0%)	152.0 (20.3%)	57.0 (7.6%)	747.0 (99.9%)
Mainlanders	0.0 (0.0%)	8.0 (7.3%)	39.0 (35.8%)	40.0 (36.7%)	22.0 (20.2%)	109.0 (100.0%)

Table 6.3

Voters' Attitude Toward the National Identity Issue (percent)

Year	Extreme independence supporters	Moderate independence supporters	Status quo supporters	Moderate unification supporters	Extreme unification supporters	Total
December 1992	6.2	6.3	30.6	30.1	26.9	100.1
January 1995	6.6	8.6	51.1	20.7	12.9	99.9
March 1996	9.1	12.4	53.5	15.4	9.7	100.1
January 1999	12.9	14.8	43.5	17.4	11.4	100.0
June 2000	6.2	15.3	46.0	22.4	10.1	100.0

Note: Row percentages may not add to 100 due to rounding. Based on surveys conducted by Opinion Research Taiwan in 1992 and the Election Study Center of National Chengchi University in other years.

more people moving toward the status quo. Indeed, the status quo became truly dominant as time went by. However, in the 1999 and 2000 surveys, the latter of which was conducted after the 2000 presidential election, there seemed to be a reverse trend moving away from the status quo and becoming a bit more polarized. Even so, the status quo remained the largest mode, attracting more people than other positions along the national identity spectrum.

Generally, even if there have been changes in the distribution of voters on the national identity issue, the broad pattern remains quite stable over the years, explaining, to a large extent, the stability in the relative strength between the pan-KMT and pan-DPP forces in Taiwan's electoral politics. The pan-KMT camp attracts most votes in the middle and on the unification side, while the pan-DPP camp gains support from the other side plus some in the middle.

Nevertheless, despite the relative stability between the two large camps, there have been significant changes within each camp as well. Within the KMT camp, there was originally only one KMT, but gradually, in addition to the KMT, the NP, DA, and PFP emerged. Similarly, on the DPP side, the one and only DPP was later joined by the TAIP and NNA.

An important factor contributing to the fragmentation within each camp is the multi-modal nature of the distribution of voters on the national identity issue. Although the status quo has been the largest mode, we can also see two smaller modes on both sides of the independence-unification spectrum. Under such circumstances, a multi-party system is, indeed, quite natural.[11]

Figure 6.1 draws the 2000 curve for the respondents on the 0–10 scale on the national identity issue. It also shows the median positions of the respondents and the four major parties as perceived by the respondents. As can be seen in the figure, the voters' position is in the middle with the KMT somewhat to their right, the NP and PFP further to the right, and the DPP very much to the left.

For a very long time, the KMT was a party advocating reunification between Taiwan and mainland China, but since the late 1980s, under the leadership of President Lee Teng-hui, it has downplayed this theme, resulting, on the one hand, in an intraparty power struggle between the less pro-unification mainstream faction and the more pro-unification nonmainstream faction, and, on the other, the split of some young turks to form the NP in 1993.

Figure 6.1 **Voters' Distribution and Voters' and Parties' Positions on the National Identity Issue, 2000**

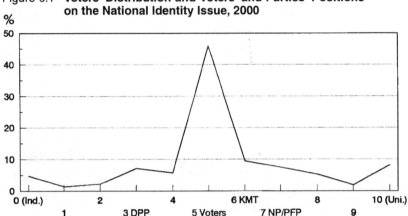

Source: The Election Study Center, National Chengchi University.
Notes: DPP—Democratic Progressive Party; KMT—Kuomintang; NP—New Party; PFP—People First Party.

Within the DPP camp, a similar trend took place. The DPP has long been known for favoring Taiwan independence. But recently, sensing the popular mood toward the status quo, it began to moderate its stance, thus alienating some staunch independence supporters who later formed the TAIP.

Apart from the multi-modal nature of voters' distribution on the national identity issue, another important factor contributing to the fragmentation of Taiwan's party structure is the electoral system used for the legislatures at various levels of government, that is the SNTV system. As noted above, such an electoral system exhibits a certain degree of proportionality, thus giving small parties or even independents a good chance to win elections. Hence, small parties may flourish. Indeed, it can be shown that the number of viable candidates will approach the number of seats available in a district (i.e., district magnitude) plus one, meaning the larger the district magnitude, the greater the opportunities for small parties to survive.[12]

Such an electoral system is very different from the method employed for electing the executive offices, under which only the two major parties are normally able to compete in elections, thus constraining, to some extent, the incentive to split in the legislative arena. Nevertheless, the use of SNTV in the legislative elections is often strong enough to bring about a certain degree of fragmentation in Taiwan's party structure.

The KMT's Strengths and Weaknesses

As is obvious from the above discussion, the KMT, as a kind of status-quo party, is, indeed, in an advantageous position vis-à-vis other political parties. There are simply more people in the middle than at any other point along the national identity spectrum. This explains, to a large extent, the KMT's success in Taiwan's electoral politics over the years.

Nevertheless, many observers of Taiwan politics often attribute the KMT's success to its superb organizational strength, its huge enterprises, its undue influence over the electronic media, its reliance upon vote buying, and so forth. This is surely true, but only to a certain extent.[13] Indeed, if the KMT relies solely upon such factors, and were very much disliked by the people, it would have collapsed long ago. As Barbara Geddes notes, when democratic transition began in many Eastern European countries, "support for Communist parties and their successors declined—dramatically in most countries" despite the fact that they "had tremendous advantages over other parties in regard to local organization, control of government resources and patronage, and control of the media."[14] Apparently, this does not apply to the KMT.

Moreover, in view of the fact that the DPP has greatly improved its organizational capability lately, but that it seems to encounter bottlenecks in further increasing its vote shares in elections against the KMT, there must be other factors that are, in a sense, more deep-rooted. In particular, because the relative strength between the (pan-)KMT and (pan-)DPP camps has been stabilized, such factors must be very resilient as well. The cleavage in society, which facilitates the emergence of political parties in the first place, is something that should not be overlooked. And as mentioned earlier, the major cleavage affecting the formation of political parties in Taiwan is national identity, which also exhibits a certain degree of stability over the years. Given the KMT's position on this issue, it does enjoy a continuing advantage vis-à-vis other political parties in Taiwan.

In this regard, Lee Teng-hui played a very important role. Being the first native Taiwanese to serve as the ROC president and the KMT chairman, he effectively changed the image of the party from one domi-nated by mainlanders, strongly supporting unification, to one better reflecting the composition of the population, giving priority to status quo with unification as a long-term goal.

A related issue is political stability insofar as deviation from the status quo on the national identity issue is often seen as provoking internal instability or even inviting invasion from China. When the respondents were asked to make a tradeoff between reform and sta-bility, an overwhelming majority chose stability (see Table 6.4).[15] In this respect, the KMT, again, as the status-quo party that has ruled the country and maintained stability for half a century, has a clear advan-tage over other political parties on the island.

In addition, the KMT's performance in the economic sphere also helps. Indeed, Taiwan's economic development is known not only for high growth rates but also for relatively equitable distribution of in-come and wealth. This certainly contributes to the KMT's success in elections.[16] However, given the fact that Taiwanese society is divided along the line of national identity, the economic issue often plays a secondary role in voters' support for political parties.[17]

Of course, the KMT has weaknesses. Perhaps the most serious one is its identification as the party closely tied to the "black and gold," namely, organized crime and big business. Moreover, the KMT's huge party enterprises, while helpful in maintaining a formidable organiza-tion and in providing money for campaigning in elections, also rein-force such an image. This, along with the image of being unresponsive, hurts the party, particularly among the young, urban, and better-edu-cated voters. Many observers attributed these weaknesses to Lee Teng-hui's handling of election affairs, arguing that he made compromises with the "black and gold" forces in order for the KMT to win the races, and to help him gain an upper hand in his struggle against the nonmainstream faction within the party. Such assertions may be true to a certain extent, but they are obviously exaggerated because, among other factors, the SNTV system may be responsible for "black and gold" politics as well (see the discussion in the next section).

Another problem for the KMT is that its internal power structure has been highly centralized—even centralized in one man. As a re-sult, it was often not adaptable enough to the changing environment. In particular, regarding the nomination of candidates for public of-fices, the lack of clear and open rules harms the party from time to

Table 6.4

Voters' Attitude Toward the Reform/Stability Issue (percent)

Year	Extreme reform supporters	Moderate reform supporters	Neutrals	Moderate stability supporters	Extreme stability supporters	Total
December 1992	1.3	2.8	15.5	31.0	49.4	100.0
January 1995	3.2	9.3	20.9	30.0	36.6	100.0
March 1996	1.7	3.2	35.1	28.2	31.8	100.0
January 1999	6.5	8.2	17.1	25.2	43.1	100.1
June 2000	4.5	9.9	15.7	28.4	41.6	100.1

Note: Row percentages may not add to 100 due to rounding. Based on surveys conducted by Opinion Research Taiwan in 1992 and the Election Study Center of National Chengchi University in other years.

time. In the 2000 presidential election, for instance, the lack of clear and open rules resulted in the division of the party between its official nominee, Lien Chan, and the popular former governor of Taiwan Province, James Soong, thus losing to the DPP's Chen Shui-bian. During his term as party chairman, Lee Teng-hui was unwilling or unable to solve this problem, and thus, to a certain degree, should be held responsible for it.

The 2000 Presidential Election and Its Aftermath

For the KMT, the 2000 presidential election is quite similar to the 1996 election in the sense that, on both occasions, the KMT was divided. In 2000, there were Lien Chan and James Soong, and in 1996, besides the KMT official candidate Lee Teng-hui, the incumbent president, there were Lin Yang-kang and Chen Lu-an, both of whom left the party to run as independents.[18] However, the results were quite different. Fortunately for the KMT in 1996, President Lee, being the first Taiwanese president and also ambiguous about his attitude toward the independence-unification issue,[19] was able to make inroads into the DPP camp. Thus, although Lin and Chen captured 24.88 percent of the vote, mostly from the traditional KMT voters, Lee was able to win the election by gaining votes from DPP supporters, ending up with 54 percent of the total vote, leaving DPP's Peng Ming-min with only 21.13 percent. Yet, in 2000, Lien lacked the kind of charisma that Lee had. He not only lost ground to Soong, but also was unable to offset the loss by gaining support from the DPP side. With the pan-DPP camp unified behind Chen Shui-bian, the KMT, for the first time, lost in a major national election.

Undoubtedly, many factors are involved that can affect an election one way or another. In addition to a long-term factor such as party configuration, other short-term factors such as candidates' personal characteristics and the specific issues raised during the election campaign may also shape the outcomes. In the legislative elections where a large number of seats are available, some of the short-term factors may be cancelled out among the candidates, and election results may be more likely to reflect, in a statistical sense, the long-term party configuration in the country. In contrast, in the presidential election where only one seat is available, short-term "accidental" factors may play a much larger role in shaping election results, thus distorting, to a certain extent, the long-term party structure.

Although in the 2000 presidential election, voters' partisan attachments, the personality of individual candidates, and the issues of the day have all affected the outcome, the vote obtained by Chen on the one hand, and the combined total by Lien and Soong on the other, conform so well to the previous pattern that it attests once again to the high degree of stability in Taiwan's party structure, and to the key role played by partisanship, which reflects the national identity cleavage, in Taiwan's electoral politics.[20]

Now, will the stability exhibited by the competition between the pan-KMT and pan-DPP camps be changed in the foreseeable future as a result of the 2000 presidential election? To some extent, yes; but not too much. It is true that, with Chen Shui-bian's victory, the pan-DPP camp may be able to gain more popular support for a time, but this hardly changes the pattern of competition between the two camps in a fundamental way. (In fact, given Chen's poor performance as president, the increased support may be eroded quickly.) So long as voters' positions on the national identity issue remain relatively unchanged (as evidenced by the survey results shown in Table 6.3, which include the data collected after the 2000 presidential election), the relative strength between the two major camps will be more or less stabilized.

Indeed, if there is any realignment in Taiwan's party politics, it will most likely take place within each camp. In the pan-KMT camp, the KMT, PFP and NP will split the traditional KMT support. Whether the KMT will be able to retain its strength depends very much upon how the PFP and NP, particularly the former, fare. Currently, it is not entirely clear where the PFP stands on the national identity issue, although the 2000 survey indicates that it occupies roughly the same position as that of the NP (see Figure 6.1). However, it is likely that such a perception may change as time goes by. Indeed, the PFP may end up in a position between the KMT and NP, even somewhere very close to the KMT.[21] As a result, the KMT may be greatly affected, but given that it has occupied its position for so long, it will be very difficult for any other party to replace it. Thus, unless the PFP is able to create a new issue dimension (e.g., the clean government issue), attracting people who are not so concerned about national identity, the PFP may not be able to take over the KMT as the leading party in the pan-KMT camp. Under the current circumstances, it will be very difficult, if not entirely impossible, to create such a new issue dimension.[22]

Moreover, whether the KMT will remain a formidable political force in Taiwan also depends upon its ability to curb further splits within its own ranks. One of the major factors contributing to previous splits was the choice made by the party leadership to move away from a more-to a less-pro-unification stance, which alienated a lot of people on the unification side, some of whom split from the party later on. Because the new KMT leadership seems more accommodative toward China, they actually turn back the party position to one that is somewhat closer to the old KMT stance. This may irritate people like Lee Teng-hui, the former party chairman, and his followers who split from the party and created the Taiwan Solidarity Union to protest against the KMT's current policy.

As mentioned earlier, even though the electoral system used in elections for executive offices, that is, the single-member district first-past-the-post system, may place constraints on the fragmentation of the party system, the electoral system adopted for legislative elections, namely, the SNTV system, will, to a certain extent, lift such constraints. Thus, in future elections, we may witness opposite trends: in the elections for executive offices, a trend toward convergence, and in the legislative elections, a trend toward fragmentation. This will certainly lead to confusion about the future direction of Taiwan's party politics. However, on balance, it is fair to say that it may not be easy to halt fragmentation in Taiwan's party structure, but there will be a certain limit imposed upon it.[23] That is, as far as the KMT is concerned, the incentive for splitting cannot always, but only to a certain extent, be ruled out. Furthermore, the KMT has a special advantage. The fact that it remains a rich party that is better organized than other parties will further limit splitting.

In general, as long as the national identity issue continues to be the major cleavage underpinning the party structure in the society, and the distribution of voters on this issue remains relatively unchanged, the KMT will continue to be a formidable force in Taiwanese politics if it is able to hold itself together.

Undoubtedly, the KMT is hurt by its "black and gold" image, which ruins its reputation particularly among the young, urban, and better-educated. However, it may be difficult for the KMT to solve this problem when its very survival in the political arena becomes the paramount concern. Indeed, although the KMT must be held responsible for its wrongdoing, an important factor causing corruption is the electoral system used for the legislative elections. The kind of electoral system adopted for such elections, that is the SNTV system, often leads to intraparty competition in election campaigns. In a district electing five seats, for instance, the KMT may nominate three candidates, and, given the relative stability between the pan-KMT and pan-DPP votes, competition among the three KMT candidates is often more fierce than that between the KMT and DPP candidates. Because the party has to remain impartial among its own candidates, the candidates cannot expect to get support from the party to fight against their co-partisans, and thus have to rely upon themselves to get elected. This provides opportunities for, say, big businesses, gangsters, and the like to intervene in the electoral process on a large scale. Moreover, all three candidates come from the same party with an identical set of platforms, making party label and campaign issues irrelevant, at least as far as the competition among the three is concerned. In order to distinguish among themselves, they may have to rely heavily upon, say, services they are able to provide to their constituents. Pork-barrel politics of one kind or another becomes almost inevitable.[24] Consequently, unless the electoral system can be changed, the "black and gold" problem cannot, in general, be easily solved.[25]

Right after the 2000 presidential election, the KMT did try to do something to alter its image in this regard. In nominating candidates to run for elections scheduled for December 2001, it deliberately tried to avoid some controversial figures. But given the incentives inherent in the electoral system, it is doubtful how far the party can go.

Also, there have been talks about holding the party enterprises in trust. Although this may increase transparency and reduce conflicts of interest in business dealings, the KMT will nevertheless remain a rich party. It is hard to imagine that the KMT would voluntarily give up its enterprises altogether under the current circumstances. While it needs money to run the organization and the campaigns, of course, the party enterprises will also damage its image in terms of fair play.

Moreover, the KMT has to reformulate its rules for resolving internal conflicts, particularly those concerning the nomination of candidates. These rules must be clear and open to placate the losers after the nomination is over. This is especially important in the elections for executive offices, where only one seat is available. Apparently, the party is still struggling to find a way to accomplish such a goal.

Conclusion

In the 2000 presidential election, the KMT lost badly, but it remains the majority party in the Legislative Yuan. In the parliamentary election scheduled for December 2001, it may lose its majority status, but will, in all likelihood, control a substantial portion of seats in the new Legislative Yuan. It will continue to be an important player in Taiwan politics as long as it is able to hold itself together. Its strength derives essentially from its unique position along the national identity spectrum, the most salient cleavage underpinning Taiwan's party structure, and will be affected mainly from within and from competition with other parties in the pan-KMT camp—the parties that split from the KMT early on.

Notes

1. Actually, this was the second time the KMT had lost an election on a nationwide basis. The first time was in the election for the county magistrates and city mayors held in 1997. But these were local elections.

2. That the ROC constitutional form of government is closer to parliamentarism can be seen in the following stipulations: The highest administrative organ in the country is the Executive Yuan (cabinet), not the presidency; the Executive Yuan is responsible to the Legislative Yuan by means of, among other things, a vote of no confidence exerted by the latter, rather than to the president; and in promulgating laws and issuing ordinances, the president shall obtain the countersignature of the premier or the countersignatures of the premier and the ministers concerned. Even though the president is now directly popularly elected and can appoint the premier without the approval of the Legislative Yuan, this does not fundamentally alter the power enjoyed by the president. Indeed, quite a few parliamentary democracies (e.g., Austria, Ireland, Iceland, and Portugal) have directly elected heads of state, and many heads of state, including the British monarch, in parliamentary countries can appoint the prime minister without a formal vote of investiture. Furthermore, many people believe that a mixed system modeled after the French Fifth Republic has been instituted in Taiwan following the recent constitutional reforms. But this is not quite right given that the ROC president cannot do many things that a French president can (e.g., dissolving the parliament in a more proactive manner, asking the parliament to reconsider a law, bypassing the parliament by appealing directly to the general public in a referendum, presiding over the Council of Ministers, etc.). For a discussion of the constitutional form of government in Taiwan, see John Fuh-sheng Hsieh, "Institutional Design for the Republic of China on Taiwan," paper presented at the annual meeting of the American Political Science Association, Boston, September 1998.

3. This change was brought about by the introduction of proportional representation (PR) for electing the Legislative Yuan members representing a nationwide constituency and the overseas Chinese communities. A peculiar feature of the operation of PR in Taiwan is that voters do not have any chance to vote directly for the party lists; instead, their votes for candidates in regular districts are aggregated according to the candidates' party affiliations, and the PR seats are distributed on the basis of such aggregated party votes. As a consequence, the candidates are asked to get the parties' endorsements prior to the election so as to facilitate the aggregation process. For the introduction of PR to Taiwan, see John Fuh-sheng Hsieh, "Manipu-

lating the Electoral System under the SNTV: The Case of the Republic of China on Taiwan," in *Elections in Japan, Korea, and Taiwan under the Single Non-Transferable Vote: The Comparative Study of an Embedded Institution*, ed. Bernard Grofman, Sung-Chull Lee, Edwin A. Winckler, and Brian Woodall (Ann Arbor: University of Michigan Press, 1999), pp. 65–84.

4. See Gary W. Cox, "SNTV and d'Hondt Are 'Equivalent,'" *Electoral Studies* 10 (1991): 118–32, and John Fuh-sheng Hsieh, "The SNTV System and Its Political Implications," in *Taiwan's Electoral Politics and Democratic Transition: Riding the Third Wave*, ed. Hung-mao Tien (Armonk, NY: M.E. Sharpe, 1996), pp. 193–212.

5. That such a system facilitates two-party competition has been dubbed Duverger's law by William H. Riker. See his "The Two-party System and Duverger's Law: An Essay on the History of Political Science," *American Political Science Review* 76 (1982): 753–66.

6. In an interesting article, Christopher H. Achen argues that Chen's vote came essentially from the traditional DPP supporters. He compares, at the township level, the distribution of Chen's vote with that of the DPP vote in the 1995 Legislative Yuan election, and finds a tremendous degree of correlation between the two. See his "Plurality Rule When Polling Is Forbidden: The Taiwan Presidential Election of 2000," paper presented at the Conference on Taiwan Issues held by the Center for Asian Studies, University of South Carolina, in Charleston, South Carolina, April 2000.

7. Seymour M. Lipset and Stein Rokkan, "Cleavage Structures, Party Systems, and Voter Alignments: An Introduction," in *Party Systems and Voter Alignments: Cross-National Perspectives*, ed. Seymour M. Lipset and Stein Rikkan (New York: Free Press, 1967), pp. 1–64.

8. See Russell J. Dalton, *Citizen Politics: Public Opinion and Political Parties in the Advanced Industrial Democracies*, 2d ed. (Chatham, NJ: Chatham House, 1996).

9. See John Fuh-sheng Hsieh and Emerson M.S. Niou, "Issue Voting in the Republic of China on Taiwan's 1992 Legislative Yuan Election," *International Political Science Review* 17 (1996): 13–27, and "Salient Issues in Taiwan's Electoral Politics," *Electoral Studies* 15 (1996): 219–35. A more comprehensive treatment of cleavages in Taiwan's electoral politics can be found in John Fuh-sheng Hsieh, "Continuity and Change in Taiwan's Electoral Politics," in *How Asia Votes*, ed. John Fuh-sheng Hsieh and David Newman (New York: Chatham House, 2002). Some people may argue that ethnicity may also be an important factor here. There is no doubt about it. But ethnicity and national identity are closely related to each other as can be seen in Table 6.2.

This is based upon National Chengchi University Election Study Center's 2000 survey (see the following discussion about this and other related surveys), and cell entries are numbers of respondents with row percentages in parentheses. Clearly, Minnan Taiwanese are more likely than others to support independence, and mainlanders are more inclined than others to be in favor of unification with Hakka Taiwanese somewhere in between. However, when we come to partisan attachments, it is national identity rather than ethnicity per se that determines how people react to political parties. A pro-independence mainlander is more likely to support the DPP or TAIP, for instance.

10. These surveys were conducted by Opinion Research Taiwan in December

1992, and by the Election Study Center in January 1995, March 1996, January 1999, and June 2000. They are all nationwide surveys in which the wordings are not always the same, but they do not deviate too much from each other.

11. See, for example, Anthony Downs, *An Economic Theory of Democracy* (New York: Harper and Row, 1957), ch. 8.

12. Steven R. Reed, "Structure and Behaviour: Extending Duverger's Law to the Japanese Case," *British Journal of Political Science* 20 (1990): 335–56; and John Fuh-sheng Hsieh and Richard G. Niemi, "Can Duverger's Law Be Extended to SNTV? The Case of Taiwan's Legislative Yuan Elections," *Electoral Studies* 18 (1999): 101–16.

13. For an alternative view, see Shelley Rigger's chapter in this book.

14. Barbara Geddes, "Initiation of New Democratic Institutions in Eastern Europe and Latin America," in *Institutional Design in New Democracies*, ed. Arend Lijphart and Carlos H. Waisman (Boulder, CO: Westview, 1996), p. 19.

15. In these surveys, the respondents were asked, similarly to the national identity issue, to pick a point between 0 for reform and 10 for stability. Again, in order to simplify the matter, I regroup the respondents into five categories: extreme reform supporters (0 to 1), moderate reform supporters (2 to 4), neutrals (5), moderate stability supporters (6 to 8), and extreme stability supporters (9 or 10).

16. In the survey conducted by the Election Study Center in January 1999, when respondents were asked which party was most capable of solving Taiwan's economic problems, 51 percent picked the KMT, followed by the DPP with only 9.1 percent.

17. For economic voting, see, for example, John Fuh-sheng Hsieh, Dean Lacy, and Emerson M.S. Niou, "Economic Voting in the 1994 Taiwan Elections," *American Asian Review* 14, no. 2 (Summer 1996): 51–70, and "Retrospective and Prospective Voting in a One-Party-Dominant Democracy: Taiwan's 1996 Presidential Election," *Public Choice* 97 (1998): 383–99.

18. Lin later got the endorsement from the NP.

19. In the Election Study Center's 1996 survey, respondents were asked to judge President Lee's position on the national identity issue. Interestingly, 22.9 percent of the respondents thought he was in favor of "unification as soon as possible" or "status quo first, unification later"; 22 percent believed he supported "independence as soon as possible" or "status quo first, independence later"; and 23 percent said he favored "status quo for good" or "status quo first, then, depending upon the situation, to move toward either unification or independence." The responses were truly divided.

20. See also Achen, "Plurality Rule When Polling Is Forbidden."

21. James Soong is a shrewd politician. He has tried very hard to change his mainlander image. On the national identity issue, he has been very cautious about not being seen as overly pro-unification.

22. When it was first formed, the NP tried to downplay the national identity issue, instead emphasizing the clean government theme. But clearly, it did not succeed. Indeed, it has been gradually "forced" to turn back to the national identity issue.

23. For a similar argument, see Matthew Soberg Shugart and John M. Carey, *Presidents and Assemblies: Constitutional Design and Electoral Dynamics* (Cambridge, UK: Cambridge University Press, 1992), ch. 10.

24. This occurred in Japan before the 1994 electoral reform, too. See J. Mark Ramseyer and Frances McCall Rosenbluth, *Japan's Political Marketplace* (Cambridge, MA: Harvard University Press, 1993).

25. The KMT has advocated the Japanese-type mixed system with as many seats reserved for the single-member district portion as possible, while the DPP, along with some other smaller parties, has opted for the German-type mixed system, essentially a variant of PR. Thus, it will be difficult for the major parties to reach an agreement regarding the electoral reform.

———— 7 ————

The Democratic Progressive Party in 2000

Obstacles and Opportunities

Shelley Rigger

From its formation in 1986 until Chen Shui-bian's victory in the 2000 presidential election, the Democratic Progressive Party (DPP) struggled without success to become Taiwan's ruling party. A year into Chen's presidency, the extent of the DPP's power remained limited, both because it lacked a legislative majority to support Chen's initiatives and because most of the executive personnel upon whom he relied were not DPP members. Nonetheless, the election of its candidate to the nation's highest office represents an enormous breakthrough for the DPP. Not least, having access to executive power may enable the DPP to dismantle some of the structures and obstacles that prevented it from winning in the past. Thus, the new century presents the DPP with both challenges and opportunities.

Obstacles to DPP Success

Given that the DPP is less than twenty years old, its accomplishments to date have been remarkable. Nonetheless, the party only recently achieved its own primary goal: capturing a branch of the national government. In this section, I will analyze the factors that prevented the DPP from

A slightly different version of this chapter was published in the *China Quarterly*, no. 168 (December 2001). The editors gratefully acknowledge *China Quarterly*'s permission to reprint the article in this volume.

attaining its goals for more than a decade. There are many ways one might conceptualize the challenges facing the DPP, but this study will focus on three categories of obstacles: contextual factors, external obstacles, and internal errors (see Figure 7.1). These categories are not specific to the Taiwan case; other opposition parties suffer from these difficulties; indeed, the analytical framework underlying this chapter is intended as a tool for comparative research on opposition parties generally.

Contextual Factors

Contextual factors are forces beyond the immediate control of political actors within a particular country. For example, if a regional hegemon, world superpower, or international lenders express a strong preference for a country's ruling party, it may be difficult for an opposition party to come to power. Likewise, external economic or security threats may persuade voters to leave a long-time ruling party in office in order to preserve stability. In Taiwan, both factors have played major roles in frustrating the DPP's efforts to become the ruling party.

To begin with, both the People's Republic of China (PRC) (Taiwan's main adversary) and the United States (Taiwan's most important friend) appear to prefer stable KMT rule over a shift to a DPP-led government. The PRC's preference is clear. Washington's preference for the KMT is much more muted than that of Beijing; nonetheless, its constant reiteration of its "one-China policy" and regular warnings to Taipei not to be "provocative" both suggest discomfort with the DPP and its policy positions. While the Chinese Communist Party is no friend of the KMT, it has long understood that the DPP—with its historic support for Taiwan independence—is even more hostile to Beijing's goals. Two weeks prior to the 2000 presidential election officials in Beijing released a policy white paper that made clear their opposition to the DPP and its candidate. Three days before the voting, the Chinese premier, Zhu Rongji, followed up this gesture with a strongly worded statement urging Taiwanese not to vote for the "wrong candidate." Zhu said, "Let me advise all these people in Taiwan: do not just act on impulse at this juncture, which will decide the future course that China and Taiwan will follow. Otherwise I'm afraid you won't get another opportunity to regret."[1] In case there was any question that Chen was the "wrong candidate," Zhang Mingqing, spokesman for China's Taiwan Affairs Office referred to Chen by name in a February 25 interview with a Japanese journalist.

Figure 7.1 **Obstacles Facing Opposition Parties in New Democracies**

Contextual factors

- international preference for ruling party
- external threats (economic or security)
- political culture

External obstacles

Negative

- flawed institutions (incomplete reform)
- ruling party's economic privileges and advantages
- ruling party's privileged access to mass media
- administrative and judicial bias in favor of the ruling party
- machine politics

Positive

- ruling party's reputation for success and competence
- ruling party's broad social base

Internal errors

Forced errors

- narrow goals and ideology
- weak economic platform
- extremism

Unforced errors

- eagerness for democratization leads to a "bad pact"
- resort to symbolic politics
- resort to regional/tribal/ethnic/religious politics
- willingness to be bought off
- poorly designed party structure and organization

After the election the Chinese leadership raised the level of its attacks, but shifted its focus from Chen himself to his vice president-elect Lu Hsiu-lien. On April 7, 2000, the Taiwan Affairs Office of China's State Council released a statement calling Lu "an extremist and hopeless independence supporter." The statement continued, "Lu's assertions of independence precisely expose the shamelessness of the small group of independence supporters in Taiwan."[2] Other statements called Lu the "scum of the nation" (*minzu bailei*) because she described Taiwan and the PRC as "close neighbors and distant relatives." In short, Beijing's opposition to the DPP both before and after the election is not hard to discern.

Another contextual factor working against the DPP's ambitions is the atmosphere of insecurity that ongoing conflict in the Taiwan Strait generates. As long as the PRC refuses to renounce the use of force to compel cooperation with its unification policy, the Taiwanese must weigh their domestic political choices against the danger of provoking the PRC. In addition to Beijing's clear opposition to a DPP government, the KMT can rightly claim to have preserved Taiwan's security and autonomy for more than fifty years. Taiwan's international isolation gives islanders little assurance that the outside world will defend the island in the event of a conflict; thus, it is hardly surprising that most voters prefer candidates linked to the KMT, which preserved stability for so long. (James Soong's KMT connections made him an heir to this record in the eyes of many who supported him in 2000, even though he technically was not a KMT candidate.)

External Obstacles

External obstacles are characteristics of the domestic political environment that are beyond the opposition party's control. They may be divided into negative obstacles—qualities of the system that suppress the opposition party—and positive obstacles—elements that promote continued ruling party success. Admittedly, the distinction between the two is blurry; both work to give the ruling party an unfair advantage over the opposition. However, they do so in slightly different ways.

The Democratic Progressive Party faces a broad array of external obstacles, both negative and positive. Some features of the political system actively discourage DPP success. Above all, the DPP finds it nearly impossible to compete with the KMT's political machine. Although direct manipulation of the electoral system through fraud is rare in Taiwan today, until very recently, the KMT controlled networks capable of mobilizing millions of votes. These networks—riddled with corruption and vote buying—undermined fair competition by making payoffs, rather than issues, party identification and candidate qualifications, the most important determinant of electoral outcomes. The networks still exist, but evidence from the 2000 presidential election suggests that their ability to channel votes to particular candidates is waning. Furthermore, the KMT can no longer count on their loyalty. Some local factions, especially in central Taiwan, supported James Soong's presidential bid. Soong's supporters included Taichung County's Red Faction, led by Liu Sung-fan (a former speaker of the Legislative Yuan) and the Lin Faction of Chiayi County, headed by former Justice Minister Liao Cheng-hao.

As long as the KMT was in power, it was impossible for the DPP to compete with the ruling party machine on its own terms. Only the KMT was in a position to deploy the political and economic resources of the state to support a pervasive system of patronage networks. In order to keep the networks loyal and compliant, the ruling party maintained a steady flow of public works projects, patronage appointments, "safe seat" nominations, and cash to its lower-level supporters. At best, the DPP could offer only nominations; candidates were on their own after that. Even with Chen Shui-bian in the presidential office, the DPP will find it very difficult to displace the KMT as the purveyor of patronage at the local level. Assuming the DPP attempts to channel public money to its supporters (which is unlikely, given the party's very public commitment to rooting out corruption), KMT and People First Party (PFP) legislators will do their best to obstruct such measures. Moreover, the DPP is weakest at the local level, where the KMT machine has its roots. For example, in the June 1998 elections for township and village offices, the DPP won only about 4 percent of the seats.

Another significant negative obstacle preventing the DPP from achieving its goals is the KMT's huge economic advantage. Taiwan's longstanding ruling party seized assets from the departing Japanese colonial regime and created some new ones from scratch. According to a *Taipei Times* report dated March 1, 2000, "The value of the KMT's assets is estimated to be between NT$200 billion (US$6.7 billion) and NT$500 billion (US$16 billion)," making the KMT one of the wealthiest political parties in the world. The DPP, by contrast, has long suffered extreme economic hardship. Until 1997, the party relied upon individual donations for most of its income; it has labored under a burden of chronic debt and economic crisis. In 1997 the situation improved with the creation of government subsidies to political parties. Nonetheless, the DPP's resources still represent only a small fraction of the KMT war chest.

Related to the KMT's riches is its privileged position in Taiwan's mass media. Until 1987, all of Taiwan's television stations were owned by party and government agencies, and the publishers of the major newspapers were KMT officials. After the Republic of China (ROC) government lifted martial law in 1987, a much wider range of voices was permitted, but the well-established KMT-linked media companies enjoyed significant competitive advantages. When cable television arrived on the scene in the early 1990s, the range of perspectives broadened, but the quality and objectivity of news reporting remains less than ideal. Finally, in five decades as Taiwan's ruling party, KMT officials made all the administrative and judicial appointments in the central government (and most of those in municipal governments), raising the specter of administrative and judicial bias against the opposition. The DPP and its predecessors have complained for years about government officials using their positions to campaign for KMT political candidates, and about harassment of opposition supporters by police, government inspectors, and tax authorities. In this election, incumbent prime minister and KMT vice presidential candidate, Siew Wan-chang raised eyebrows more than once when he attended events in his prime ministerial role—including a Taipei City ceremony honoring volunteers and a Kaohsiung City-sponsored cycling race—wearing campaign garb.

In addition to these negative obstacles, the DPP's progress also has been retarded by a powerful positive obstacle: Many voters simply prefer the KMT. On the political issues they find most important, Taiwanese generally rate the KMT above the DPP. For example, a 1998 DPP survey found that 35.6 percent of voters thought the KMT was the party most able to enhance economic prosperity, while only 10.3 percent believed the DPP was most able to do so. On the issue of national security, the KMT enjoyed an even larger advantage with 46.5 percent of voters believing that the KMT was best able to ensure national security, compared to only 6.4 percent for the DPP.[3] Even Chen Shui-bian can claim only 39 percent of the vote; his victory almost certainly rested on the division of KMT votes between Lien and Soong.

The KMT's support base is extraordinarily broad, thanks to its long-standing strategy of incorporation. Over the decades, the KMT built a cross-class coalition that included farmers (first mobilized through the land reform and then through Farmers' Associations), labor (organized into state-sponsored unions), government employees, military personnel, and entrepreneurs (granted special access to the state through party-sponsored business associations). The only significant groups left out of this coalition were independent professionals and entrepreneurs in small and medium-sized businesses. Until the 1970s, the former sector was relatively small, and the latter was brought under the KMT umbrella through patronage networks (local factions). Thus, the opposition movement was initially a coalition of independent intellectuals and professionals existing outside the KMT's corporatist structures, along with disgruntled local politicians whose personal ambition or ideological preferences could not be satisfied inside the KMT.

Given the KMT's widespread support and broad social base, even after more than a decade of two-party competition, the DPP still relies on the collapse of the KMT to bring about its biggest successes. The DPP's triumph in the 1997 municipal executive races was due less to a shift toward the DPP by the electorate than to a breakdown of KMT discipline in many districts. Thanks to the presence of KMT mavericks in many districts, the DPP was able to capture twelve out of twenty-one municipal executive seats with only 43 percent of the votes cast. Likewise, Chen Shui-bian almost certainly would not be the president-elect today had James Soong not wrenched away key KMT constituencies: mainlanders, urban moderates, and local factions in central Taiwan. A final consequence of this dynamic is the DPP's consistently disappointing performance in legislative elections, where multimember districts promote KMT unity and discipline.

Internal Errors

Internal errors are characteristics and actions of an opposition party that make it difficult for that party to win. Some errors are inevitable, so I have called them forced errors. Perhaps the most important forced errors stem from opposition parties' tendencies to try to unite under a single roof all those who wish to overturn the ruling party. Their efforts have two results. First, during the democratization process, the opposition may find that it grows fastest when it limits its demands to a single issue dimension: democratization. This limits the party's appeal, especially when the ruling party meets some or all of its reform demands. Second, because the ruling party's coalition includes a broad spectrum of social and economic interests, the opposition may be unable to articulate a package of economic and other public policies that differentiate it from the ruling party, especially if the broad-based ruling party is willing to coopt popular opposition proposals. (The KMT has used this strategy to a fault, perhaps the best example being its decision in 1993 to take over a DPP-initiated effort to regain Taiwan's United Nations representation.)

Unforced errors are understandable, but they are not inevitable. They are mistakes that move the opposition party away from its goal of winning power. Often, unforced errors result from frustration and impatience. After decades of struggle, an opposition party may become so eager for democratization that it agrees to an incomplete reform package. Or, frustrated by the ruling party's cooptation of its popular proposals, the opposition may resort to symbolic, ethnic, regional, or religious politics. These strategies help to solidify the opposition's base, but they limit its appeal to the broader public—often to the point of preventing it from ever becoming the majority party.

The DPP has made both forced and unforced errors. Its major forced error was the decision to embrace all anti-KMT elements in Taiwanese society. Because the KMT is a cross-class coalition of social groups, the DPP had no choice but to adopt the same model, pulling together the anti-KMT members of all social groups. Each DPP supporter had his or her own constellation of reasons for opposing the KMT. Groups that supported the opposition included intellectuals, founders of small and medium-sized firms, local politicians, feminists, and environmentalists. All that most DPP supporters had in common were a preference for democracy (whether for ideological reasons or out of personal ambition) and a desire to remove the KMT from power. Beyond issues of regime change, DPP members shared very few interests or ideas.

As the major elements of the DPP's democratization agenda were implemented, the party had difficulty finding new issues that would unify its existing supporters and attract new members and voters. In the absence of other issues with equally broad appeal, the opposition party made an unforced error: It chose a political strategy based on ethnic mobilization. Ethnic politics solidified the DPP's core, but it drove away pro-democracy mainlanders, who came to see the DPP as an antimainlander party, and also nervous moderates who found the DPP's positions on cross-strait and national identity issues too provocative and risky.

The logical conclusion of the DPP's shift toward ethnic mobilization arrived in 1991, when ideological hardliners pushed through a charter revision calling for Taiwan independence. The moderates in the DPP knew that most Taiwanese did not favor independence, but they gave in, in part to extract concessions from the hardliners, and in part because they hoped to strengthen the party's base. The downside of the charter revision was that many voters came to view the DPP as reckless, willing to endanger national security for its own quixotic goal. The DPP compounded its problem when it nominated Peng Ming-min, a strong independence advocate, as its presidential candidate in 1996. These decisions all but guaranteed that the DPP would not win the presidency or gain a legislative majority, at least until it convincingly repudiated the strong pro-independence position.

The DPP also suffered from the effects of another unforced error. In its eagerness to achieve democratization, the party allowed the KMT to retain many of its prereform structural advantages. Rather than continuing to fight for political reform in extraconstitutional channels, the DPP decided to work through the electoral process, even though doing so might slow the pace of reform. For example, the pact reached at the National Affairs Conference (NAC) in 1990 opened the national parliamentary bodies to electoral renovation, and laid the groundwork for direct presidential elections. However, it did nothing to dismantle the KMT's political machine; in fact, election-related corruption and violence have increased since the NAC. Some NAC recommendations aimed at ending machine politics, such as eliminating the Provincial Assembly and replacing elected grassroots officials with appointed ones, were carried out slowly or not at all. It was only in 1997 that a fourth television station began broadcasting, offering the first on-air challenge to the existing stations' pro-KMT message. Meanwhile, the KMT's financial advantage remains enormous. In short, during the transition to democracy, the DPP accepted a pact that addressed the technical issues of institutional reform, but left in place many of the unfair practices that helped preserve the KMT's dominant position.

Finally, the DPP's organization has contributed to the party's problems. The DPP is modeled on the KMT's Leninist structure—it has a central committee, party congress, and so on. However, it lacks the strong central leadership that has been the KMT's most significant organizational feature for more than fifty years. Instead, the DPP is a highly democratic party, offering abundant opportunities for individual party members to promote their opinions and ideas. Strong personalities and a political star system dominate the DPP, while factional struggle and negotiation drive its decision-making process. As a result, the DPP has not been able to respond effectively to new policy opportunities and challenges. Without a strong central leadership to guide it, the party tends to fall into embarrassing public squabbles and weak policy consensus.

Overcoming Obstacles in the 2000 Presidential Election

Given this litany of reasons for the DPP's weakness, is not its failure already overdetermined? How can this author account for Chen Shui-bian's victory in March 2000? Three factors are most important. First, the DPP faced a divided KMT in the 2000 presidential election, greatly reducing the number of votes Chen needed to win. Second, many of the phenomena I have called "external obstacles" ended up working against the KMT in this election, helping to divide the KMT vote and push some undecided voters into the DPP camp. Third, the DPP corrected some of its own errors. Working together, these factors gave the DPP the edge it needed to overcome its long-standing disadvantages, at least in this election. In order to increase its share in the next legislative election, the DPP will have to push these trends even further forward. The prospects for progress in this direction are outlined in the conclusion.

The reasons for the KMT split in this election are beyond the scope of this chapter. However, the DPP did play a role in the KMT's disintegration, in the sense that pressure from the opposition helped undermine KMT unity and discipline. The loyalty of the patronage networks on which the KMT machine depends has been diminishing since the DPP came on the scene. When DPP candidates began to attract significant numbers of votes, they introduced a "wild card" into an electoral system that had long depended on the predictable, orderly allocation of votes among KMT candidates. Once local politicians and factions realized the KMT could not guarantee their success, they increasingly acted as free agents. They used the presence of DPP candidates in their districts as a source of leverage over the ruling party, in some cases helping to elect DPP candidates.[4]

Once the KMT's patronage networks came to see themselves more as free agents than as team players, holding the party together was nearly impossible. Taiwan's electoral system for legislative races masks party disunity by permitting nominations of candidates from each of several factions. However, this option is not available in executive races, in which each party must present only one nominee. The KMT has faced defections in municipal executive elections since 1977; as we have seen, the DPP's victory in 1997 was due in large part to rebellious local factions. The 2000 presidential race provided another opportunity for the leaders of patronage networks to flex their political muscles. James Soong skillfully exploited their ambitions in his presidential campaign, appropriating numerous KMT networks for himself. Soong laid the groundwork for this strategy back in the mid-1990s, when he was the governor of Taiwan Province. The peripatetic governor visited each of Taiwan's 309 towns and townships at least once, forging intimate personal connections with a vast number of local faction leaders. Although it is impossible to prove without more detailed data, the election results suggest that many of these local bosses returned Soong's favor, encouraging their grassroots supporters to vote for the maverick candidate in the 2000 presidential race.

The transformation of external obstacles into DPP advantages was a key component of the 2000 presidential election. Negative obstacles such as KMT wealth, machine politics, and administrative and judicial impartiality—once the cornerstones of KMT electoral dominance—provoked a popular backlash in 2000.

The KMT's economic wealth still bought considerable access to the voters in 2000, but it also became something of an embarrassment. The DPP's years of complaining about the KMT's unfair financial advantage finally bore fruit in this campaign. On January 2, the KMT's presidential candidate, Lien Chan, promised to put his party's business holdings in trust, in order to eliminate suspicions that the KMT might use its business assets to manipulate the economy for political advantage. Although many hailed the gesture, some suspected the KMT would not carry out its promise. According to Wu Jau-hsieh, a political scientist at National Chengchi University, "What Lien promised today was nothing new, as some have perceived. The problem is that the promises have never been realized. . . . It would be a good thing if the KMT put its party assets in trust, or even returned all its assets to the state and put itself on an equal footing with other parties in competing for voters." Wu continued, "But I still doubt whether the KMT is going to do it."[5] In the end, the KMT-dominated Legislative Yuan failed to pass the necessary legislation to carry out Lien's promise, confirming the cynics' expectations.

One of the key issues in the 2000 election was political corruption, known in Taiwan as *heijin zhengzhi*, or "black and gold politics." Voters were especially up in arms about political abuses such as vote buying, bid rigging in public construction, political violence, and the penetration of elected bodies by criminal organizations. Each of these phenomena is

linked, directly or indirectly, to the KMT's machine politics. Vote buying is a key component of the patronage networks' strategy for mobilizing votes for KMT candidates. Bid rigging is one of the ways local
political bosses are rewarded for supporting the KMT and cooperating
with its strategy, either because they themselves operate construction
companies or because friendly construction firms pay kickbacks to them.
Political violence has increased in recent years, in part because the money
to be made through the manipulation of public policy has grown. Several high-profile cases—including the execution-style murders of a
Taoyuan County executive and his aides—highlight this increase. Finally, Taiwan's mass media recently have called attention to the gang-
land connections of many elected officials, especially county and city
council members, but also including national parliamentarians.[6]

A December 5 *Taipei Times* article described a report issued by DPP
legislator Chien Hsi-chieh. According to data Chien compiled from a
police report on gangster involvement in bid rigging on construction
projects, "at least 100 elected politicians in Taiwan have an organized
crime background." Said Chien, "The elected representatives include
88 deputies sitting on county or city councils, five legislators, and seven
National Assembly deputies . . ." Information released by the ROC
government reinforced Chien's claims. According to the same *Taipei
Times* report, a former justice minister estimated that about a third of
Taiwan's 800 elected officials had criminal records, while statistics released by the Judicial Yuan listed more than 200 politicians involved in
ongoing legal disputes, both criminal and civil.

Media favoritism and administrative and judicial bias also prompted
criticism of the KMT. Media watchdog groups publicized accusations
of bias. Meanwhile, civil servants from both parties accused one another of engaging in partisan activity on city time. For example, Chen
Shui-bian criticized the KMT mayor of Taipei City for disciplining the
local police chief who introduced Chen to the officers under his command. (During his term as Taipei mayor, Chen had similarly disciplined
police officials who showed favoritism to KMT candidates.)

A month before the 2000 election, police raided the home of a prominent Soong supporter, former Legislative Yuan speaker Liu Sung-fan.
Although the search was part of a long-standing bank scandal investigation, many observers interpreted it as evidence of judicial bias. What
troubled observers most was the timing of the raid, which followed hard
upon Liu's endorsement of Soong. Wang Shih-si, the director of Taiwan's

Judicial Reform Foundation, denied that the search was politically motivated. However, she spoke for many Taiwanese when she added, "I think there is one thing the judges have to think about: When the courts have acted so slowly in handling criminal charges against over 200 lawmakers, and when prosecutors have delayed so long in investigating a questionable multimillion dollar loan made by Vice President Lien Chan, how could you expect us to have faith in you?"[7] In sum, instead of hindering the DPP's progress, these "external obstacles"—KMT wealth, machine politics, and administrative, judicial, and mass media bias—all ended up embarrassing the KMT in 2000.

Another important development in the 2000 presidential race was Chen's retreat from the DPP's pro-independence charter provision. By pulling away from that stance, Chen Shui-bian made his candidacy acceptable to many Taiwanese who otherwise would have been unwilling to support him. In this sense, he corrected the error his party made in 1991 and reinforced in 1996. Nor was Chen's strategy on this issue a radical departure from the DPP mainstream. At least as early as 1993, other DPP leaders were using the same tactic. As Shih Ming-teh put it in 1995, the position of the party leadership (if not the party charter) was that if the DPP came to power, "we will not need to, nor will we, declare independence."[8] Throughout the campaign, Chen Shui-bian stressed his moderation on this issue, promising to eschew independence unless Taiwan were under military attack. At the same time, he called for a higher level of cross-strait economic integration than even the KMT was willing to accept, including opening the three direct links. Chen also avoided another of the DPP's past errors: His campaign maintained good relations with the DPP headquarters throughout the race. Chen provided the ideological leadership and focus the party needed to stay together throughout the campaign season, while party chairman Lin Yi-hsiung kept the organizational apparatus functioning well in support of Chen's presidential bid. The two organizations ran on parallel tracks, each playing to its strength in a way that facilitated cooperation rather than competition, while individual members of the DPP staff—including the long-time DPP administrator Chiou Yi-jen—held key positions in Chen's campaign.

The DPP's Opportunities and Continuing Challenges

Now that the DPP has captured the presidential office, a new set of challenges awaits. At the same time, however, Chen's victory offers the first real opportunity to remold Taiwan's political system in a way that will improve his party's chances for future success. Under Chen it may be possible to dismantle some of the roadblocks that have obstructed the DPP's progress in the past. Overcoming these obstacles will not be easy, however. Improving the quality of Taiwan's democracy seems like an unimpeachable goal, but concrete measures aimed at accomplishing this objective are sure to provoke controversy, both from those whose privileges will be reduced and from those who hope for more thorough-going reform. If the DPP is to make the most of the opportunity Chen's presidency presents, it will need to address the contextual problems, external obstacles, and internal errors that have hampered its performance in the past.

Minimizing Contextual Problems

The Chen administration should continue to give priority to overcoming the resistance of Beijing and Washington and convincing the Taiwanese people that the DPP is capable of safeguarding peace and stability. If Chen cannot persuade the voters that he can handle cross-strait relations, he is unlikely to make much progress toward his other policy objectives. Initial indications suggest that Chen may achieve at least some success in this area. U.S. reaction to his election has been favorable; although before the election, many American officials suspected that Chen's moderate stance on cross-strait issues was insincere, they appear more inclined to believe him now. Beijing's reaction is more complex. On the one hand, the tide of anti-Chen rhetoric that peaked in Zhu Rongji's March 15 speech receded after the ballots were cast. The Chinese leadership promised to take a "wait and see" attitude toward the new leader. However, Beijing's vituperative attacks on the vice president-elect and its refusal to back down on the one-China principle as a precondition for cross-strait talks reflect its desire to keep pressure on Chen Shui-bian. In the first year of his presidency, cross-strait relations saw little in the way of renewed tensions, but Chen's gestures to the mainland—including opening direct transportation between two Taiwan-held islands and the PRC—met with little enthusiasm in Beijing.

Overcoming External Obstacles

Whether or not the DPP can dismantle the structural advantages the KMT has enjoyed in the past will be an important determinant of its success. Unless it can make the political system fairer, the DPP is unlikely to increase its share of legislative seats significantly or win a second presidential term in 2004. To avoid becoming a "one-term wonder," Chen Shui-bian must address Taiwan's institutional flaws.

Already, there is evidence of progress toward political reform. Soon after the 2000 presidential election, the National Assembly decided to reduce its own power drastically and downgrade its status to that of an ad hoc body. Getting rid of the National Assembly is a long-standing DPP goal. The party views the Assembly as an unnecessary, wasteful institution rooted in an obsolete notion of Taiwan's identity. Moreover, the Assembly traditionally was an important resource for the KMT's patronage networks. Up-and-coming KMT politicians used Assembly seats as stepping stones to higher offices, while the votes they mobilized on their own behalf reinforced the KMT's power. The National Assembly districts tend to be very small, increasing the efficacy of traditional KMT mobilization. Thus, eliminating National Assembly elections may help to weaken the KMT machine.[9]

Another measure that would help undermine machine politics is action to reverse the trend toward "black and gold politics." Rolling back corruption and gangsterism in the political realm was one of Chen Shuibian's most important campaign promises; he could not ignore this issue after he took office. The most immediate way to attack black and gold politics was to launch criminal investigations and prosecute corrupt public officials and their private-sector cronies. In interviews I conducted immediately after the election, several DPP officials used the phrase "kill some chickens to scare the monkeys" to describe this strategy. To facilitate these prosecutions, the DPP planned to reorganize aspects of the judicial process that have protected politically connected criminals and criminal organizations in the past.

Criminal prosecution is not the only weapon available to fight corruption. The DPP also planned corruption-fighting legislation. For example, most analysts agree that Taiwan must establish the rule of law in the bidding process for public works projects. The money to be made off public construction is a key motivation for black and gold politics. Similarly, some have suggested that individuals convicted of certain crimes should be forbidden to run for public office. Given that a large proportion of Taiwan's county and city council members have criminal records, such a rule would significantly reduce the criminal element's role in politics. Other measures to discourage black and gold politics include eliminating elections for basic-level offices (the patronage networks' roots), decreasing the size of the Legislative Yuan, and implementing a single-member district system. These measures are unlikely to pass without a fight, because the black and gold politicians at whom they are aimed hold a significant share of seats in the legislature. According to a DPP strategist, the party will strive to establish a firm public consensus in favor of its reform measures before introducing them in the legislature, in the hope of increasing the pressure on legislators to pass the bills.

As we have seen, the KMT enjoys a large financial advantage over its competitors, as well as privileged access to mass media, administrative personnel, and the judiciary. The proposal offered by the KMT before the election to put its business assets into a trust failed; a similar bill—perhaps one with even farther-reaching consequences—will be required if the KMT's economic headstart is to be shortened. Working for a DPP president, under a multiparty cabinet, surely will be a new experience for Taiwan's bureaucrats, who in the past have worked for the KMT exclusively. Whether they will abandon their political role, shift their loyalty to the DPP, passively resist the new regime, or actively oppose it remains to be seen. The DPP is counting on the professionalism of central government bureaucrats to carry out its instructions.

Correcting Internal Errors

To a great extent, the DPP's troubles are of its own making. As an organization cobbled together from diverse anti-KMT elements, the party inevitably must face internal conflict and struggle. During the presidential campaign, the DPP's internal controversies were muted, as the DPP's factions put aside their differences to concentrate on winning the election. Now that the victory has been won, however, the party leadership must preserve that fragile unity. In particular, the DPP must avoid public internecine squabbles over positions and policy. The first year of Chen's administration was marred by frequent criticisms of the president by members of his party. As the 2001 legislative elections approached, however, the DPP was able to rekindle the unity that played such an important role in 2000. The DPP also needs to address its other major unforced error—the endorsement of Taiwan independence—by bringing its official platform into synch with the preferences of the electorate and the position of its most influential leader, Chen Shui-bian. Efforts to do so have foundered on the party's reluctance to give up what many see as an important bargaining chip without the promise of compromise in Beijing.

Chen Shui-bian and his party face many challenges as they set out to realize their goals. Lacking a firm popular mandate, and forced to work through Taiwan's imperfect political institutions, Chen's proposals struggled in both the legislative and executive branches of government. And given the KMT's broad, patronage-based foundation, the DPP's policy options are constrained from the outset; it never has had a chance to develop a fully-articulated set of issue positions. Meanwhile, Beijing opposes Chen and the DPP, and both the PRC government and many Taiwanese politicians have worked hard to undermine popular confidence in the new administration. The nadir seemed to have been reached, however, in the fall of 2000 when KMT and PFP legislators joined together in an effort to recall Chen from office. The move failed, due in large part to popular opposition, but it illustrated the Chen administration's weakness, and the reluctance of KMT and PFP politicians to cooperate with a DPP-led executive. Nonetheless, Chen's presidency offers the DPP its best opportunity to date to break through the structural obstacles that have frustrated Taiwan's democracy for more than five decades.

Notes

1. *Taipei Times*, March 16, 2000.
2. *Taipei Times*, February 27, 2000.
3. Democratic Progressive Party Survey Center, "Survey on Party Images in Taiwan," July 23, 1998.
4. See Chen Ming-tong, *Paixi zhengzhi yu Taiwan zhengzhi bianqian* (Factional politics and Taiwan's political evolution) (Taipei: Yuedan, 1995), p. 190. See also, Shelley Rigger, *Politics in Taiwan: Voting for Democracy* (New York and London: Routledge, 1999), pp. 114–16, 144–46.
5. *Taipei Times*, January 3, 2000.
6. Just after the March election, Yunlin County was declared the leading municipality for gangster participation in politics. Liu I-chou, a professor of political science and Yunlin native who specializes in the study of grassroots politics, observed that the designation was incomplete, because it counted only county council members, and omitted the county's most important gangster politician, the county executive. Another well-known example is Luo Fu-chu, a member of the Legislative Yuan who has called himself the "spiritual leader" of a major Taiwanese crime gang.

7. *Taipei Times*, January 3, 2000.

8. Shelley Rigger, *From Opposition to Power: Taiwan's Democratic Progressive Party* (Boulder: Lynne Rienner, 2001), p. 127.

9. The reason for the National Assembly's abrupt self-destruction is not as admirable as this discussion may make it seem. The DPP struggled to carry out this reform for years, but it could not persuade KMT Assembly members to cooperate. After Lien Chan's presidential defeat, however, the KMT recognized that a National Assembly election in the near future would give Soong a venue in which to strengthen his People First Party. By downgrading the National Assembly, the KMT denied its new antagonist a critical opportunity to build its organization and popular base.

8

The March 2000 Election in Historical and Comparative Perspectives

Strategic Voting, the Third Party, and the Non-Duvergerian Outcome

Tun-jen Cheng and Yung-ming Hsu

The March 18, 2000, direct presidential election in the Republic of China (ROC) on Taiwan was definitely a watershed event, as it dislodged the Kuomintang (the Nationalist Party or KMT) from political power after half a century of uninterrupted rule, and set in motion a new round of party realignment. A less noticeable but equally significant result of this milestone election was that it revived Taiwan's three-party system and contradicted the prediction of "Duverger's law." A single-member district election, according to Duverger,[1] is conducive to the making of a two-party system. Rational voters tend to choose between the incumbent and the most viable challenger, often from the government party and the main opposition party, rather than waste votes on candidates from third parties. Where district magnitude (*M*) is larger than one, the number of parties is still expected to be *M* plus one.[2] Yet, the case

Tun-jen Cheng and Yung-ming Hsu would like to thank the Chiang Ching-kuo Foundation for Scholarly Exchange and Taiwan's National Science Foundation (NSC 89–2414-H-194–017) for research support, especially for the collection of poll data. They are also grateful to Bruce Dickson, Szu-yin Ho, Ogasawara Yoshiyuki, and two anonymous reviewers for their helpful comments on earlier drafts of this essay.

of newly democratized Taiwan often presents a non-Duvergerian equilibrium in its executive elections (where $M = 1$), enhancing rather than undermining the third party. This past election epitomized such an outcome.

Since its democratic transition, Taiwan has had four major chief executive elections, two gubernatorial ones (1994, 1998) and two presidential ones (1996, 2000). A significant third party—the New Party (NP)—emerged in 1993 and did extremely well in the 1994 Taipei mayoral election. While this third party fared poorly in the 1994 Taiwan governor's race, it performed well in the 1996 presidential race. The third party was, however, weak in the 1998 Taipei mayoral race, much in line with the Duvergerian logic that the third party suffers in a one-on-one contest. Yet, the recent presidential election reasserted a three-party system. The magnitude of "electoral correction" was so strong in this past election that an independent candidate, James Soong, supported by the existing third party, nearly tied the winner. This past election permitted Soong to form a new party—the People First Party (PFP)—that is, poised to overshadow, and even absorb, the existing third party, the NP, and may even threaten to replace the KMT as the principal opposition party. Moreover, in this past election, the KMT no longer served as the "coordination point" for strategic voters as was the case in the 1996 presidential election. Instead of being the primary beneficiary of strategic voting, the KMT candidate turned out to be its victim in the 2000 presidential race in Taiwan.

Strategic voting—an act of defection from a voter's most preferred candidates to support a less preferred one so as to prevent the least preferred one from being elected—often occurs in Taiwan's executive elections. The strategic voting of mainlanders, an ethnic minority, is particularly noticeable and consequential, affecting electoral outcomes and the fate of the third party. Comparing five of the most recent national-level executive elections in Taiwan, this chapter analyzes the swings of strategic voting and the vicissitude of the third party in Taiwan's one-on-one elections; identifies the ethnic minority as third-party voters and outlines the logic of their collective action; presents a model of directions and the magnitude of strategic voting; explains the fate of the significant third party in light of the ethnic minority's strategic choice at the elite and mass level; and shows how strategic voting debilitated the age-old ruling KMT in the 2000 presidential election and instilled new life into the third party.

Ethnic Voters and the Third Party

The third party under a single-member district, plurality-based electoral system can be ephemeral if it is composed mainly of estranged voters who are only protesting against the two mainstream parties. Yet, a third party can also be quite long lasting if it has a stable social basis. In the United States, the third party—supported by alienated voters[3]—can quickly evaporate, if the two main parties adjust policies to accommodate the aspirations and demands of these protest voters. In contrast, social democrats in postwar Canada and liberals in post-1970s Britain have persistently defied predictions of their demise, thanks to the sustained activism of intellectuals and their social allies in these two polities.[4] Third-party voters in Taiwan were initially estranged voters, but they quickly learned to act collectively and strategically, and, if necessary, to serve as the backbone of a new and more promising third party. Despite the ebbs and flows of its electoral fate, the third party proves to be resilient in Taiwan's political contours.

The elasticity of the third party appears to be attributable to the electoral system for Taiwan's legislature. Eighty percent of Taiwan's legislators are chosen by single-nontransferable votes in multiple-seat districts, the so-called SNTV system. This system is a hybrid between the single-member district system and the proportional representation (PR) system.[5] The larger the average district magnitude an electoral system has, the more akin it is to a PR system, the smaller the district magnitude, the more akin it is to a single-member system. Most electoral districts for Taiwan's legislature are large, making its SNTV system more like a PR system, and, presumably, giving third parties ample living space. As chief executive elections and legislative elections are not held concurrently in Taiwan, the former cannot possibly generate coattail effects on the latter. Other things being equal, one would then expect the third party to "contract" in chief executive elections, but to "expand" in legislative elections. However, contrary to this theoretical prediction, the third party in Taiwan has often done well in one-on-one elections, while its electoral performance in SNTV-based legislative elections has often been dismal.

We contend that the third-party phenomenon in newly democratized Taiwan has less to do with electoral systems than with ethnic politics. To begin with, numerous studies have established that the principal political cleavage in newly democratized Taiwan is forged primarily along ethnic fault lines rather than based on class, religious, regional, or rural-urban divisions.[6] The Minnan group—which speaks a dialect of southern Fujian—constitutes about 71 percent of the total population in Taiwan, the Hakka 15 percent, the mainlander 13 percent, and the natives 1 percent. The Minnan and Hakka arrived centuries ago, make up the ethnic majority of the island, and are called "native Taiwanese," while mainlanders, as latecomers and as the backbone of the pre-democratic KMT regime, are the ethnic minority. The ethnic divide in Taiwan is primarily based on differences in the spoken languages and the timing of immigration rather than on races, written languages, or religions as in the case in South Africa, Malaysia, or the Balkan Peninsula. Intermarriage, education, and urbanization are blurring ethnic distinctions, but ethnicity remains a powerful predictor of electoral choice, as shown in nearly all the studies on Taiwan's elections. Mainlanders have rarely voted for DPP candidates, while the NP has drawn support primarily from mainlanders. Mainlander voters basically shift loyalty between the KMT and the NP, while "native" Taiwanese choose mainly between KMT and DPP candidates.

Next, the emergence of the NP as the first significant third party in Taiwan was a result of the dynamics of ethnic politics during Taiwan's transition to democracy. The DPP as the prime mover for Taiwan's democratization initially exploited the issue of ethnic cleavage and hoped to mobilize "native Taiwanese" for its electoral gain. In contrast, the KMT has always proclaimed itself as a catchall party for all social and ethnic groups. Prior to recent democratic change in Taiwan, the KMT was firmly in the hands of mainlanders who controlled 85 percent of key government and party positions. With President Lee's ascension to its chairmanship and his recruitment of local political and business elites into the KMT, mainlanders began to lose their grip on political power. For awhile, mainlanders acquiesced to Lee's leadership, as the KMT was the only party able to cope with challenge from the DPP. The DPP's appeal to ethnic support forced the KMT to further dilute its mainlander quotient and policy orientation, which, in turn, drove a group of mainlander elites to bolt from the KMT to form the NP, ushering in an era of a three-party system.[7] The NP was established to become a political arm of the mainlander minority. Yet, not all mainlander elites defected from the KMT, and mainlander voters do not necessarily reject KMT candidates or support NP candidates. Thus, ever since the formation of the NP, mainlander voters have become a crucial factor in determining electoral outcomes as well as the changing fate of all three parties.

Collective action by the ethnic minority is often understood as an expression of distinct cultural identity, political beliefs, emotional attachment, and even altruism, much in the way that nationalism is construed.[8] Seemingly "irrational" behavior (e.g., Chechnya's futile pursuit of independence without external assistance) is often attributed to patriotic commitment to a cause that an ethnic group presumably embraces. But, as David Laitin convincingly argues, beneath the veneer of heroism and passion in ethnic politics may lie self-interest-based motivations and rational political calculus.[9] Indeed, collective action may even impart more instrumental utility than expressive utility to the ethnic minority in Taiwan. On the one hand, the emotional and expressive dimension of ethnic politics in Taiwan has been decreasing. For awhile, the highly emotionally charged issue of national identity has driven many mainlanders to embrace the NP (which takes a proactive stand for unification with the mainland), to reject the DPP (which, until recently, took a proactive stand for creating a Republic of Taiwan), and to suspect the KMT (which, in its views, at best wavers between the two stands and at worst colludes with the DPP). However, the clash between the two competing identities (Taiwanese vs. Chinese) is ameliorating, while the tendency toward multiple identity is gaining strength in Taiwan,[10] especially since President Lee called for redefining mainlanders as "new Taiwanese," thereby transforming the national identity issue from an "either-or" proposition into a "more or less" one. On the other hand, collective action by the ethnic minority in Taiwan has always created high instrumental value. Democratization in Taiwan has inevitably reversed the preexisting imbalance of power between an ethnic majority that used to be in a subordinate position and an ethnic minority that used to be in a dominant position. Hence, it is utterly rational for mainlanders in Taiwan to undertake calculated collective actions if only to avoid being marginalized in a new political game. Playing ethnic politics is simply smart politics, as it minimizes costs that the new political game may impose while also ensuring or even enhancing group benefits that the new political game no longer confers automatically.

Collective action makes sense for both the masses and the elite. For rank-and-file members of a minority, a solidarity movement can compel the leadership of the ethnic majority to adopt public policies that serve the interests of the minority. For the political elites of a minority, group solidarity strengthens their bargaining position vis-à-vis leadership of the ethnic majority. Indeed, it is to the advantage of minority leaders to keep the minority group culturally and politically distinct, for they would otherwise lose their representative function.[11] And if the ethnic majority is politically divided, a unified minority can even play the role of a critical balancer. This is clearly the case of the ethnic minority in Taiwan, as the ethnic majority has split its loyalty between the DPP and KMT.[12] Hence, mainlander leaders who can deliver minority votes *en bloc* are in an excellent position to bargain with KMT majority leaders, and, not inconceivably, DPP leaders, for political gains. Mainlander leaders are always in need of support from the mainlander community to take collective action, and they are always competing among themselves for the position of standard bearer of the community.

There are hurdles to collective action. The well-known free-rider problem is one.[13] This is, however, not an intractable problem for the ethnic minority in Taiwan, given their relatively small number, residential proximity, dense social ties, and fairly similar occupational choices. With the political ascension of "native Taiwanese," a keen sense of crisis (*weiji yishi*) has also developed in the mainlander community, alleviating the free-rider problem. The main problem lies in coordinating the elite and the masses, as the two sides may differ cognitively in assessing collective interests and prescribing the optimal political strategy for the group.[14] Nearly all mainlander leaders were initially groomed within the KMT, a party that had nearly unconditional electoral support from mainlander voters. Those mainlander leaders who bolted from the KMT to form a third party (as in the case of the NP founding fathers) or to become independent candidates (as in the case of James Soong in the 2000 election) are, by definition, defectors, creating centrifugal forces and potentially undermining the welfare of the mainlander community. These defectors often have to endure group pressure, absorb the cost of blazing a new course, and bear the burden of persuasion that their strategic choice might create long-term benefits for the group. In Moe's terminology,[15] they are risk takers and political entrepreneurs acting on behalf of, but not at the behest of, group members, and trying to educate the followers in the art of political arbitrage. Leaving the KMT does not mean not cooperating with the party any longer; and the mere existence of a third party makes it even more likely for the KMT leadership to make good offers to the mainlander community. However, for rank-and-file mainlanders, the main concern is whether their leaders, now split into two camps, will take concerted action to enhance group interests or will be pitted against each other to put group interests at risk.

Mainlander elites who have bolted from the KMT and those who remain within the fold of the KMT do not always converge in their expectations. On the one hand, mainlander KMT elites obviously benefit from the existence of the NP because it means that, if necessary, they can credibly threaten to exercise the option of exit from the KMT. Moreover, if the KMT is to collaborate with the NP to cope with the challenge from the DPP, then KMT mainlander elites will serve as an honest broker, and, indeed, a guarantor, for the NP's credible commitment. This bridge-making function strengthens KMT mainlander elites' bargaining position vis-à-vis KMT majority leadership. Without a third-party option, both mainlander elites and the masses would be taken for granted by the KMT majority leadership and become the KMT's captured second-class constituency. On the other hand, the existence of the NP poses the danger of splitting mainlander votes and pitting mainlander elites within and outside the KMT against each other. Mainlander KMT elites need to persuade NP elites and mainlander voters of the utility of their collaborating with KMT majority leadership. Their persuasive power hinges on the resources and opportunities they can obtain from KMT majority leadership to benefit the minority community. As KMT mainlander elites cannot always deliver benefits to mainlander voters, there is no reason for the NP elites to play second fiddle to KMT mainlander elites. Hence, NP and KMT mainlander elites may be collaborating to promote the well-being of the mainlander community, but they may also be competing for the leadership of this political community.

To sum up, while minority leaders may split and diverge, their ability to negotiate with the majority group hinges on their ability to maintain solidarity in the minority group. Group cohesiveness determines whether minority elites will be politically recognized and rewarded with status, benefit, and influence commensurate with, if not exceeding, the electoral strength of the minority. As such, minority elites have every incentive to solidify the minority group and to use internal policing to deter defection. However, successful internal policing is based on unity and collaboration at the elite level. When minority elites in the NP and the KMT are coordinated, minority voters are easily congealed into bloc votes. If the minority elite splits or fails to coordinate, then the internal policing mechanism will malfunction, minority solidarity will weaken, and minority voters may take individual actions. The task for the competing minority elites then becomes one of persuading as many minority voters as possible to form a voting bloc, and then to try to shape the direction of such a "moving pack." Strategic voting often becomes a selling point. Yet, elites propose, voters dispose.[16] Minority voters are free agents, not the instruments of their leaders. They may or may not vote strategically, irrespective of the elite's advice.

Strategic Voting

Strategic voting refers to a voter's decision to switch support from his/her first preference to second preference, in order to prevent the third or the least preferred candidate from winning. There are three necessary conditions for strategic voting. First, the expected winner is not a voter's most preferred candidate. Second, a voter's next preferred candidate is not very different from his/her most preferred candidate in terms of policy stands and personal attributes. In short, a voter can also accept his/her second best choice. Third, the distance between one's next preferred candidate and the third (least) preferred candidate is wide, again, in terms of policy stands and personal attributes. In short, a voter really dislikes the third candidate. If all three conditions are met, this voter has an incentive to vote strategically.

If we assume a voter's preference order as $U(A) > U(B) > U(C)$, then the first condition for strategic voting can be denoted as $P(A) < \min \{P(B), P(C)\}$. That is, while candidate A is the best choice for this voter, B the second best, and C the worst, this voter predicts that A is less likely to win the race than either B or C. The second and third conditions can be depicted as $U(A) - U(B) < U(B) - U(C)$. That is, to this voter, the distinction between A and B in policy stands or personal attributes is smaller than that between B and C. If all three conditions are met, then this voter *may* abandon A to rescue B (*qi-A-bao-B*) from being defeated by C. To summarize,

$$\text{If } U(A) > U(B) > U(C),$$
$$\text{and } P(A) < \min \{P(B), P(C)\},$$
$$\text{then } U(A) - U(B) < U(B) - U(C) \Rightarrow \text{vote} \sim A.$$

William Riker argues that strategic voting is quite prevalent in single-member district elections and that, in a sense, it is a motivational basis for the making of a two-party system.[17] However, a potential strategic voter does not always vote strategically. A voter may simply stick to his/her first preference and be a sincere (or protest) voter rather than a strategic voter. For example, supporters for third-party candidates in U.S. executive elections are mostly sincere or protest voters. Ross Perot voters in 1992 and 1996 might have preferred George Bush or Robert Dole to Bill Clinton, or vice versa, but they voted for Perot even though his chances of winning were slim.[18] In fact, most American voters, Raymond Wolfinger argues, neither calculate rationally nor act in accordance with expectations about the likely margin of the electoral victor.[19] Similarly, in newly democratized South Korea, the necessary conditions for strategic voting were met in two of the three most recent presidential elections, 1986 and 1997, but entrenched regional cleavages prevented voters from acting strategically.[20]

Strategic voting did occur in newly democratized Taiwan in a few national-level chief executive elections covered in this chapter.[21] We advance three propositions to explain the patterns and magnitudes of strategic voting in Taiwan. First, strategic votes tend to shift between candidates with the same ethnic background. Assume a voter's preference order as $U(A) > U(B) > U(C)$. If A and B, but not C, are from this voter's ethnic group, then this voter is more likely to vote strategically. But if only A, that is, a voter's most preferred candidate is from this voter's ethnic group, then this voter is more likely to be a sincere voter, even if A is unlikely to win the race. For example, Minnan voters were more likely than mainlander voters to engage in strategic voting in the 1994 Taipei mayoral race between two Minnan candidates, Hwang Ta-chou of the KMT and Chen Shui-bian of the DPP, and a mainlander candidate, Jaw Shao-kang of the NP. For Minnan voters, Huang and Chen were either the most or next preferred candidates (i.e., either A or B) and the difference between them was narrow, while Jaw as the least preferred candidate (C) was very distinct from the other two. Given that $U(A) - U(B) < U(B) - U(C)$, Minnan voters were in a position to act strategically. Conversely, mainlander voters were expected to be sincere voters loyal to their most preferred candidate, as they were very likely to be indifferent to the other two candidates, B and C, that is, $U(A) - U(B) > U(B) - U(C)$. The ethnic combination of candidates for the 1998 Taipei mayoral election was reversed, now with two mainlanders, Ma Ying-jeou of the KMT and Wang Jian-hsuan of the NP, but one Minnan, Chen Shui-bian of the DPP, in the race. In this race, mainlander voters were more likely to vote strategically than were Minnan voters. Occasionally, there is ambiguity about a candidate's ethnic background, making it possible for this candidate to play both sides, becoming either the coordination point or departure point for both mainlander and Minnan strategic voters. Lien Chan, the KMT's presidential candidate in 2000, is a typical example. Lien is from a prominent family in Tainan, Taiwan, but he was born on the mainland and raised by a mainlander mother.

The second proposition, not unique to Taiwan, is that the dimmer the prospect of one's most preferred candidate, or A, is, and the more competitive one's second preferred candidate, or B, is (vis-à-vis the least preferred one, or C), the more likely this person will be to vote strategically. Polls—which attempt to measure the support levels for various candidates—are likely to form voters' expectations of the electoral outcome. Opinion leaders' endorsements are likely to reinforce this expectation, and these endorsements should be crucial in the final period of campaign during which the release of any poll is usually interdicted. Two conditions are essential to the decision to vote strategically. First, the gap in polls between the second preferred candidate (B) and the least preferred candidate (C) should not be too wide, otherwise a voter will not be motivated to act strategically. B has to remain competitive with C. If B is far behind or far ahead of C in the poll ratings, then a voter is likely to remain loyal to A, given that his/her strategic vote is not likely to bridge the gap between B and C. Second, if C is leading in the poll ratings, then the rating for B should be significantly higher than that for A (at least by a margin of error) in order to motivate a voter to abandon A to rescue B. Any voter would hesitate to switch from his/her top choice to the second best, unless the latter is substantially more "electable" than the former.

The third proposition is that the People's Republic of China's intimidation makes strategic voting even more likely in Taiwan, but such voting tends to go against Beijing leaders' wishes. China staged a war game during Taiwan's first democratic presidential election in 1996, and issued a stern warning during its second presidential election in 2000. The intention was to deter Taiwan voters from embracing the KMT candidate in 1996 or the DPP candidate in 2000, both *personae non gratae* for Beijing. By and large, the threat from Beijing failed to achieve its purpose. It might have scared some risk-averse voters into dumping the candidate blacklisted by Beijing, but it might even have provided more risk-neutral voters with a stronger motive to cast strategic votes for this candidate.

The first proposition helps us to identify the main patterns of strategic voting, while the second and third propositions allow us to assess the magnitude of strategic voting. Ethnic majority voters would exercise arbitrage between the DPP and the KMT, while ethnic minority voters between the KMT and the NP or non-KMT mainlander candidates. In terms of magnitude, the wider the gap in polls between A and B, and the narrower the gap between A and C, the larger the volume of strategic voting. And the harsh words from Beijing reinforce strategic voting, irrespective of the expectation of Beijing leaders. Based on the raw data in Appendices 8.1 through 8.5, Table 8.1 summarizes the magnitude and suggests the directions of strategic voting in five executive elections in newly democratized Taiwan. We use aggregate data—polls and ballots—to specify the thrust of strategic voting, even though the model presented above is based on individual voters' preferences and expectations. This is a second-best solution. Panel data recording individual preferences before and after the 1994 Taiwan gubernatorial election and data for the 1996 presidential election simply do not exist. Moreover, given that we attempt to use the calculus of strategic voters to explain the electoral outcome in all five elections and the evolution of the party system, it is probably justifiable to use aggregate data.

The first five rows of Table 8.1 present a general profile of five elections covered in this chapter regarding the number of contenders and party affiliation of the obvious leader or loser in polls. One candidate emerged as the obvious leader in the polls in all but the 2000 elections. No candidate was hopelessly lagging behind in polls for the 1998 and 2000 elections. We then compute the gap in the polls between the two front runners (row 6) and the gap in the votes they actually received (row 7). The next two rows in Table 8.1 show the corresponding gaps between the two last runners. We propose that the discrepancies between the average preelection polls and the actual votes received by candidates reveal the magnitude of strategic voting. We also distinguish the two dimensions of strategic voting at the aggregate level; one is the shift of strategic voters toward the most viable candidate (Dimension I), the other is the shift away from the least viable candidate or the obvious loser (Dimension II). The magnitude of strategic shift in Dimension I (row 10) can be denoted by the difference between two gaps, the gap in polls between the front runner and the candidate ranked second (row 6), and the gap in actual votes received by these two candidates (row 7). The difference between the last and next to last ranked candidates in polls indicates the magnitude of strategic shift in Dimension II, as shown in row 11, which is the difference between row 9 and row 8. We define

Table 8.1

Two Dimensions of Strategic Voting

	1994 Taipei mayor	1994 Taiwan governor	1996 President	1998 Taipei mayor	2000 President
(1) Number of major contenders	3	3	4	3	3
(2) The obvious leader in polls	Chen	Soong	Lee	Ma	n.a.
(3) This leader is from KMT	no	yes	yes	yes	n.a.
(4) The obvious loser in polls	no	Chu	Chen	Wang	no
(5) This loser is from the third party	yes	yes	yes	no	n.a.
(6) Gap between the two front runners in polls	11.5	29.0	26.3	5.3	6.9 (Soong-Chen)
(7) Actual vote gap between these two front runners	13.5	17.5	32.9	5.2	2.0 (Chen-Soong)
(8) Gap between two last runners in polls	5.0	8.2	4.3	28.0	4.6 (Chen-Lien)
(9) Actual vote gap between these two last runners	4.3	34.4	4.9	34.8	14.0 (Chen-Lien)
(10) Type I strategic shift = (7) − (6) if larger than +5 percent, big swing	2.0 small	−11.5 big	6.6 big	0.2 small	−8.9 big
(11) Type II strategic shift = (9) − (8); if larger than +5 percent, big swing	−0.7 small	26.2 big	0.6 small	6.8 big	9.4 big

Source: Compiled and computed by the authors based on the raw scores in the appendices.

Notes: The contenders for the 1994 Taipei mayoral election were Chen Shui-bian (DPP), Huang Ta-chou (KMT), and Jaw Shao-kang (NP). The contenders for the 1994 Taiwan governor's race were James Soong (KMT), Chen Ting-nan (DPP), and Chu Kao-cheng (NP). The contenders for the 1996 presidential election were Lee Teng-hui (KMT), Peng Ming-min (DPP), Lin Yang-kang (a KMT rebel), and Chen Lu-an (a KMT rebel). The contenders for the 1998 Taipei mayoral race were Chen Shui-bian (DPP), Ma Ying-jeou (KMT), and Wang Jian-hsuan (NP). The contenders for the 2000 presidential race were Lien Chan (KMT), James Soong (independent), and Chen Shui-bian (DPP).

a strategic shift of 5 percent or more as a big swing, a shift less than that a small swing. If the magnitudes in shift for the two dimensions are symmetrical, that is, both swings are big or both are small, then strategic voters have abandoned the obvious losers and gravitated toward the winner of the first two front runners. If the swing in Dimension II is big, and the swing in Dimension I is small, then strategic voters have abandoned the least hopeful candidate and shifted their support to both the front runner and the second ranked candidate. If the swing in Dimension II is small, but the swing in Dimension II is big, then strategic votes have not come from the supporters of the least viable candidate, but rather from the independent voters, the so-called undecided voters in the polls.

Table 8.1 shows that, except in the 1994 Taipei mayoral election, strategic voting has been significant in one-on-one elections in Taiwan. In the 2000 presidential election, most mainlander voters supported independent candidates James Soong instead of the KMT or NP candidates early during the campaign, as Soong appeared to have the best chance of preventing a DPP victory. The mainlander voters' strategic move was, however, overwhelmed by a massive shift of Minnan voters—9.4 percent of total voters (see column 5 of Table 8.1)—away from the KMT candidate toward the DPP candidate. Consequently, the ranking of the first two front runners (Soong vs. Chen) was reversed, and Chen eventually beat Soong by 2 percent of votes. Unlike the other four elections listed in Table 8.1, the 1994 Taiwan governor's race had, for some unknown reasons, an exceptionally high level of "undecided" voters (see Appendix 8.5). Comparing the polls and actual votes received, we find that the gap between the two front runners, the KMT candidate, Soong, and the DPP candidate, Chen, was greatly narrowed (11.5 percent of total votes, see column 2 of Table 8.1). Furthermore, the gap between the two last runners, Chen, and the third party candidate, Chu, widened. This indicates that many "undecided" (most likely Minnan) voters weighed in to attempt to avert a landslide for Soong. Both the 1996 presidential race and the 1998 Taipei mayoral race show asymmetry between the two dimensions of strategic voting. In 1996, the shift was from the second ranked candidate, Peng of the DPP, to the front runner, Lee Teng-hui of the KMT. Obviously, Minnan voters, not mainlander voters, were the prime movers here. The shift of strategic votes in 1998 is the only one that did not fit our model. For that race, the KMT candidate, Ma Ying-jeou, a prominent mainlander with an illustrious record of government service, had a slim lead in polls over an extremely popular DPP candidate, Chen Shui-bian, the incumbent Taipei mayor. The third candidate, Wang Jian-hsuan of the NP, was a distant third in polls. According to Table 8.1, about 6.8 percent of voters might have shifted away from Wang. Given that Wang's supporters were primarily mainlander voters, these strategic votes should have flowed to Ma only and should have widened the gap between Ma and Chen. And yet, the gap between Ma and Chen remained the same (see column 4 of Table 8.1). Either KMT supporters acted strategically in Chen's favor or undecided voters threw their weight to Chen to offset the mainlander voters' strategic move.

Mutation of the Duvergerian Outcome

As mentioned earlier, the DPP draws its support predominantly from the ethnic majority or "native Taiwanese," and it competes with the KMT for their votes. In the case of all national elections, executive and legislative, the DPP has never been able to receive more than 40 percent of total votes cast.[22] Mainlanders as an ethnic minority can thus affect electoral outcome and the rise and fall of the third party. However, their political impact varies from election to election, depending on whether mainlander elites coalesce or split, and on whether mainlander voters act strategically. Mainlander elites inside and outside the KMT may cooperate to forge solidarity among mainlander voters, or mainlander elites may compete to divide up the votes. When mainlander elites do well within the KMT (such as winning the party nomination), they usually are able to establish a high reputation among mainlander voters, thus convincing mainlander elites outside the KMT to lend them at least tacit support during the electoral campaign. Otherwise, mainlander elites within the KMT will have to compete with those outside the KMT for the loyalty of mainlander voters. Mainlander voters may or may not respond accordingly. When called upon by mainlander elites within the KMT to support their candidate strategically, they may cast sincere or protest votes for the third-party candidate, resulting in a KMT defeat and a DPP victory. When called upon by non-KMT mainlander elites to support the third party, they may cast strategic votes to support the KMT candidate, thereby dealing the third party a fatal blow. The interaction of mainlander elites' coalition behavior and minority voter's choice can therefore determine the fate of the third party and often decisively shape

Table 8.2

Executive Elections and Non-Duvergerian Outcomes in Taiwan

		Minority Elite	
		Division	Unity
	High level	A	C
		Third party at its peak	Third party languished
		2000 presidential	1998 Taipei mayoral
Minority voters' strategic choice			
	Low level	B	D
		Third party competitive	Third party vanished
		1996 presidential	1994 Taiwan provincial
		1994 Taipei mayoral	

the electoral outcome, as demonstrated in the four possible conditions or cells in Table 8.2.

Cell A depicts a situation in which mainlander elites split, mainlander voters act strategically, and the third party is in full swing. The 2000 presidential election is a good example. KMT Chairman Lee Teng-hui did not permit James Soong, a popular mainlander elite, to seek the party's nomination, driving the latter out of the KMT to run as an independent. Mainlander elites split into two subgroups, cutting across the party line between the NP and the KMT. Ma Ying-jeou, John Kuan, Hsu Li-teh, and Chen Lu-an endorsed Lien Chan, while Hau Pei-tsun, Chao Yau-tung, and most NP leaders sided with James Soong. Earlier, an overwhelming majority of mainlander voters had strategically turned against the NP and the KMT to support James Soong, who had the best chance of preventing the DPP candidate from winning. However, on election day, a significant number of Minnan KMT supporters shifted to shore up DPP's Chen who won the presidency by a narrow margin. Aside from solid support from mainlander voters, Soong also managed to garner a high level of support from Hakka voters and former KMT voters in "peripheral counties" (giving Taiwan's minority politics a new twist; see details below). A new third force—later formalized into the PFP under James Soong—was in full swing, nearly on an equal footing with the two main parties.

Cell B depicts a situation under which mainlander elites split, mainlander voters cast sincere or protest votes, and the third party remains strong. As in the Cell A situation, mainlander elites' choice again fails to win the KMT nomination and competes with mainlander elites outside the KMT for the leadership among mainlander voters. Yet, unlike the situation in Cell A, mainlander voters in Cell B are not engaged in strategic voting, either because they are indifferent to the other two candidates or because one of these two candidates has an absolute lead in polls. Mainlander voters are riveted to their most preferred candidate from the third party. The third party is able to remain a significant political force, neither powerful enough to win nor marginalized by the two major parties. The 1994 Taipei mayoral election and the 1996 presidential election are the two examples presented in Cell B. In 1994, NP leaders and KMT mainlander elites did not collaborate. The former presented a party candidate, Jaw Shao-kang, while the latter—most notably, James Soong, then the KMT party secretary—was obligated to support the party candidate, Huang Ta-chou, a Minnan. Nearly all mainlander voters supported Jaw while many Minnan KMT voters sided with the DPP's Chen Shui-bian, who won with a plurality of votes. While Jaw as the third-party candidate was defeated, he received more votes than the KMT candidate. Had mainlander voters acted strategically and sided with Huang, the DPP would not have had a chance to win. In the 1996 presidential race, mainlander elites within the KMT were not even given a chance to bid for the running mate position on the party ticket. Mainlander elites again split, and those siding with the KMT lost the leadership of the mainlander community to NP elites. Mainlanders voted for their most preferred candidates, either Lin Yang-kang (who teamed up with Hau Pei-tsun) or Chen Lu-an (who teamed up with Wang Ching-feng), both of whom were KMT insurgents. The NP formally endorsed Lin, but mainlanders split their votes rather evenly between Lin and Chen, instead of voting strategically for one of them. For his part, Lee, a clear-cut front runner from the very beginning of the campaign, emerged as a majority winner, thanks to the strategic voting of many "native" Taiwanese voters who might otherwise have sided with the DPP candidates. The third-party votes—the combination of votes amassed by the two KMT insurgents, exceeded the votes amassed by the DPP candidate. In both the 1994 Taipei mayoral and the 1996 presidential elections, the third party clearly demonstrated its ability to compete with at least the lesser of the two main parties.

Cell C depicts a situation in which mainlander elites coordinate, mainlander voters strategically support the KMT candidate, and the third party wanes. In this case, the mainlander elites succeed in becoming the leaders within the KMT and are poised to replace NP elites as chief of the mainlander voters. Many NP cadres acquiesce to the leadership of KMT mainlander elites, while mainlanders abandon the NP candidate to prevent an upset victory by the DPP. The coalescing of mainlander elites and the strategic choice of mainlander voters turn the third party into an insignificant player in the political market, totally marginalized and barely visible or audible. The 1998 Taipei mayoral election provides the best example. In this race, the KMT nominated a popular mainlander, Ma Ying-jeou, to face an equally popular incumbent DPP mayor, Chen Shui-bian. The tight race between Ma and Chen motivated mainlanders to turn away from an extremely respectable NP candidate, Wang Jian-hsuan, a competent, former technocrat of the KMT government. As mainlander voters sided with the KMT electorally, the NP as the third party began to lose its raison d'être. The third party was conspicuous for its redundancy in the political market.

Cell D depicts a situation in which mainlander elites unify, mainlander voters do not have to act strategically, and the third party vanishes from the political market. The best example is the 1994 election for Taiwan provincial governor. The KMT leadership rejected the bid from an "ethnic Taiwanese," instead nominating a mainlander, James Soong, who was obviously the most preferred choice for mainlanders. In this lopsided two-way race, the polls show that James Soong, fully supported by KMT elites, mainlander, or "native Taiwanese," was far ahead of a respectable, but frail DPP candidate, Chen Ting-nan, a most competent and honorable magistrate from I-lan County. There was no motivation or need for mainlander voters to cast strategic votes. While the DPP candidate eventually narrowed the gap on election day, the "strategic votes" he amassed came mainly from the independents. The third party simply abdicated the electoral space.

The above analysis of four types of situational logic and five episodes of electoral competition among major parties in Taiwan allow us to identify a cyclical pattern of change in Taiwan's party system. Mainlander elites' coalition behavior and mainlander voters' strategic choice can lead to two equilibria, the Duvergerian and the non-Duvergerian. Whenever we see a non-Duvergerian outcome, the third party ascends, a three-party system emerges, and, more often than not, the DPP wins a narrow victory. The 1994 Taipei mayoral election illustrates this situation. Given this suboptimal outcome, the ethnic majority and the ethnic minority in the KMT leadership have a strong incentive to coalesce to entice mainlander voters, thereby weakening the third party. A

Duvergerian equilibrium may be restored, as was vividly demonstrated in the 1994 Taiwan governor's and the 1998 Taipei mayoral elections. However, whenever the ethnic majority within the KMT is tired of compromising with mainlander leaders and begins to assert its primacy at the expense of the mainlander community, the Duvergerian equilibrium may be upset. The third party can be revitalized and may even overshadow the KMT, if mainlander voters' strategic withdrawal from the KMT triggers a massive defection of "native Taiwanese" from the KMT to the DPP. The 2000 presidential election illustrates this suboptimal, non-Duvergerian outcome again. The incentive for KMT and PFP elites to coordinate to restore the Duvergerian equlibrium will be strong in 2004.

To sum up, electoral competition in Taiwan has vacillated between two equilibria, which forms a cyclical pattern of change in Taiwan's party system. The KMT leadership's treatment of mainlander elites within the KMT has largely shaped the direction and duration of the swing between the two equilibria. Mainlander voters have responded in a tit-for-tat manner, "penalizing" or "rewarding" the KMT leadership, and fully displaying the power of collective rationality. The DPP had been unable to influence the shift between two equilibria of electoral competition. It could only make a third decision in responding to the grand plan of the KMT leadership, and then to the strategic calculation of mainlander voters. The DPP's electoral fortune was, in a sense, a dependent variable. The challenge for the DPP as the incumbent party is to prevent the restoration of a Duvergerian outcome in the next election by forming an innovative coalition with either the KMT or the PFP, thereby consolidating the resurfaced three-party system.

Like the DPP, the PRC had little impact on the shift between the Duvergerian and the non-Duvergerian electoral outcomes in the ROC on Taiwan. Obviously, the PRC has a strong incentive to coalesce the KMT and the PFP, in order to make Chen Shui-bian a single-term president. However, the PRC neither nominates presidential candidates nor selects political appointees in Taiwan; it possesses no capacity to frame the structure of party competition. It can, however, affect the magnitude of strategic voting, as it did in the 2000 presidential race, to which we now turn.

The 2000 Presidential Election and Beyond

Elite dissension plagued the KMT in the first two popular presidential elections, in 1996 and 2000, but the party had a stunning victory in the first race and a crushing defeat in the second. In both races, mainlander elites split rather than unified, but mainlander voters engaged in strategic voting only in the 2000 election, a collective action matched by significant Minnan voters. In 1996, mainlander voters were "sincere voters," spreading their votes between the third and fourth candidates (Lin and Chen), rather than siding with KMT candidate Lee in order to prevent DPP candidate Peng from winning. In that race, Lee Teng-hui was the obvious leader in polls from the very beginning of the campaign (see Appendix 8.2). As there was widespread rational expectation of his winning the race, there was no viable second most likely candidate for mainlander voters to gravitate to *en bloc*, as indicated by a low value in row 11 and column 3 of Table 8.1. Yet, quite a few potential DPP voters shifted to swell Lee Teng-hui's votes, as demonstrated by the relatively high value in row 10 and column 3 of Table 8.1. Given that Lee was leading by a wide margin in the polls, there was little need for DPP supporters to vote strategically for Lee. That many eventually did can probably be attributed to the PRC factor. Due to the PRC's blatant military threat to Taiwan (most notably, its firing of missiles at Taiwan's territorial waters), the national security issue dominated the 1996 election. Already with unsurpassed popularity, the KMT candidate Lee Teng-hui took a firm position and showed an ability to command the security issue, further reinforcing his position as the only viable choice for most voters. Indeed, for some voters, a yes vote for Lee was also a way to defy the PRC's intimidation of Taiwan.

As to the 2000 presidential election, most third-party voters made an early strategic decision to support James Soong, an independent candidate, rather than the NP's nominee, Li Ao. The polls indicated a three-way race among three major candidates, Lien Chan from the KMT, Chen Shui-bian from the DPP, and James Soong (see Appendix 8.1). Given uncertain electoral prospects, the motivation for strategic voting was expected to be strong and the magnitude large. However, directions of strategic voting were more difficult to predict. As it turned out, strategic voting took the shape of two directional shifts away from the KMT candidate. As Table 8.1 shows, about 9.4 percent of voters strategically switched their support from Lien to Chen, hence leading to the narrow victory of the DPP candidate. The KMT candidate thus lost most mainlander voters to James Soong and most Minnan voters to Chen.

Given the situation that, among the three major contenders, the KMT's Lien was the second preferred candidate for most voters, mainlanders and Minnan alike, Lien could have become the beneficiary of strategic voting. However, consistently lagging behind the other two contenders in polls rendered Lien a nonviable alternative, and eventually he became the victim of strategic voting. Aside from his alleged stiff personality, the issue of clean politics—probably the most salient issue during the 2000 campaign—greatly contributed to Lien's inability to surpass the second front-runner. Many reasons account for the rise of this issue: widespread corruption, lingering political interference with the judiciary branch of government, financial scandals (which even implicated James Soong and the KMT management team), and an electoral system tainted by organized crime and business influence (the so-called black and gold politics). The flaws in the judiciary system were primarily a legacy of the authoritarian past. But the rampant financial scandals and the penetration of business and even organized crime into politics were side effects of Taiwan's democratization.[23] In an attempt to outmaneuver the conservative elements of the party bureaucracy and leadership stratum, President Lee entered into a sort of alliance with businesspeople, many of whom were well connected with organized crime.[24] In a sense, financial scandals also stemmed from the very process of incremental democratization, pensioning off the old guard and recruiting support from business. In this dire political climate, Chen Shui-bian and, prior to the exposure of his own scandal, James Soong injected this issue into electoral domains, claiming issue ownership.[25]

The KMT hoped to use the national-security issue to dampen the salience of the clean-politics issue, thus lifting its candidate out of third place in the polls. National security was indeed an issue in the 2000 election. While the PRC did not lob missiles in 2000 as it had in 1996, it did launch incessant vitriolic attacks on Taiwan and attempt to intimidate Taiwan voters to keep them from supporting the DPP candidate. However, the national-security issue was either neutralized by the DPP or mismanaged by the KMT. Chen Shui-bian had long shelved a venturesome, pro-independent position, and instead embraced President Lee's assertive position of defending the status quo, thereby consolidating his hold on traditional DPP voters while catering to the KMT voters. James Soong, for his part, took an extremely well-crafted pro-unificationist stand that did not appear to be undermining Taiwan's interest. In contrast, Lien, as the KMT candidate, wavered between Lee's assertive position and James Soong's more pro-unificationist stand, thereby losing the confidence of centrist voters. Finally, when one week before the election, the PRC's Premier Zhu Rongji issued a stern warning about the use of force against Taiwan under a DPP presidency, the KMT instantly equated a DPP victory with war and a KMT victory with peace. Using this occasion, the KMT attempted to revive the saliency of the national-security issue to direct strategic voting away from the DPP candidate and James Soong. However, Dr. Y.T. Lee, the president of Academia Sinica and a tremendously popular Nobel laureate, in timely fashion, threw his weight behind the DPP candidate just prior to the election, underscoring again the centrality of the clean-politics issue to the future of Taiwan. Y.T. Lee's endorsement effectively neutralized the KMT's effort to undermine Chen's credibility in dealing with the cross-strait relations.

The defection of KMT supporters in both directions greatly enhanced the vote share of the DPP candidate and the independent candidate, James Soong. Unable to prevent Chen Shui-bian from gaining the presidency, Soong was nonetheless able to dwarf Lien in terms of voting share. Chen's share of total votes in the 2000 presidential race stood at 39 percent, a level that the DPP candidate reached in the 1994 Taiwan governor's race, and a level below what it achieved in the Taipei mayoral election in 1998 (44.2 percent).[26] Not only did Soong collect votes from all preexisting third-party supporters and emerge as their new leader, he has also created new support bases for the third party, most notably many Hakka voters in North Taiwan and most voters in the "belt of the periphery," mainlanders and Minnan alike. Hakka voters supporting James Soong reside primarily in three counties, Taoyuan, Hsinchu, and Miaoli, while the "periphery voters" are from four small outlying counties, Hualien, Taitung, Lienchiang, and Quemoy, as well as the only landlocked county, Nantou (see Table 8.3). These two "minorities"—the Hakka as a subset of "native Taiwanese" and the "periphery voters" as a sort of political minority—used to be among the KMT's support base (see Table 8.4). Thanks to James Soong's political entrepreneurship, these two political groups may be discovering the instrumental value of minority politics. Only time will tell whether they can forge collective rationality, undertake group action, and exercise political arbitrage for joint gains. But a more variegated type of minority politics seems to be emerging. The mutation of the Duvergerian outcome and the vicissitude of third parties are likely to continue in Taiwan.

Table 8.3

Vote Distribution in Hakka Counties/Cities and in Peripheral Counties During the 2000 Election

	Soong (Ind.)	Chen (DPP)	Lien (KMT)
Hakka-concentrated areas			
Miaoli County	49.6	26.8	22.2
Hsinchu County	51.6	24.8	20.7
Hsinchu City	42.8	33.8	22.4
Taoyuan County	43.8	31.7	22.1
Peripheral areas			
Hualien County	58.8	21.4	19.3
Taitung County	52.8	23.2	23.7
Nantou County	46.9	34.5	28.2

Source: Compiled by the authors from the statistics provided by the Central Election Committee.

Table 8.4

Partisan Support of Hakka Voters

	KMT	DPP	NP	
Legislative election				
1983	53	13	—	
1986	63	22	—	
1989	52	16	—	
1992	48	27	—	
1995	43	16	7	
1998	44	19	5	
Taipei mayoral				
1994	24	40	15	
1998	46	38	5	
Presidential			KMT rebel	KMT rebel
1996	64	9	4	6

Source: The Election Study Workshop at National Taiwan University.

Notes

1. Maurice Duverger, *Political Parties: Their Organization and Activity in the Modern State* (New York: Wiley, 1954).

2. Gary Cox, *Making Votes Count* (Cambridge, UK: Cambridge University Press, 1997); Steven R. Reed, "Democracy and the Personal Vote: A Cautionary Tale from Japan," *Electoral Studies* 13, no. 1 (1994): 17–28; Reed and John M. Bollan, "The Fragmentation Effect of SNTV in Japan," in *Elections in Japan, Korea, and Taiwan Under the Single Non-Transferable Vote*, eds. Bernard Grofman et al. (Ann Arbor: University of Michigan Press, 1999).

3. Steven Rosenstone and Roy Behr, *Third Parties in America: Citizen Response to Major Party Failure* (Princeton: Princeton University Press, 1996); see also Ronald Rapopport, L. Atkeson, J. McCann, and W. Stone, "Citizens for Perot: Assessing Patterns of Alienation and Activism," in *Broken Contract? Changing Relationships between Citizens and their Government in the United States*, ed. Stephen C. Craig (Boulder: Westview, 1996), 147–76.

4. Pippa Norris and Ivor Crewe, "Did the British Marginals Vanish? Proportionality and Exaggeration in the British Electoral System Revisited," *Electoral Studies* 13, no. 3 (1994): 201–21.

5. Arend Lijphart, *Democracies: Patterns of Majoritarian and Consensus Government in Twenty-one Countries* (New Haven: Yale University Press, 1986).

6. Alan M. Wachman, *Taiwan: Nationality Identity and Democratization* (Armonk, NY: M.E. Sharpe, 1994), and Hung-mao Tien, ed. *Taiwan's Electoral Politics and Democratic Transition* (Armonk, NY: M.E. Sharpe, 1996).

7. Tun-jen Cheng and Yung-ming Hsu, "Issue Structure, the DPP's Factionalism, and Party Realignment," in Tien, ed., *Taiwan's Electoral Politics*.

8. Milton I. Esman, *Ethnic Politics* (Ithaca: Cornell University Press, 1994).

9. David Laitin, "Marginality: A Micro Perspective," *Rationality and Society* 7, no. 1 (1995): 31–57.

10. Szu-yin Ho and Liu I-chou, "The Taiwanese/Chinese Identity of the Taiwan People," *Issues and Studies* 35, no. 3 (May/June 1999): 1–34.

11. David A. Lake and Donald S. Rothchild, eds., *The International Spread of Ethnic Conflict* (Princeton: Princeton University Press, 1998); Kanchan Chandra, "The Transformation of Ethnic Politics in India," *Journal of Asian Studies* 59, no. 1 (2000): 26–61.

12. Yung-ming Hsu, "A Tale of Two Cities (1994 and 1998): Mass Choice under Uncertainty," *Soochow Journal of Political Science*, no. 12 (March 2001): 75–112 (in Chinese).

13. Mancur Olson, *The Logic of Collective Action* (Cambridge, MA: Harvard University Press, 1965).

14. Dennis Chong, *Collective Action and the Civil Rights Movement* (Chicago: University of Chicago Press, 1991).

15. Terry Moe, *The Organization of Interests* (Chicago: University of Chicago Press, 1980).

16. Edward Carmines and James Stimson, *Issue Evolution: Race and the Transformation of American Politics* (Princeton: Princeton University Press, 1989).

17. William H. Riker, *Liberalism Against Populism* (San Francisco: Freeman, 1983).

18. See Ronald Rapoport and Walter Stone, forthcoming, *Perot Voters*.

19. Raymond R Wolfinger, "The Rational Citizen Faces Election Day or Why Rational Choice Theorists Don't Tell You Much About American Elections," in *Elections at Home and Abroad; Essays in Honor of Warren E. Miller*, ed. M. Kent Jennings and Thomas E. Mann (Ann Arbor: University of Michigan Press, 1994).

20. Tun-jen Cheng and Mihae Tallian, "Bargaining over Electoral Reform during the Democratic Tansition," in *Rationality and Politics in the Korean Peninsula*, ed. Hee Min Kim and Woosang Kim (Osaka: Committee on Politics and Law, International Society for Korean Studies, 1995); Byung-Kook Kim, "The Politics of Crisis and a Crisis of Politics: The Presidency of Kim Dae-Jung," in *Korea Briefing 1997–1999*, ed. Kongdan Oh (Armonk, NY: M.E. Sharpe, 2000).

21. John Fuh-sheng Hsieh, Emerson M.S. Niou, and Philip Paolino, "Strategic Voting in the 1994 Taipei City Mayoral Election," *Electoral Studies* 16, no. 2 (June 1997).

22. Yung-tai Hung, "The Distributions of DPP Votes," *China Times* Feature Section, 2000.

23. T.J. Cheng and T.C. Chou, "Informal Politics in Taiwan," in *Informal Politics in East Asia*, ed. Lower Dittmer, Haruhiro Fukui, and Peter N.S. Lee (New York: Cambridge University Press, 2000).

24. Cal Clark, "Taiwan's Elections in 2000," *Asia Society Briefing Paper*, 2000.

25. For issue ownership, see John Petrocik, "Divided Government: Is It All in the Campaigns?" in *The Politics of Divided Government*, ed. Gary Cox and Samuel Kernell (Boulder: Westview, 1991).

26. Hung, "The Distributions of DPP Votes."

Appendix 8.1

Polls Conducted During the 2000 Presidential Election

Date	Democratic Progressive Party	Soong	Kuomintang	Remarks
2/20	26	25	21	Policy platform released on television
2/22	25	26	21	Three days after the PRC White Paper was released
2/29	24	25	24	Chen Lu-an endorsed the KMT ticket
3/5	26	24	25	Ten days before ballot day
3/10	26	26	26	Y.T. Lee endorsed the DPP ticket
3/13	30	—	23	Y.T. Lee resigned from the academy
3/15	24	—	—	Zhu intimidated Taiwan
3/16	23	—	—	Zhu's warning widely reported
3/17	26	25	20	Election eve
3/18	39	37	23	Breakdown of total votes cast
3/19	+4	+5	−9	Post-ballot poll on strategic voting
	35	32	32	If without strategic voting

Source: Based on polls conducted by the *China Times* and TVBS (TVB Super Channel).

Note: The Election and Recall Law, effective May 16, 1999, prohibits the release of any poll data on candidates, parties, and campaigns during the two weeks prior to election day.

Appendix 8.2

Polls Conducted During the 1996 Presidential Election

Date	Lee (KMT)	Peng (DPP)	Lin	Chen	No reply	Remarks
1995						
June	—	—	—	—	—	China fired missiles
October	—	—	—	—	—	China staged military maneuver
11/6	49.4	5.2	5.0	5.7	34.7	—
11/15	31.9	4.1	7.9	4.8	51.3	Lin teamed up with Hau
11/25	41.2	5.0	10.1	6.0	36.7	Lin-Hau launched campaign
12/2	—	—	—	—	—	DPP did well in legislative election
12/4	39.0	5.2	10.7	3.8	40.4	—
12/19	5.5	14.9	6.4	34.2	39.0	—
1996						
1/24	—	—	—	—	—	*New York Times* reported China's plan to attack
1/26	37.7	5.4	11.3	4.3	41.3	—
2/1	40.9	5.4	12.1	4.3	37.3	China prepared military maneuver
2/11	27.6	4.0	8.0	3.6	56.8	Debate without Lee
2/12	25.8	4.9	8.5	4.5	56.3	Debate without Lien (deputy)
2/23	33.9	7.6	6.3	3.3	56.7	One month before election
3/6	33.9	4.9	6.5	4.5	50.2	China announced missile test
3/8	—	—	—	—	—	China fired missiles
3/18	—	—	—	—	—	United States dispatched two carriers
	54.0	21.1	14.7	9.8	—	Breakdown of votes cast
	41.0	16.0	11.2	7.4	—	Percent of total voters; Turnout rate, 76 percent

Source: Based on polls conducted by the *China Times* and TVBS (TVB Super Channel).
Notes: KMT—Kuomintang; DPP—Democratic Progressive Party.

Appendix 8.3

Polls Conducted During the 1998 Taipei Mayoral Election

Date	Ma (KMT)	Chen (DPP)	Gap	Wang (NP)	Unde-cided	Remarks
5/30	51.00	30.00	21.00	4.90	14.1	Ma decided to run
6/30	41.10	36.40	4.70	5.80	16.7	Five months before election
7/30	40.80	37.30	3.05	4.30	17.6	Four months before election
8/31	39.50	36.50	3.00	4.30	19.7	Three months before election
9/29	40.30	37.70	2.60	4.70	17.3	Two months before election
10/6	43.10	35.20	7.90	5.20	16.6	Chen's adviser quit
10/20	44.70	35.40	9.30	6.50	13.4	Eve of public debate
10/24	38.30	36.70	1.60	9.10	15.9	After the first debate
11/4	39.50	36.00	3.50	8.30	16.3	Chen verbally attacked
11/12	39.10	35.30	3.80	9.20	16.4	After second debate
11/19	40.90	37.10	3.80	8.30	13.7	Six weeks before election
11/24	37.80	38.00	0.20	6.70	17.6	Ten days before election
12/3	40.90	36.90	4.00	6.60	15.6	Two days before election
12/4	43.70	38.30	5.40	3.70	14.4	One day before election
	51.13	45.91	5.22	2.97	—	Breakdown of votes cast
	41.40	37.20	4.20	2.40	—	Percent of total voters; turnout rate, 81 percent

Source: Based on polls conducted by the *China Times* and TVBS (TVB Super Channel).

Notes: KMT—Kuomintang; DPP—Democratic Progressive Party; NP—New Party.

Appendix 8.4

Polls Conducted During the 1994 Taipei Mayoral Election

Date	Chen (DPP)	Jaw (NP)	Huang (KMT)	No response	Remarks
7/23	34.0	22.1	14.2	29.7	
9/18	42.1	23.3	16.5	18.1	
9	32.9	17.4	13.5	36.2	
10/1	36.2	19.3	16.2	28.3	Public debate
10/3	35.8	24.7	12.7	26.8	Public debate
11/5	27.9	21.6	21.7	28.8	
11/4	27.2	20.8	19.1	32.9	
11/6	22.9	20.6	16.0	40.5	
	43.7	30.2	25.9	—	Breakdown of votes cast
	34.3	23.7	20.3	—	Percent of total voters; turnout rate, 78.5 percent

Source: Based on polls conducted by the *China Times* and TVBS (TVB Super Channel).

Notes: DPP—Democratic Progressive Party; NP—New Party; KMT—Kuomintang.

Appendix 8.5

Polls Conducted During the 1994 Taiwan Gubernatorial Election

Date	Soong (KMT)	Chen (DPP)	Chu (NP)	Undecided or others	Remarks
9/7	44.0	10.0	3.0	43.0	
10/10	38.0	11.0	3.0	48.0	Registration
11/8	41.0	11.0	2.0	46.0	Campaign began
11/13	36.0	10.0	2.0	52.0	Party platform announced
11/22	39.0	11.0	2.0	48.0	Rally in Pingtung
	56.2	38.7	4.3	24.5	Breakdown of votes cast
	42.8	29.5	3.3	—	Percent of total voters; turnout rate, 76.15 percent

Source: Based on polls conducted by the *China Times* and TVBS (TVB Super Channel).
Notes: KMT—Kuomintang; DPP—Democratic Progressive Party; NP—New Party.

Part IV

Lee Teng-hui's Impact on Taiwan's External Relations

—————— 9 ——————

The Republic of China's Foreign Relations Under President Lee Teng-hui

A Balance Sheet

Chien-min Chao

In the past half century, the Republic of China (ROC) has successfully built a market economy and a liberal democracy that is the envy of many less-developed countries. The end of the cold war, the gradual thaw in relations between the two sides of the Taiwan Strait, and the transformation of its internal structures have heightened the international stature of this heretofore isolated island country.[1] Since the 1990s, under the stewardship of President Lee Teng-hui, Taiwan has unveiled a new chapter in its diplomatic relations with the United States, Western Europe, the Southeast Asian countries, and even its former rival, the People's Republic of China (PRC).

But, on the other hand, diplomatic endeavors undertaken by the ROC have evoked strong reactions from Beijing, straining relations across the Taiwan Strait, and, in turn, pressurizing Taiwan's international space. The visit made by President Lee to his alma mater, Cornell University, in June 1995 was seen as "splittist." Missile-firing intimidation ensued in the following year, prompting the United Sates to send two aircraft carrier battle groups to the waters near Taiwan. As a gesture to calm tensions, Washington conceded to Beijing's demand of forming a "strategic partnership" when President Jiang Zemin visited the United States at the end of 1997. A new "three-no's policy"—the U.S. government would not lend support to Taiwan independence, or to one China–one Taiwan or two Chinas, or to Taiwan's effort to join international organizations with statehood as a requirement—was announced in June 1998 when President Clinton reciprocated with a visit to China, dealing a blow to President Lee's "pragmatic foreign policy." The unexpected turn toward rapprochement reinforced Taipei's apprehension over its legitimacy as a sovereign state, leading President Lee to make the controversial announcement that the two sides of the Taiwan Strait were in a "special state-to-state relationship" and further straining the already tense condition of trilateral relations.

Beijing is adamant that its "one country, two systems" framework, in which Taipei is not allowed to engage itself with any official activities in the international arena, be maintained. Taipei's bid for membership in the World Trade Organization was delayed pending the results of Beijing's eventually successful membership application. Taiwan, even after being stricken with several contagions such as the deadly foot-and-mouth disease, had its bid for membership in the World Health Organization rejected outright. Although an important trade partner and capital supplier to the Southeast Asian countries, Taiwan has not been allowed to participate either in the discussions of the ASEAN Regional Forum or in a second-track dialogue mechanism known as the Council for Security Cooperation in the Asia Pacific (CSCAP).[2] At present, Taiwan maintains official relations with a paltry twenty-nine, mostly small and insignificant countries, and is a member of only sixteen intergovernmental organizations (IGOs).[3]

Confronting this daunting reality, President Lee made foreign policy one of his key concerns and pledged to take charge personally upon assuming office in 1988. As a result, developments during the past decade have resembled a roller coaster ride. At the same time, President Lee made restructuring and democratization of the aging quasi-Leninist regime the main theme of his administration, a move that ultimately won him international acclaim as "Mr. Democracy." Taiwan's own transformation contrasted sharply with the Beijing regime's rigidity, leading many countries to reexamine their policies toward the island democracy in the early 1990s. But the tensions that subsequently developed in the area eroded Taipei's relations not only with Beijing but also with Washington. On the other hand, Washington's rapprochement with Beijing and the latter's threatening deployment of missiles on the mainland side of the Taiwan Strait have caused concerns in the United States that have resulted in some compensatory policies in favor of Taipei. The passage of the Taiwan Security Enhancement Act in the House of the U.S. Congress, the security situation report in the Taiwan Strait released by the Pentagon, proposals to include Taiwan in the development of the Theater Missile Defense system, and the sale of more advanced arms to the ROC are convincing evidence of this policy shift.

This chapter reexamines the costs and benefits of pragmatic foreign policy under the leadership of President Lee Teng-hui, and concludes that President Lee has left deep marks in Taipei's quest for more international space but that these were made at the expense of increasingly unstable Taipei–Beijing relations and an uncertain diplomatic future.

A Review of the Past

The ROC's foreign endeavors in the past fifty years can be divided into the following four stages.[4]

Period of Expansion

The Korean War and the subsequent consummation of the Sino-U.S. Defense Treaty in 1954 reversed the adverse trend that the ROC had experienced in the international arena after suffering a defeat in the Chinese civil war. The country, with the help of its major ally, the United States, successfully warded off the military offensives of the PRC and managed to retain its UN seat. The signing of the treaty with the United States reestablished the confidence that had been shaken during previous years. Friendship with America and Japan as well as the maintenance of its permanent member status in the United Nations Security Council (UNSC), became the three pillars of ROC diplomacy. Taipei even mobilized support in the UNSC to censure the Soviet Union for its invasion of China, and, in a separate deal with Japan, the ROC signed a peace treaty.[5] The 1958 Taiwan Strait crisis brought the country ever closer to its U.S. ally, with that country providing its most up-to-date weaponry.[6] With U.S. economic assistance on the way and a military alliance in place, Taipei–Washington relations became institutionalized.[7] During the 1960s, the ROC turned its attention to Africa and Central and South America to woo support for its ever more tenuously held UN seat.[8] Consequently, the ROC was poised to expand its influence in

Africa and achieved what would come to be regarded as the "golden era" of its diplomatic history,[9] gaining the recognition of nearly seventy countries.

Period of Retreat

Entering the 1970s, it was as if a dark shadow was falling over the ROC's diplomatic skies. The post–World War II international system was undergoing dramatic changes at the turn of the decade as détente with the communist camp displaced containment as the key component of U.S. foreign policy. The traditional cold war dichotomy was about to be changed as a new U.S.–China policy came to be articulated during President Richard Nixon's trip to Beijing in February 1972. The unexpected visit caught the ROC off guard and fundamentally destroyed the three pillars of the ROC's foreign policy. Before the end of the decade, around fifty nations had shifted their loyalties, relocating their embassies to Beijing and leaving a meager twenty-two countries in Taipei's diplomatic corpus.

Period of Recuperation

After succeeding his father as the new president of the country in 1978, President Chiang Ching-kuo immediately initiated what was known as the "flexible foreign policy." The new policy shifted to unorthodox tactics to counter the adverse tide in ROC foreign relations. Consequently, trade, economic assistance, and person-to-person exchanges were emphasized in the hope of using "people power" to offset losses incurred in the official diplomatic arena. The augmentation of the ROC's economic strength and the inception of democratic processes resuscitated some of the confidence lost during the previous decade. Retaining membership in major international organizations was another area of concentration. Symbols proclaiming or indicating statehood, such as the national flag and anthem, were no longer uncompromising issues. In 1984, a compromise was reached with the International Olympics Committee to use the name "Chinese, Taipei" for its athletes to compete in the Los Angeles games, breaking a ten-year standoff. Five years later, instead of leaving the Asian Development Bank (ADB), Taipei opted to remain in attendance with the name "Taipei, China" forced on it instead of boycotting the annual meeting held in Beijing. In January 1990, Taipei applied for membership in the General Agreement on Tariffs and Trade (GATT) with the title of "Separate Customs Territory of Taiwan, Penghu, Kinmen, and Matsu."

In a policy that reversed its former position of not making contacts with the communist world, Taipei started to relax restrictions on trading with former Eastern European communist states.[10] By the time Lee took the helm as president, the ROC was ready to develop relations with all countries and regions of the world except Cuba and North Korea.[11] The country was desperately trying to break out of the diplomatic darkness that had beset it since the beginning of the 1970s (see Table 9.1).

In the meantime, Taipei suffered a drastic setback when a joint communiqué was issued between Washington and Beijing in August 1982 that limited Taipei's ability to acquire arms that were desperately needed for its defense against possible attacks from Beijing. In Taiwan the communiqué further rocked what tenuous confidence was left in its U.S. ally after the rupture in relations with its former ally occurred in January 1979.

Readjustment of Diplomatic Strategies

Heralding a new era in the ROC's diplomatic history, President Lee Teng-hui made foreign policy one of his top priorities after assuming office in 1988. President Lee set out to amend the diplomatic strategy first and the so-called pragmatic diplomacy was inaugurated accordingly. The country was finally able to shake off its ideological onus by engaging with all countries regardless of their ideological hue. Along with the continual enlargement of its economic power and a high-powered drive toward democratization, the ROC was able to project a new image in the global community.

Before the Period of Mobilizational for Suppressing the Communist Rebellion was abrogated in 1991, mainland China was treated as an enemy to be eliminated. As a consequence, Taipei's foreign policy was based on the conviction of noncoexistence (*han-zei bu liang li*) with Beijing. In order to retain exclusive representation of China, Taipei would not tolerate allies that developed relations with its enemy, nor would it accept recognition from countries already recognizing China. After the policy was repealed and China was no longer considered an enemy, Taipei replaced its policy of exclusive representation with an inclusive one that

Table 9.1

Changes in the Diplomatic Map of Taipei and Beijing, 1969–1998

	ROC	PRC
1969	67	49
1970	67	54
1971	54	69
1972	41	87
1973	37	89
1974	31	96
1975	27	105
1976	27	109
1977	23	111
1978	22	113
1779	22	117
1980	22	121
1981	23	121
1982	23	122
1983	24	125
1984	25	126
1985	23	127
1986	23	127
1987	23	127
1988	22	136
1989	26	136
1990	28	136
1991	29	139
1992	29	153
1993	29	156
1994	29	157
1995	30	158
1996	30	158
1997	27	160
1998	27	160

Sources: Lang Kao, "Diplomatic Competitions Across the Strait of Taiwan in the Past Decade," in *Hou lengzhan shiqi de Zhongguo waijiao*, ed. Yu-suo Cheng (China's diplomacy in the post-cold war era) (Hong Kong: Cosmos Books, 1999), p. 328; ROC Ministry of Foreign Affairs, *ROC Diplomatic Yearbook, 1998* (Taipei: Ministry of Foreign Affairs, 1998), p. 587; Quansheng Zhao, *Jiedu Zhongguo waijiao zhengce* (Interpreting Chinese foreign policy) (Taipei: Yuedan Books, 1999), p. 108.

put forth the idea of "one divided China." The huge personnel and commodities exchanged between the two sides following the relaxation in Taipei policy further attested to the fact that a new chapter in cross-strait relations was about to be opened.

With the inception of the "pragmatic diplomacy," a debate was fomented that pitted the country's mainland China policy against its foreign policy in early 1996. The debate was so fierce that it dominated the presidential campaigning of that year. One viewpoint in this debate suggested that priority should be given to mainland policy while other elements of foreign policy should be subordinate. Given the fact that China had been the major obstacle to the heightening of Taipei's international standing, Minister of Foreign Affairs Frederick Chien suggested in January 1996 that "mainland policy should have precedence over foreign policy." The statement was reaffirmed by Premier Lien Chan. Advocates of this theoretical position argue that the "pragmatic diplomacy" caused tensions in the Taiwan Strait area and damaged the country's interests. Given the size of the PRC and the overwhelming concern this causes for stability, the international community was unlikely to extend a helping hand by lending support to Taiwan's course. Taiwan's pursuit of interests in the international arena should be predicated on a Taipei–Beijing rapprochement.[12]

A second perspective in this debate suggested that mainland policy be but one part of an integrated global strategy. For those who promote local Taiwanese values over the "imported values" transplanted from mainland China, it is rather difficult to accept a policy agenda that places mainland policy at center stage. For this group of people, the long-standing mainland-first policy has hampered the ROC in its foreign relations endeavors. It is erroneous to argue that the deterioration of relations with Beijing was caused by Taipei's own diplomacy. Taiwan should not be hamstrung by the "one-China principle" nor should its foreign policy be constrained by mainland policy because this, too, is tantamount to agreeing to the sovereign status defined and insisted on by China.[13]

A third school argues that, while it is true that to compromise Taiwan's needs with Beijing's demands would render diplomacy exceedingly difficult, and that cross-strait relations should have no bearings on Taiwan's diplomatic performance, it is to the benefit of this country to maintain workable relations with the PRC. Beijing should not be allowed veto power over Taiwan's external affairs, however, cross-strait relations and foreign policy can be complementary in nature.[14]

President Lee's legacy has been to reposition Taiwan's status vis-à-vis that of China, and, henceforth, to alter the relationship between foreign policy and mainland policy. What he so strenuously aimed to do—in ways that range from the abandonment of the principle of sole representation of China and putting forth the idea of a "divided China," to the invention of the "special state-to-state relationship" concept—was to follow neofunctionalist teachings to resolve the cross-strait quagmire. With the "German model" in mind, Lee seemed to be putting foreign policy on a par with mainland policy. But the fact that cross-strait relations stalemated during his second term in office somehow upset Lee's priorities, and foreign policy seemed to surpass mainland policy in degree of importance for his administration.

Economic- and Trade-Oriented New Pragmatism

President Lee adopted a two-pronged strategy that cashed in on the economic and democratic advancements made during the past decade. Taiwan's economy was thoroughly transformed and the island emerged as one of the largest economies in Asia. Huge volumes of trade and outward foreign investment added leverage to Taiwan's resolve to promote its overseas profile. The metamorphosis to democracy inspired popular expectation for higher international standing and brought a closer sense of psychological intimacy with the major democracies of the West.[15] Moreover, the transformation to democracy rid foreign policy thinking of its last vestiges of ideology.

Riding a new internationalist tide where economics superseded the politico-ideological factor as the most important element in determining a nation's external behavior, President Lee maximized and perfected economics and trade as a means of carrying out his foreign policy goals. While keeping official relations with less than thirty countries, the ROC has maintained healthy commercial ties with almost all countries and regions of the world. The ROC is one of the most economically dynamic countries on earth, and plays a significant role in both commodity exchanges and capital movement. Economic advancement means overseas investments for its sunset industries, which once dominated the world with labor-intensive goods. Beginning in the second half of the 1980s, Taiwan has emerged as a major capital exporter, with Southeast Asia and mainland China being the two prime beneficiaries. Taiwan's capital investment in the Southeast Asian area started in 1986 and accelerated in 1991 and 1992. By the beginning of the 1990s, Taiwan displaced the United States and rivaled Japan as the largest source of foreign direct investment in that region. Investment constituted a major part of what has been known as the "southward policy," accounting for roughly 35 percent of Taiwan's total outbound capital. In the decade from 1986 to 1996 Taiwan was estimated to have pumped US$42 billion worth of capital into that region to help with its development. The ROC government has established industrial zones in the Subic Bay area of the Philippines, Batan Island in Indonesia, and the Mekong Basin development-cooperation project in Vietnam. While two-way trade between Taiwan and Southeast Asia totaled slightly less than US$3 billion in 1980, this figure rose to a whopping US$38.26 billion in 2000 (see Table 9.2).

The Asian financial crisis starting in 1997 rendered Taiwan new opportunities. In an Asia-Pacific Economic Corporation (APEC) finance minister meeting held in November 1997, Taiwan proposed the creation of an "Asian Foundation." Closer regional cooperation was called for to preempt similar mishaps from recurring. These economic and commercial linkages developed into what has been referred to as an era of "summit diplomacy," a period when President Lee was first invited to Singapore in 1989 and later to Thailand, Indonesia, and the Philippines in 1993. During the same period Vice President Lien Chan also paid a visit to Singapore and then to Malaysia. Taipei's diplomatic missions in those countries were also upgraded in both name and function.[16]

Taiwan's economic relations with China started in 1987 when Taipei unilaterally lifted the ban and allowed its citizens, separated by the civil war in the 1940s, to pay humanitarian visits to their relatives on the mainland. Over the years, Taiwanese businessmen have poured over US$30 billion into the Chinese market hoping to reap the benefits of the largest economic reforms ever implemented in human history.[17] Over the same period, two-way trade has blossomed to a colossal US$25 billion in the short span of slightly over a decade.

Rising personal income in the ROC also helps raise aggregate purchasing power. External trade in 1991 totaled US$140 billion, a 330 percent increase over the totals from the previous decade, while this figure increased to US$215 billion by 1998. Taiwan has emerged as an important market for agricultural products as well as industrial machinery. Huge public projects such as the six-year national development plan, plans for a north–south high-speed railway system and nuclear power plants have all attracted large multinational corporations to participate in the bidding.

Economic assistance has played an important role in the implementation of the ROC's diplomatic objectives. In the 1960s, "Project Pioneering" was initiated to help with the diplomatic work in Africa. Later

Table 9.2

Trade and Investment Between Taiwan and ASEAN (Unit: US$ million)

	Thailand	Indonesia	Philippines	Malaysia	Vietnam	Singapore	Total
Taiwan's investment							
1987	885.0	2,295.1	16.9	141.4	N.A.	465.3	3,803.7
1988	859.9	913.0	109.9	313.0	N.A.	6.4	2,202.2
1989	892.2	513.2	148.7	799.7	1.0	5.2	2,360.0
1990	782.7	618.3	140.7	2,347.8	251.0	47.6	4,188.1
1991	583.5	1,057.3	12.0	1,326.2	520.9	12.5	3,512.4
1992	289.9	563.3	9.1	574.7	561.6	8.8	2,007.4
1993	215.4	127.5	5.4	331.2	421.3	69.5	1,170.3
1994	477.5	2,487.5	267.8	1,122.8	518.6	100.7	4,974.9
1995	1,803.9	567.4	13.6	567.8	1,239.7	31.6	4,224.0
1996	2,785.2	534.6	7.4	310.4	534.3	165.0	4,336.9
1997	414.3	3,419.4	13.1	480.4	247.8	230.3	4,805.3
1998	253.6	155.4	5.4	263.4	440.6	158.2	1,276.6
1999	211.1	1,180.3	5.0	70.3	172.9	324.5	1,964.1
2000	437.4	131.2	1.0	241.1	280.5	219.5	1,310.7
Total	10,891.6	14,563.5	756.0	8,890.2	5,190.2	1,845.1	42,136.6
Trade							
1996	4,460	3,840	2,780	6,520	1,490	7,370	26,550
1997	4,490	4,320	3,620	7,260	1,690	8,040	29,520
1998	3,890	3,150	3,760	5,910	1,560	5,950	24,280
1999	4,490	3,590	4,780	6,730	1,730	7,130	28,470
2000	5,330	4,750	6,630	8,940	2,130	10,470	38,260
2001	4,306	3,998	5,399	7,275	2,146	7,418	30,542

Sources: There is a great discrepancy between investment data released by Taipei and the ASEAN countries. The amount of investment used in this table prior to 1988, see Zhao-zhen Song, *Taihai Liangan yu Dongnanya* (The two sides of the Taiwan Strait and Southeast Asia) (Taipei: Wunan Publishing Co., 1999), p. 52. For the rest of the investment data, see Industrial Development and Investment Center, Ministry of Economic Affairs, http://www.idic.gov.tw/html/c3408.xls; trade data between 1996 and 2000, see Board of Foreign Trade, Ministry of Economics, http://www.trade.gov.tw; for 2001 data, see http://cus.trade.gov.tw.

on the plan was renamed the "Sino-Africa Technological Cooperation Plan." The plan successfully helped to raise the ROC's international standing in that part of the world and was instrumental in the country's bid to maintain its UN seat.[18] In an effort to reactivate the program, the ROC Ministry of Foreign Affairs created the Fund for International Economic Cooperation in 1988, endowed at slightly more than US$1 billion. An International Humanitarian Fund was also established in 1990 with eleven countries, including South Korea, Malawi, and the Philippines, receiving assistance the following year.[19] US$10 million was donated to the European Bank for Reconstruction and Development in 1991, and Taipei was awarded observer status accordingly. After endowing the Fund for the Economic and Social Development of Central America, a creation of the Central American Development Bank, with US$150 million, the ROC was permitted to become a member of the bank with its official name retained.[20] As of 1998,Taiwan has given away nearly US$3 billion in economic assistance. In sum, the reinvigorated economic and trade instruments have enabled an unprecedented period of "summit diplomacy." President Lee traveled to Asia, Central America, Africa, the Middle East, and eight other countries, but his travels peaked in his visit to Cornell University in June 1995. However, the tour enraged China, and the brief history of ROC "summit diplomacy" ended.

The new pragmatism, based on economic and trade interests, has brought the ROC to waters never before navigated. Under the guidance of the pragmatic foreign policy, seventeen countries have established diplomatic ties with the ROC and seven countries severed these ties.[21] In 1972, the ROC had forty-one overseas embassies and twelve representative offices; ten years later, the number of embassies was reduced to twenty-three while representative offices increased to thirty-eight; in 1996, the number of embassies increased slightly to thirty and the representative offices increased to sixty-five. Under President Lee's leadership reins, the ROC has opened unofficial representative offices in nearly half of the countries in the world.[22]

Not only has the number of representative offices been on the rise, but their names and functions have also been elevated. In the past, the ROC was constantly asked to use names that were not representative of this country to avoid irritating Beijing. Instead, names such as "commercial office," "Far East Trading Company," "Sun Yat-sen Association," "Chinese Travel Agency," "relations association" or "coordination council" and so on are common examples. Foreign diplomatic missions in Taiwan have also reflected this diversity in obscurity. Influenced by the ROC's newly expanded economic and trade relations, Western Europe led the way in a dramatic wave of change. Traditionally, Western Europe had been quite apathetic to the ROC, but, spurred by the new commercial tide, efforts were undertaken to upgrade unofficial bilateral ties. The ROC has established some twenty-one representative offices and four commercial offices in Western Europe, with most of them enjoying semi-official status. Eighteen European countries have established twenty representative offices in Taiwan charged with the authority of handling consular affairs. There are twenty-two European banks operating in Taiwan, and five Taiwanese banks operating in Europe.[23] The United States and Japan decided to change the names of the ROC missions in their respective countries, deciding on and adopting a more representative title, the Taipei Economic and Cultural Office. The 1990s also saw visits by high-level officials from abroad. After a long wait, the United States finally sent Assistant Secretary of Commerce Thomas Duesterberg in February 1992, breaking a taboo set by Washington and in place since 1979, when the United States established official ties with the PRC. A few days after the visit, Great Britain sent John Redwood, State Minister for Corporate Affairs, to Taipei. Redwood was the highest British official to visit Taipei since relations were broken in the 1950s.[24] Retired heads of government have increasingly been seen walking in the streets of Taipei.

A New Multilateralism

Integration into the new global and Asian regional order was essentially part of the president's endeavors. Having gradually shaken off the nightmare of the preceding couple of decades, the ROC is now a member of sixteen intergovernmental organizations (IGOs) and enjoys observer status in another five.[25] Since the 1990s, the ROC has joined a number of highly important IGOs as well as a growing number of non-governmental organizations (see Table 9.3).[26] In 1989 the ROC became a dialogue partner of the Organization for Economic Cooperation and Development (OECD), a group composed of twenty-six of the most economically advanced countries in the West. In June 1991, the ROC joined the Central American Development Bank, grouping with Guatemala, Salvador, Costa Rica, Nicaragua, and Honduras. Taipei has also become a member of the important Asia-Pacific Economic Cooperation,

Table 9.3

The Republic of China's Membership in Non-Governmental Organizations

Year	Number of memberships
1988	728
1989	747
1990	747
1991	766
1992	778
1993	795
1994	816
1995	867
1996	901
1997	917
1998	943

Source: ROC Diplomatic Yearbook, various years.

an organization acclaimed as one of the most important economic organizations in the world, and boasting a membership-list of twenty-three countries, including the United States, Japan, Canada, South Korea, Australia, and ASEAN. After some haggling, the three Chinese communities, Taiwan, Hong Kong, and mainland China, were admitted as a package.[27] Taipei enjoys all the privileges of that organization, except participation in summit meetings and the foreign ministers' meeting. Taipei's rights were further compromised when the "Olympics model" was imposed as a condition for membership under which the ROC was to be addressed as "Chinese Taipei." The same year Taipei became a member of the European Bank for Reconstruction and Development and linked through a special foundation affiliated with the bank. The foundation was created in 1990 to help former communist countries in Eastern Europe to establish a market order within their countries' societies. In January 1991, Taipei opted for "Separate Customs Territory of Taiwan, Penghu, Kinmen, and Matsu" to apply for membership in the GATT and was awarded observer status a year later. The organization has since been renamed the World Trade Organization and, during negotiations for accession, the Taipei delegation has been addressed as "Chinese Taipei." Taiwan has completed negotiations with all twenty-six countries and territories that have requested meetings, and its membership is pending the outcome of Beijing's accession talks.

Since 1993, the ROC has been trying to rejoin the United Nations.

Lately, Taipei has changed tactics by asking the world body to form a committee to study the possibility of its readmission. But the economic/trade-oriented diplomacy has not brought success to that mission. Taiwan's bid has yet to pass the procedural committee and remained off the agenda. Since 1997, Taipei has also been trying to retain observer status in the World Health Organization (WHO), signaling a shift to an incremental approach by turning attention to the more peripheral organizations of the UN.

However, Taipei has made great breakthroughs in the area of arms procurement. Restrained by the August 17 communiqué, Taiwan had not been able to acquire the high-performance military hardware necessary for its defense. But the situation was reversed in the 1990s. France relented on its Taiwan arms sales policy and sold six Lafayette-class frigates to Taiwan in 1991. The sale was followed by another sale of sixty Mirage 2000–5 fighter jets. In a "commercial sale" Germany also granted sales of four minesweeping vessels.[28] Spurred by the French sales, and in a move to woo domestic voters for his presidential bid, U.S. President George Bush finally conceded to the sale of 150 F-16s, fulfilling a request that the ROC had pursued for over a decade.

Challenges to the New Pragmatist Foreign Policy

The new pragmatist foreign policy under President Lee has broadened the dimensions of the ROC's international horizons. However, instead of creating an equal partnership across the Taiwan Strait, which seemed to be his objective, Lee had succeeded in destabilizing further the already fragile bilateral relationship as the exasperated and sometimes hysterical Beijing leadership not only suspended all communications with Taiwan but also tightened the screws against a possible ROC "breakthrough" on the international scene. In view of the facts that the PRC's GDP has quadrupled in the past two decades and that the disputes over political sovereignty between Taipei and Beijing have heightened, the tasks faced by Lee, especially toward the end of his tenure, were daunting to say the least.

The pragmatic diplomacy is premised on the understanding that the cross-strait rivalry can be held constant. This assumption is part of the grand strategy that President Lee undertook to ease tensions across the Taiwan Strait. Ending the Period of Mobilization marked an important step toward that end. However, the new modus operandi had to meet with Beijing's reciprocation to be successful. Unfortunately, the new policy was condemned by Beijing as nothing less than a "conspiracy to split the motherland."

Lee's "frontal attack" tactics led Beijing to the belief that Taiwan intended to seek a permanent separation from China under the pretense of internationalization. In a new bid to obliterate the ROC's presence from the international political configuration, Beijing has strengthened its hold on the "one-China principle," and, consequently, the sovereign status of the ROC is even more gravely at risk. Externally, there appears to be less room for the ROC to make its claim to sovereignty. During the cold war era, the two Chinas were engaged in a fierce contest for sovereignty recognition and the bipolar system granted at least partial legitimacy to each's claim. Capitalizing on the new developments in the post–cold war era, President Lee wanted to create a cross-strait order in which both sides could coexist and prosper, ridding the area of the specter of imminent confrontation. Models proposed by Taipei, ranging from "one country, two governments," "one divided China," "two political entities," to "special state-to-state relations," testify to the conviction that this could have been achieved. However, Taipei's overtures have yet to be reciprocated by Beijing, which has insisted on nothing less than full acceptance of its version of a unification model—the "one country, two systems" formula. News began to surface in 1997 that a new "three empties" policy (*sanguang zhengce*) to rid the ROC of all diplomatic allies, to block every formal venue, and to exhaust all resources was secretly passed down to Beijing's foreign service personnel with the year 2000 set as a target.[29] Consequently, four countries, including South Africa, broke relations with the ROC between December 1997 and November 1998. At a press conference following the annual APEC meeting held in Auckland in September 1999, the moderator, the New Zealand foreign minister, in the presence of the ROC's delegation, placed Taiwan in the same category as Hong Kong and implied that sovereignty was a nonnegotiable issue.[30] At about the same time, in a move that reversed its previous stand of noninterference, the U.S. delegation to the UN spoke for the first time in opposition to Taiwan's reentrance bid.[31]

Lee's policy of ambiguity to circumvent politics and concentrate on economic and cultural exchanges had not only not eased tensions across the strait as he had hoped, but also intensified a debate both at home and across the strait about his determination to stick to the ROC's original national identity. The invocation of the "state-to-state" theory had exacerbated the spar. The increasing inconsistency between his foreign and mainland policy goals had also thwarted his other ambitions. For instance, the proposal for the creation of an Asia-Pacific Regional Operations Center to build this country into a center for regional finance, transportation, technology, production, information exchange, and the like was commendable. And yet, the grand strategy could not possibly get off the ground without first cultivating a wholesome environment of dialogue with China. A lack of coordination between economic and mainland policies has hounded the development strategy from the beginning.

Similarly, a foreign policy designed first and foremost on the defense of sovereignty would inevitably opt to seek out breakthroughs. Summit meetings with foreign leaders have become a national obsession. The quest for nomenclature has not only exhausted the limited resources of this country and made the meetings more difficult, but has also taken transparency out of the foreign policy decision-making process, causing resentment.

Second, unaccompanied by similar overtures across the Strait, the new pragmatic diplomacy has been eyed by Beijing with suspicion. Consequently, efforts made by Taiwan to engage other countries have often been misinterpreted as a divergence from the "one-China principle" and a sign of vying for independence. In a move to thwart this deflection, Beijing has increasingly resorted to intimidation as a means to pressure Taipei into submission, putting Taiwan's security, an important foreign policy goal, at risk. Beijing has deployed hundreds of short-range and medium-range missiles, M-9 and M-11, along its Taiwan-facing coast. Its newly acquired SU-27 Russian-made jet fighters are also based in an airport near the potential flashpoint. Other purchased weapons such as marine-based Sunburn surface-to-surface missiles are construed by Taiwan as a means of neutralizing the Seventh Fleet lest it seek to come to Taiwan's rescue. In a white paper released by the State Council on the eve of Taiwan's March 2000 presidential elections, Beijing added a new condition to the use of force against the island on top of the two conditions proclaimed in the past. According to this new ultimatum, violence cannot be ruled out if the island resists *sine die* (i.e., indefinitely) unification talks.[32]

Facing increasing pressure on its security, President Lee had been hard at work trying to knit together a net of countermeasures. The Asian Collective Security system was briefly proposed, but seemingly abandoned owing to a lukewarm international response.[33] Later, the issue of join-ing the U.S.-proposed Theater Missile Defense (TMD) system has drawn much attention with pros and cons being vigorously debated to this date. Taiwan has enormous economic stakes in Southeast Asia and has been one of the chief foreign capital suppliers to that region. And yet, despite these interests, the country has still not been able to obtain access to the ASEAN Regional Forum, a major venue for the discussion of security issues in the Asia-Pacific region. Among the six regional security fo-rums currently in existence, Taiwan has only been allowed to partici-pate in the Workshop on Managing Potential Conflicts in the South China Sea.[34] Without Beijing's acquiescence, it is highly unlikely that the is-land will be included in the joint development of the TMD currently under way between the United States and Japan.

A foreign policy stressing the importance of economic instruments and the maintenance of sovereignty would inevitably lead to the politicization of economic decisions that would, in turn, diminish their effects. The southward policy was undoubtedly a policy move made from the political consideration to diversify risks lest overdependence of the mainland market cripple Taiwan's economic autonomy. Taiwan's economic and financial links with South Africa and the Caribbean have likewise been shaped largely by government policies. However, politi-cally abetted investments suffered a great deal during the Asian finan-cial crisis. Since President Lee made a historic journey to the United States and tensions subsequently increased in the Taiwan Strait area, ASEAN countries have been under pressure to relent to Beijing's de-mands and have given up whatever slight ambiguity those countries formerly held to in order to reap the maximum benefits from the cross-strait quagmire. Taipei, naturally upset by this response, retaliated with a reduction in economic links. In 1997, Taiwan's investments in the area were considerably reduced and bilateral relations suffered considerable setbacks. After these disappointments, the ROC's economic attention turned to South Africa into which it poured half of its economic assis-tance in a bid to maintain the last "big" country in its diplomatic corpus. Unfortunately, owing to domestic and international concerns, President Nelson Mandela decided to break ties in December 1997. Taipei retali-ated again by cutting economic assistance and induced Taiwan busi-nessmen to boycott the country after its decision. Future ties were damaged as a result. After the loss of South Africa, Taipei shifted its economic focus to Central and South America where nearly half of its

Table 9.4

Taipei and Beijing's Economic Relations with Panama

	Commercial vessels registered in Panama	Vessel passage in Panama Canal	Trade US$ 100 million	Investment US$ 100 million
PRC	1,200	Third	22.0[a]	Hong Kong and China are catching up
Taiwan	270	Ninth	2.1	5.6

Source: Far East Economic Review, October 21, 1999, pp. 28–29.
[a]Including Hong Kong.

diplomatic friends reside. A Free Trade Agreement was signed with Panama and the five other Central American countries with which Taiwan had diplomatic ties. Taipei helped with the creation of the Central Development Fund and shared the costs of half of the fund's endowment for the development of the region's economy. Among the ten overseas industrial parks that Taipei has helped create thus far, half of them are located in this area. As a result, President Lee was invited to attend the ceremony heralding the U.S. transfer of authority of the Panama Canal back to the Panamanian government. However, the close economic and trade ties were not enough to deter the Bahamas from breaking ties with the ROC. Worse, Panama, the largest country in the ROC's diplomatic corpus at present, has shown signs of wanting to shift recognition to Beijing as the two are tinkering with commercial and other exchanges (see Table 9.4). Similar reports have been heard about Haiti and the Vatican as well. Where would the economic-oriented and sovereignty-maintaining diplomacy be heading if the Central and Caribbean countries fall from the fold? Although this scenario may seem unlikely, it is not impossible, and should cause the future leadership of this country to act quickly and intelligently to find possible solutions.

Over the years, Taiwan has emerged as an economic powerhouse. The ROC is the twentieth largest economy in the world, the thirteenth exporter of commodity goods, the ninth biggest capital exporter, and a major supplier of computer periphery products. Yet, this impressive economic clout has not been able to catapult the ROC into major international economic and financial organizations such as the International Monetary Fund (IMF) and the World Bank.

The new pragmatic policy has broadened the ROC's diplomatic perspectives, but it has also resulted in tremendous pressure from Beijing. After both South Korea and South Africa withdrew recognition, the only countries to retain ties with the ROC were generally both poor and small in size. Nauru and Tuvalu in the South Pacific are less than thirty square kilometers in size with a population of 10,000 each. Among the twenty-nine countries maintaining official relations, there are eight under 1,000 square kilometers in size. Twelve of them have populations of less than 500,000 (see Table 9.5).

The ROC has relied heavily on unofficial and unconventional means in handling relations with the outside world, and with some success. This is especially evident in its relations with the less developed and relatively small countries of the Caribbean and the African continent where economic assistance has been almost the sole viable linkage. However, the economic reforms implemented in China since the 1980s have greatly elevated the national power of that country, placing strong pressure on the economics-oriented foreign policy undertaken by Taipei. Presidential candidate Bill Clinton criticized George Bush for coddling the dictators in Beijing and pledged that unless China improved its human rights practices, he would not separate the human rights issue from trade matters. However, swayed by economic concerns as president, Clinton did delink these two issues and even adopted what has come to be known as the policy of "comprehensive engagement."[35] Moreover, President Clinton's decision to make an official announcement on what has been dubbed the new "three-no's policy" on his visit to China in June 1998 was also to some extent attributable to these commercial concerns.

The new tensions in the Taiwan Strait area have furthered the ROC's dependence on the United States for the advancement of its diplomatic course. The United States is not only the biggest market for Taiwanese manufactured goods and a major source of technology and investment capital, but also the main supplier of Taiwan's defense needs. The ROC has to rely on the United States for its voice to be heard in major international organizations. For example, without U.S. support Taipei would not have gained membership in international organizations such as the ADB, APEC, and CSCAP. In the future, Taipei must continue to count on that support for its admission into such international bodies as the WHO, IMF, and the World Bank. This overdependence undoubtedly renders Taiwan vulnerable should the interests of the two countries become incompatible. The three communiqués signed by Washington and

Table 9.5

Countries Maintaining Official Relations with the Republic of China (ROC)

	Size (1,000 square kilometers)	Population (million) 1997	Per capita (US$) 1997	Trade (US$ million) 1996	Trade with ROC (US$ 1000) 1998	Date of establishing relations
Asia-Pacific						
Republic of Nauru	0.021	0.011 (1996)	1,000.00 (1992)	113.00	200	May 4, 1980
Solomon Islands	28.896	0.391 (1996)	689.00 (1995)	265.00 (1994)	1,122	Mar 24, 1983
Tuvalu	0.026	0.01 (1996)	800.00 (1995)	12.71 (1995)	8	Sep 19, 1979
Republic of the Marshall Islands	0.181	0.061	1,600	94.80	0	Nov 20, 1998
Republic of Palau	0.487	1.8	—	—		1999
Africa						
Burkina Faso	274.000	11	240	999.00	12,133	Dec 14, 1961 (ties established); Oct 23, 1973 (ties severed); Feb 2, 1994 (ties resumed)
Republic of Chad	1,259.000	7	240	1,341.00	3,711	Jan 31, 1962 (ties established); Dec 27, 1972 (ties severed); Aug 12, 1997 (ties resumed)
Republic of Gambia	11.295	1.2	300 (1998)	142.4 (1995)	1,840	1968 (ties established); Dec 28, 1974 (ties severed); July 13, 1995 (ties resumed)
Republic of Liberia	111.369	2.10 (1996)	765	238.12 (1997)	77,055	Aug 19, 1957 (ties established); Feb 23, 1977 (ties severed); Oct 9, 1989 (ties resumed)

Republic of Malawi	118.484	10.00	220	1,188.00	10,496	Jul 11, 1966
Democratic Republic of Sao Tome and Principe	0.964	0.13 (1995)	317.00 (1998)	34.00	130	May 6, 1997
Republic of Senegal	196.722	9	570 (1996)	2,600 (1995)	64,28	Sep 23, 1960 (ties established); Nov 8, 1964 (ties severed); Jul 16, 1969 (ties resumed); Apr 12, 1972 (ties severed); Jan 3, 1996 (ties resumed)
Kingdom of Swaziland	17.360	0.90 (1995)	1,200 (1996)	1,625 (1995)	2,656	Sep 6, 1968
Europe						
Vatican	0.44	0.001	—	—	483	Jul 1942
Republic of Macedonia	25.713	2.19 (1996)	1,090	3,060.00	2,462	Jan 27, 1999
Central and South America						
Belize	22.963	0.222	2,308	468.00	19,389	Oct 13, 1989
Republic of Costa Rica	51.100	3.48 (1998)	2,640	6,753.00	58,935	—
Commonwealth of Dominica	0.751	0.071 (1996)	3,182	186.82	3,130	May 10, 1983
Dominican Republic	48.442	0.767 (1996)	1,670	10,193.00	88,747	—
Republic of El Salvador	21.040	50.900	1,810	3,693.00	68,786	—
Grenada	3.440	0.090	2,985 (1996)	171.400	210	Jul 20, 1989
Republic of Guatemala	108.889	10.0 (1998)	1,500	5,177.00	76,561	—

(continued)

Table 9.5 *(continued)*

	Size (1,000 square kilometers)	Population (million) 1997	Per capita (US$) 1997	Trade (US$ million) 1996	Trade with ROC (US$ 1000) 1998	Date of establishing relations
Republic of Haiti	27.750	7.490	330	1,045.00	13,027	Apr 25, 1956
Republic of Honduras	112.088	5.900	700	2,767.00	57,392	Was put under the ROC consulate to Panama 1944; consulate office established in 1957; upgrade to embassy in 1965
Republic of Nicaragua	127.664	4.140	410	1,729.00	57,312	Dec 7, 1985 (ties severed); Nov 6, 1990 (ties resumed)
Republic of Panama	75.517	2.710	3,080	3,336.00	212,907	A General Consulate was established in 1909; a legation was established in 1922 and was upgraded to embassy in 1954.
Republic of Paraguay	406.752	4.83	2,010	4,150.00	68,492	Jul 8, 1957
Saint Christopher and Nevis	0.261	0.042	4,918	152.00	140	Oct 9, 1983
Saint Vincent and the Grenadines	0.380	0.11	2,570	178.30	1,979	Aug 15, 1981

Source: ROC Ministry of Foreign Affairs network, www.mofa.gov.tw/; World Bank, *World Development Report* (Oxford University Press, 1998), pp. 190, 191, 228, 229; ROC Ministry of Foreign Affairs, *Shijie geguo jianjie ji zhengfu shouzhang mingce* (Brief introduction to countries in the world and names of government heads) (Taipei: ROCMOFA, 1999).

Beijing, as well as the new "three-no's policy," are products of this conflict of interests.

Pragmatic foreign policy has been at the center of the dispute between Taipei and Beijing. Taiwan is increasingly alienated and agitated by Beijing's containment policy. Beijing obviously perceives Taiwan's striving for more international space as a sign of "splittism." The democratization and localization processes that began in Taiwan at the end of the 1980s have sharpened the disparities across the Taiwan Strait, further straining relations. Take, for example, the record earthquake that hit Taiwan on September 21, 1999. Thousands of people perished and the initial damages were estimated at US$30 billion. Beijing's response was less than spontaneous, presumably hampered by dissatisfaction over recent developments in Taiwan's political stance. Local residents were further angered when the International Red Cross was asked to seek permission from Beijing before extending aid and assistance. It was even reported that Moscow's relief efforts were also aborted after Beijing refused to grant aerial passage. It was suggested that the two sides of the Taiwan Strait had squandered the rare opportunity which was, unfortunately, provided by the natural disaster, to promote goodwill and cooperation and to reestablish the links broken by President Lee's visit to the United States.

Conclusion

The economic-and trade-oriented pragmatic policy was designed to break Beijing's containment and, hence, to maintain the sovereign status of the ROC. This policy has yielded the country some diplomatic fruits, but it has also sharpened the differences between the two sides of the Taiwan Strait. The policy has too often been mistaken by Beijing as an attempt to vie for independence and, consequently, the sovereignty of the country has been overshadowed. The obscurity that ensued has, in turn, brooked inconsistency and caused confusion over Taipei's national objectives, particularly with regard to policies regulating its foreign and mainland affairs. While it is true that the ROC has become more actively involved in the global community, this activism has in no way concealed the harsh reality that this country has become more isolated at the official level. The pragmatic foreign policy has also inadvertently intensified strife in cross-strait relations and vilified the domestic effects of the "stability card"—played by the KMT in past election campaigns to good effect but, as we have seen, ultimately backfiring in the loss of the 2000 presidential election.

President Lee seemed finally to realize the limits of his "pragmatic policy" and the prickly reality that cross-strait relations should probably take precedence over Taiwan's quest for more international space. In an unparalleled move, during an informal visit to Shanghai in October 1998, Koo Chen-fu, head of Taiwan's semi-official Strait Exchange Foundation, explored the possibility that Beijing allow Taiwan to participate in the Korean Energy Development Organization and that a summit meeting be held between Lee Teng-hui and Jiang Zemin on the sidelines of the APEC annual meeting. But both proposals were rejected by his counterpart Wang Daohan, head of the Association of Relations across the Taiwan Strait.[36]

Looking to the future, the new administration has less room for maneuvering. Chen Shui-bian's administration will be facing the same dilemmas that haunted President Lee during his second term in office. The new president has to forge a new national identity, and only then can a new balance between foreign policy and mainland policy be found. In a way, it is unlikely that President Chen Shui-bian will go beyond President Lee's diplomatic legacy in both ideological and policy terms. If past policy is any indication, the DPP will face more challenges in pushing its diplomatic agenda ahead than had the KMT before them. The Lee administration's agenda of ranking foreign policy before mainland policy has to be amended to avoid a further deterioration in relations with Beijing. If President Chen continues the past policy that China and Taiwan are two separate states, and insists that the "one-China" policy clung to by the KMT is responsible for the country's setbacks in the international arena, then foreign policy will be very hard to retain. Beijing has continually refused to back down from the "one-China" principle and insists that President Chen respond to this demand in his administration's dealings with foreign and mainland policy.

In a dramatic move to end hostility, President Lee repositioned the relations of the two adversaries with the model of "one country with two different political entities." Under the new framework, the ROC would forsake the original claim of sole representation of China in exchange for "de facto sovereignty" status. Over time, the term "ROC on Taiwan" (ROCOT) gradually emerged. For the DPP, the issue of national identity has gone through a three-stage metamorphosis. In the first stage, it was suggested that Taiwan be entitled to its own sovereignty. In the second stage, it was argued that Taiwan is already a sovereign state. Lately a third voice has appeared, arguing that the ROC is already a sovereign state so there is no need for further declarations of independence. The likely outcome will be something like "Taiwan in the ROC." At the ethnic level, the ruling DPP has refused to be identified as "Chinese." What has been proposed, instead, has witnessed an evolution moving from "the new Taiwanese race" to "Taiwanese." Recently, Chen Shui-bian has coined the term "Chinese community" and "ethnic Chinese" as alternatives. These developments are encouraging, but are still far from meeting Beijing's expectations. Before new ground is found with Beijing at the national identity level, as well as at the ethnic level, Taipei's diplomatic future is still destined to be precarious.

Nevertheless, there are people who argue that the new ruling party is in a better position than the KMT to mobilize the country and reach a new consensus with regard to its future direction. These people suggest that Chen, like Richard Nixon, is free from the onus of the historic Kuomintang-Chinese Communist Party rivalry and, hence, is better poised to revolutionize bilateral relations. It is further argued that saying Taiwan is a sovereign country is no different from saying that the ROC is a de facto country, and there is thus no need to worry.

Nevertheless, before President Chen could make a drastic change the rivalry between Taipei and Beijing had already widened. The real challenge for Taiwan's pragmatic foreign policy has just begun.

Notes

1. Robert G. Sutter, "Taiwan's Role in World Affairs: Background, Status, and Prospects," in *Taiwan in World Affairs*, ed. Robert G. Sutter and William R. Johnson (Boulder: Westview Press, 1994), p. 1.

2. Taiwan is allowed to participate in the discussion only on an individual membership basis.

3. They are the Asian Development Bank, Association for Science Cooperation in Asia, Food and Fertilizer Technology Center for the Asian and Pacific Region, Asian Productivity Organization, Afro-Asian Rural Reconstruction Organization, Asian Vegetable Research and Development Center, Study Group on Asian Tax Administration and Research, Asia-Pacific Economic Cooperation, Central American Bank for Economic Integration, Conference of Governors of South-East Asian Central Banks, International Cotton Advisory Committee, International Office of Epizootics, International Seed Testing Association, Asia/Pacific Group on Money Laundering, Association of Asian Election Authorities, and Egmont Group of Financial Intelligence Units of the World.

4. The division is borrowed from Chien-min Chao, "1990 niandai Zhonghua

minguo de wushi waijiao." (The ROC's pragmatic diplomacy in the 1990s), *Wenti yu yanjiu* (Issues and studies) (Taipei) 32, no. 1 (January 1993): 1–16.

5. The motion was initiated by the ROC government at the fourth United Nations plenum session on September 27, 1949. The bill was passed on February 1, 1952, at the Sixth Plenum meeting. See Ralph N. Clough, "The Republic of China and the World, 1949–1981," in *China: Seventy Years after the 1911 Hsin-hai Revolution*, ed. Hungdah Chiu and Shao-chuan Leng (Charlottesville, VA: University Press of Virginia, 1984), pp. 525–32.

6. During and after the crisis, the United States started to provide the ROC with weapons such as F-100, F-104, and F-5E fighter aircraft for the latter's defense. See Harvey S. Feldman, "U.S.-Taiwan Relations, 1948–1987," in *Mei Tai guanxi yu Zhongguo de tongyi*, ed. Li Da (U.S.-Taiwan relations and the unification of China) (Hong Kong: Wideangle, 1987), pp. 12–14.

7. Michel Oksenberg, "The Dynamics of the Sino-American Relationship," in *The China Factor: Sino-American Relations and the Global Scene*, ed. Richard H. Solomon (Englewood Cliffs, NJ: Prentice-Hall, 1981), p. 57.

8. Before 1961, the motion to replace the ROC's UN seat with the PRC never made it to the floor. But the issue was designated an "important issue" that year, which requires two-thirds of the votes for approval, signaling a sea change was in the offing. It was becoming harder to get a simple majority to support the ROC's UN course. See Clough, "The Republic of China and the World," p. 529. "Project pioneering" was initiated that year. Over the next decade, thirty-five teams were sent to twenty-three African countries with 1,220 agricultural experts responding to the call.

9. Chao, "1990 niandai Zhonghua minguo de wushi waijiao."

10. *Ziyou shibao* (Liberty times) (Taipei), April 16, 1989, p. 15.

11. *Zhongguo shibao* (China times) (Taipei), January 23, 1980, p. 2.

12. "Rank Mainland Policy Before Foreign Policy," *Lianhe bao* (United daily news) (Taipei), January 3, 1996, p. 3

13. Parris Chang, "How Can We Continue Expanding Our Foreign Space?" *Ziyou shibao*, January 15, 1996, p. 7.

14. "Pragmatic Foreign Policy and Cross-strait Relations Can Coexist," *Taiwan shibao* (Taiwan times) (Taipei), January 9, 1996, p. 2.

15. On Taiwan's democratization, see Tun-jen Cheng, "Democratizing the Quasi-Leninist Regime in Taiwan," *World Politics* 41 (July 1989): 471–99; Hung-mao Tien, ed., *Taiwan's Electoral Politics and Democratic Transition: Riding the Third Wave* (Armonk, NY: M.E. Sharpe, 1996).

16. For example, the mission to Indonesia was changed from the "China Commercial Office" to the "Taipei Economic and Trade Office" in 1989. The "Center for Far East Trade and Travel" in Malaysia was renamed the "Taipei Center for Economics and Culture" in 1988 and changed again in 1992 to the "Taipei Economic and Cultural Office."

17. Mainland Affairs Council, *Liangan tongji yuebao* (Cross-strait statistics monthly), January 2000.

18. Chung-hen Hsu, "An Analysis of the ROC's Foreign Technological Cooperation," *Wenti yu yanjiu* 30, no. 10 (October 1991): 124

19. Frederick Chien, "New Orientations of the ROC's Foreign Policies in the 1990s," *Wenti yu yanjiu* 30, no. 10 (October 1991): 8.

20. *Washington Post*, June 29, 1992, p. A1.

21. The sixteen are Bahamas, Grenada, Liberia, Belize, Lesotho, Nicaragua, Republic of Central Africa, Niger, Burkina Faso, Gambia, Senegal, the Marshall Islands, Papua New Guinea, Chad, Sao Tome and Principe, and Macedonia. In the meantime, Uruguay, Saudi Arabia, South Korea, Lesotho, Niger, Bahamas, Guinea-Bissau have broken ties with the ROC during the same period.

22. Lang Kao, *Zhonghua minguo waijiao guanxi zhi yanbian* (The evolution of ROC foreign relations) (Taipei: Wunan, 1994), pp. 117–19.

23. Ralph N. Clough, "The Republic of China and the International Community in the 1990s," paper prepared for the Sino-American-European Conference on Contemporary China, Taipei, August 1992, p. 1.

24. *Japan Times*, February 26, 1992, p. 1.

25. The five are: WTO, Inter-American Development Bank, Inter-American Tropical Tuna Commission, International Commission for the Conservation of Atlantic Tunas, Convention for the Conservation of Southern Bluefin Tuna.

26. David S. Chou, "Tactics for Participation in International Organizations," in *Guoji kongjian zai tupou zhi celüe*, ed. Si-an Chen (Tactics for breaking wide international space) (Taipei: Foundation for National Development, 1997), pp. 112–35.

27. When an annual meeting was held in Australia in 1989, the chairman of the meeting, prime minister of the host country, Bob Hawke, wanted to include the three as members. Beijing opposed the idea and insisted on sovereignty as a condition for membership. When that proposal was rejected, Beijing then proposed the three be given observer status. Again, the proposal was rejected.

28. Clough, "The Republic of China and the International Community," p. 11.

29. *Ziyou shibao*, October 18, 1998, p. 6; "Interview with Foreign Minister Chen Chien-jen," *Zhongyang ribao* (Central daily) (Taipei), January 2, 2000, p. 4.

30. *Zhongguo shibao*, September 14, 1999, p. 3.

31. *Wenhui bao* (Hong Kong), September 17, 1999, p. A5.

32. "White Paper on the One-China Principle and the Issue of Taiwan," *Lianhe bao*, February 22, 2000, p. 1.

33. President Lee tinkered with the idea in the early 1990s, suggesting that a regional security mechanism could prompt arms reduction and sharing of resources within the region. See *Zhongyang ribao*, November 9, 1992, p. 2; April 1, 1993, p. 2.

34. The other five are: ASEAN Regional Forum, Council for Security Cooperation in the Asia Pacific, Asia-Pacific Roundtable, Western Pacific Naval Symposium, and Conference of Asia-Pacific Center for Security Studies. Scholars from Taipei can participate in one of the four group discussions, that on confidence-building and security of the CSCAP only in an individual capacity. See Cheng-I Lin, "Tactics to Build a Relationship of Security Cooperation," in Chen, ed., *Guoji kongjian zai tupou zhi celüe*, pp. 142–50.

35. James Mann, *About Face: A History of America's Curious Relationship with China, from Nixon to Clinton* (New York: Alfred A. Knopf, 1999), ch. 16.

36. *Lianhe bao*, November 3, 1998, p. 2.

—— 10 ——

Cross-Strait Relations

Buying Time Without Strategy

Julian J. Kuo

During the twelve years of President Lee's rule, Taiwan entered a zig-zagging course of policy change on cross-strait relations. On the face of it, Taiwan's mainland policy has gone a long way from zero-sum struggle in the era of two Presidents Chiang toward positive-sum engagement in the period of President Lee. But in probing deeper, we find that not only the evolution of mainland policy has often been off the track of its intended goals, but policy shifts have tended to occur in a dramatic way beyond what was anticipated. Worse, policy changes have sometimes even jeopardized cross-strait interactions and led to political deadlocks on the brink of confrontation. In retrospect, Taiwan's vacillating position and strategic ambiguity on cross-strait relations are particularly impressive as compared with Beijing's everlasting resoluteness and strategic clarity.[1]

As Steven Goldstein put it, Taiwan's mainland policy is best characterized as "pseudo-engagement." In this variant, the purpose is to buy time and security on the assumptions that mutual goals are basically irreconcilable, but that talk and some contact is better than conflict. In so doing, Taiwan hoped to lower tensions, avoid crisis situations, and stave off further demands from the People's Republic of China (PRC). The policy focus is on the *process* of diplomacy rather than its *substance*. In the end, however, it does not really ameliorate the non-status quo elements of Beijing's position in that it merely seeks to evade or, at least, to ease the pressure on Taiwan from the PRC without addressing substantive issues.[2]

Lacking a strategic doctrine and a coherent policy, it is inevitable that Taiwan's mainland policy shifts tend to be fitful. We are in no position to know whether a given policy enhances national interest, detracts from it, or is simply irrelevant, because the hardcore concept of national interest is never clarified or subject to debate. As a consequence, new policies were often proposed by President Lee as ad hoc methods of crisis management in the face of external pressure, but ended up without an overall sense of purpose—in short, without a sense of national strategy.

Unworkable Guideline

To be sure, President Lee did not make mainland policies in a political vacuum. He often appealed to the National Unification Guideline (NUG), as the Kuomintang's (KMT) strategic plan, at least during his earlier presidency. But the NUG was essentially a product of political compromise in 1991 when the KMT was still mired in factional struggle. Insofar as the KMT's factions were split along national identity cleavage, the NUG was inevitably replete with ideological contradictions and unworkable preconditions.

The NUG applies a three-stage model to characterize Taiwan's national strategy toward cross-strait relations. The first stage is called "reciprocal exchanges," and is directed toward establishing rules of cross-strait interactions and intermediary institutions, lowering tensions and hostility, and so forth. The second stage is called "mutual trust and cooperation," and is directed toward establishing official channels, opening three links, jointly participating in international organizations, promoting high-level visits, and the like. The third stage is called "negotiating unification," and is directed toward establishing cross-strait units to work out a common constitution based on political democracy, economic freedom, and social justice.

In appearance, the NUG endorses a gradualist and functionalist approach to cross-strait integration, hoping to avoid a sovereignty debate and postpone the unification issue for as long as possible. But in substance, the NUG is not immune from political presumptions that betray its alleged functionalism and expose diametrically opposed contradictions. Besides the functionalist terminologies, the NUG also sets up three political preconditions for the first stage to move toward the second: The PRC does not deny the Republic of China (ROC) as a political entity, the PRC renounces the use of force against the ROC, and the PRC respects the ROC's right to join the international community.

In other words, if Beijing wants to establish official channels, open three links, or promote high-level visits, it must first acquiesce to Taiwan's political status, renounce the use of force, and accept Taiwan's international presence. But for the PRC, these three political concessions amount almost to an endorsement of de facto "two Chinas," which is a pill too bitter for Beijing to swallow.

The PRC thus takes the NUG's three political preconditions as unfriendly barriers, set up deliberately to block direct exchanges and cross-strait integration, and particularly to thwart political dialogues and negotiation across the strait. On the other hand, however, Taiwan insists on three political preconditions as fundamentals for national survival, without which the ROC's equal status is susceptible to Beijing's slant and Taiwan's future is not immune from the PRC's encroachment. In short, mutual goals are basically irreconcilable.

In effect, the implicit contradictions of the NUG are destined to restrain cross-strait exchanges and hinder the institutionalization of bilateral orders. Moreover, the NUG's three political preconditions for cross-strait economic deregulation also compel Beijing to take a politics-first stance, forcing the PRC's softliners to stand together with hardliners on the idea that cross-strait breakthroughs are impossible without dealing with political issues.

As a result, even in seeking solutions to practical problems, it proved difficult to avoid political implications. The PRC was determined not to imply recognition of Taiwan as a separate political entity, while the ROC was equally determined not to accept agreements implying that Taiwan was part of the PRC. Thus, negotiations on seemingly simple matters such as the authentication of legal documents or the handling of registered mail could drag on for many years.[3]

Unfortunately, the overpoliticizing trends became even more dominant as President Lee consolidated power in February 1993, when the mainlander Premier Hau Pei-tsun stepped down and the first Taiwanese Premier Lien Chan took over. It became increasingly apparent that Lee had little interest in Chinese unification. Before Lee revealed his true colors, however, Taipei and Beijing jointly held the first Koo-Wang talks in Singapore on April 27–29, 1993, where the PRC relented on its attitude toward sovereignty by signing four bilateral agreements without mentioning the "one-China" principle, at least in written documents.

But the good times did not last long. The PRC's softliners were soon confronted with challenges. Hardliners criticized the Koo-Wang talks as insubstantial, as having made no progress in political negotiation, and as potentially even creating an international illusion that the PRC tacitly accepted the ROC as an equal political entity. To highlight the PRC's politics-first position, the Foreign Ministry published a white paper called "The Taiwan Problem and Chinese Unification" on August 31, 1993, raising the irreconcilable "one-China" issue as the most critical, putting cross-strait relations once again on an overpoliticized path.[4]

In response, Taiwan's Mainland Affairs Council issued a white paper called "Explanations of Cross-Strait Relations" (ECSR), after almost a whole year (July 5, 1994). It showed President Lee's determination to shy away from the irreconcilable sovereignty debate by changing the definition of "one China" from a political concept to a nonpolitical one, meaning the "historical, geographical, cultural, ethnic China." But this did not mean that President Lee also shied away from Taiwan's political presumptions. Following the model of two Germanys and two Koreas, ECSR proposed a "divided-nation" model for the first time, emphasizing that the source of cross-strait tension was not sovereignty, but institutions and way of life, and showing no interest in dealing with the "one-China" principle. As expected, Beijing replied with a loud no.

Beijing's disappointment turned into furor because Taiwan's white paper was issued right after President Lee's personal interview with a Japanese writer, Shima Ryotaro. During this famous interview (May 6, 1994), Lee revealed his true anti-Chinese national identity sentiments in such a straightforward manner that it appalled Beijing's nationalist leaders. Lee disclosed his repugnance toward identifying himself as Chinese and labeled the KMT as an "emigrant regime." Furthermore, as a devout Christian, he also expected to act as Taiwan's Moses to lead the Taiwanese people as if it were the "exodus from Egypt," which was understood by Beijing as a "separatist confession."

In retrospect, 1994 became a turning point for cross-strait relations. The official redefinition of "one China" as a nonpolitical concept, together with President Lee's personal declarations against Chinese history and identity, finally cast an indelible impression upon Beijing that the NUG was a mere unification façade for Lee in covering his de facto "splittist movement." The three political preconditions of the NUG were later even labeled as Lee's "conspiracy" to invalidate the progress of cross-strait integration and unification.

On January 30, 1995, the PRC issued its last moderate appeal to Taiwan as "Jiang Zemin's eight points," stressing the primacy of a single Chinese sovereignty and promising to open all issues for dialogue and negotiation if Taiwan accepted the "one-China" principle. In return, President Lee proposed six points on April 8, reiterating the PRC's acceptance of Taiwan's separate jurisdiction as a political precondition for discussing the implication of "one China," and refusing to deal with "one China" as a principle. At best, Lee would only accept that "the definition of one China is subject to respective interpretations by each side," and hoped to shelve the sovereignty dispute for the time being.

The irreconcilable goals of Taipei and Beijing are quite clear: Taipei's priority is to earn equal status, confidence in peace, and international space, worried that if it accepts the "one-China" principle first, Beijing might confuse it with the PRC and reduce Taiwan to subordinate status. In contrast, Beijing's priority is to achieve symbolic unification, worried that if Beijing recognizes the ROC or renounces the use of force first, Taipei might immediately postpone unification talks indefinitely.

The question is: If political concessions proved so difficult for both sides, why not skip over them and turn to substantive and constructive issues, such as three links, economic deregulation, joint development, and so forth? However, it was apparent from the beginning (i.e., the NUG) that President Lee did not prefer this choice. Lee's emphasis on three political preconditions prior to the mid-term stage of the NUG reiterated his "postpone and wait for changes" approach toward cross-strait relations. Lee would rather stay put if the PRC did not compromise in political terms. He would rather go slowly and be inactive on cross-strait affairs if the PRC pushed too hard on political negotiation. Most of Lee's actions and reactions were directed toward buying time and waiting for chances, presuming that time was on Taiwan's side. In so doing, Lee believed that Taiwan's status quo and security were at least guaranteed and would not be traded away.

Unrealistic Assumptions

Although President Lee has never specified what "status quo" means, the sanctified words "status quo" were taken for granted in Taiwan as the highest strategic value without careful examination. Lee's approach was based on three assumptions:

1. Before Taiwan acquires political parity with the PRC, Taiwan's status quo is better served if Taiwan stays at arm's length from mainland China. Taiwan should postpone the sovereignty deal with the PRC for as long as possible.
2. As a weaker state vis-à-vis the PRC, Taiwan is at a disadvantage on political issues unless it first highlights the ROC's equal status and sovereignty internationally, thus drawing global backing to forestall the PRC's downgrading of the ROC.
3. It is therefore inevitable for Taiwan to confront diplomatic struggles with the PRC before cross-strait negotiation on political issues.

Lee put these three assumptions into practice on two fronts: As to economic exchanges, both the NUG's three political preconditions and "go-slow" policies were designed to decelerate the pace and restrict the scope of cross-strait cooperation. As to political interactions, the KMT's persistent refusal to initiate political dialogues and negotiation was also a dodging tactic aimed at delaying the sovereignty discussion and lessening bilateral institutionalization. Moreover, Lee also embarked on a sovereignty promotion campaign after 1993, in an attempt to publicize Taiwan's political appeals in the hope of gaining international support.

Unfortunately, Lee's double-edged tactics of cross-strait shirking and international diplomatic struggle proved incapable of holding the cross-strait status quo under control. On the contrary, Lee's tactics backfired beyond his expectations and jeopardized the cross-strait balance in Beijing's favor, putting Taiwan repeatedly into an increasingly awkward position.

Though it was true that Lee could retain the ROC's de jure status quo if he refused to deal with the PRC on sovereignty issues, he could not expect to protect Taiwan's de facto status quo if he failed to withhold international politics from tilting toward Beijing. However, this dire trend is exactly what Taiwan has been forced to confront since 1997, especially after President Clinton's reference to the three no's during his visit to China in June 1998. As Andrew Nathan noted, "What was novel (of Clinton's three no's) was the manner and context of their articulation—on Chinese soil, clustered together as a package of negatives directed at Taiwan, framed as a reassurance to China, devoid of the other elements of U.S. policy that were favorable to Taiwan, and given canonical status by public presidential utterance."[5] Clearly, Clinton's calculatingly devised shot dealt a blow to President Lee, which has surely caused the de facto downgrading of Taiwan's international status.

Ironically, the U.S. blow to Taiwan was brought forth by a long process of political chain reactions triggered by President Lee himself. Clinton's return visit to China and his talk of three no's were viewed as a soothing gift to Beijing after Jiang's visit to the United States in October 1997. The two U.S.–China summits were prompted by increasing military tensions in the wake of Lee's trip to Cornell in June 1995, culminating in the PRC's military exercises and missile tests on the eve of the 1996 presidential election. With this series of events from 1995 to 1998 as the backdrop, Lee's trip was viewed as the event that triggered the whole chain reaction.[6]

It is worth noting that Lee's trip to Cornell occurred only two months after his having returned six points to President Jiang. The PRC's ARATS president, Wang Daohan, was also scheduled to visit Taiwan during autumn of the same year. Worried that Wang might force the opening of political talks upon his arrival, President Lee resorted to a diplomatic offensive by making his historic trip. But the PRC reacted violently by aborting Wang's trip, suspending U.S.–China exchanges, and launching military drills against Taiwan's presidential election. Contrary to Lee's wishes, Taiwan ended up pushing the United States closer to the PRC for a constructive partnership via two U.S.–China summits, and receiving a blatant three no's from President Clinton on his unprecedented state visit to China.

Regretfully, the 1995–96 backfire did not teach President Lee a lesson. Similar misfortune occurred again on July 9, 1999, when Lee proposed his "special state-to-state relationship" to redefine Taiwan's political status vis-à-vis the PRC, again as a bid to forestall political pressures from the U.S. proposal of a cross-strait "interim agreement" and Wang's planned visit to Taiwan. Almost a replica of the 1995–96 situation, the PRC aborted Wang's trip, accused the United States of tacit support, and resorted to military threats against Taiwan's presidential election in 1999–2000. Contrary to Lee's wishes, Taiwan was accused even more vehemently in the United States as a "troublemaker" and the post-1992 tacit consensus of "one China, respective interpretations" across the Strait was also aborted in its wake. To Lee's dismay, cross-strait sovereignty was neither shelved nor abolished by Lee's assertive remark, but was forced upon both sides, coming into full effect, out of line with Lee's strategic plan.

Lee's opponents often accused him of spoiling Wang's visits on purpose, in an attempt to mar the summit meetings with the PRC to decelerate the pace of cross-strait interactions. Some opponents even charged that Lee did it deliberately in an attempt to aggravate cross-strait tensions for political profit, whether by stirring up contradictions within the United States, or by playing the United States against the PRC, or by antagonizing ethnic and national identity struggles domestically. In whatever versions, Lee was portrayed as a "great conspirator" masterminding an overall strategic plan against the progress of cross-strait relations and Taiwan–U.S.–China rapport, to create favorable conditions for Taiwan's independence movement.[7]

Judging from the dire international consequences in opposition to Taiwan, however, we find that President Lee was no master of strategy. He seriously miscalculated the unintended outcomes of international politics, especially the big power politics of the United States and the PRC. He also overestimated Taiwan's room to maneuver for U.S. support in the cross-strait dispute over sovereignty issues. His indirect approach in the face of the PRC's "one-China" offensive, that is, his transfer of the combat zone to the international arena was disproportionate to Taiwan's limited strength. The international realpolitik reacted against Taiwan like a boomerang. President Lee's attempt to internationalize Taiwan's sovereignty problem was vehemently reacted to twice in an effort to throw the problem back upon Taiwan, and with an increased trend toward pushing Taiwan to deal with the sovereignty issue directly with the PRC, and to treat it as a cross-strait problem. Ironically, Lee's endeavor to shirk cross-strait sovereignty talks and internationalize Taiwan's sovereignty problem has instead led to a more urgent political face-off across the Strait, aided by an apprehensive United States as an intermediary.

President Lee often claimed that he appealed to the sovereignty promotion campaign more as a defensive reaction than as an aggressive action. In other words, it was not an orchestrated and cumulated action with long-term strategic goals, but more an improvised and episodic response to cope with a short-term crisis. Even so, Lee's ad hoc defensive measures of crisis-management were not effective in terms of the adverse consequences against Taiwan.

After all, as a weaker state vis-à-vis the much stronger PRC and the United States, Taiwan was in no position to play high-risk diplomatic games, especially when democratic Taiwan was still mired in national identity struggles, and while a cross-strait policy of strategic ambiguity was tacitly endorsed by both the PRC and the United States. Even worse, in both the cases of Lee's Cornell trip and his proposal of a two-state theory, he went so far as to abuse the U.S. trust in Taiwan, without prior notice to or consultation with the United States about his provocative moves. Lee's unilateral and assertive action inevitably turned the U.S.-Taiwan relationship sour and produced distrust and antipathy among U.S. elites toward Taiwan, sometimes even stirring up unsympathetic voices that accused Taiwan of being a new "troublemaker."[8]

Losing Ground

In international affairs, the status quo is more a dynamic political concept than a static legal one. In seeking international recognition of a nation's status, the political struggle over power and interest is often more significant than the legal debate over discursive legitimacy. For a small state to protect itself from a big power's encroachment, it often chooses to join that big power's bandwagon or seek alliance with other big powers for balance.[9]

It needs to be emphasized that to bandwagon with a big power does not mean to become a dependent or a client state, but refers to choosing a strategy that tacitly reduces one's political autonomy and complies with the big power's interests, at least to the extent of not explicitly offending the latter. On the other hand, for a strategy of balancing against a big power to be effective, there must be fundamental antagonisms between two big powers, thus making an alliance with one side sustainable.

In the case of cross-strait relations over his twelve years as president, Lee was apparently inclined toward a strategy of balancing against the PRC, choosing to ally with the United States as before. However, Lee was confronted with a political and economic cross-strait reality that was totally different from that of both President Chiang Kai-shek and President Chiang Ching-kuo. Politically, the PRC arose rapidly as a new giant in Asia, achieved normalization with all major powers, was well engaged in global activities as one of the world leaders, and widely recognized as the only legitimate government of China. Economically, the PRC ranked top in the world in terms of GDP growth during the past two decades, succeeded in becoming the fastest growing market for world investors, and became a major trade partner of the United States. In spite of these unprecedented changes, the PRC stuck to its ideological principles, at least formally, and remained the largest authoritarian state ruled by a single communist party. It was in response to the complexity of the PRC's uneven development that the United States has been eager to find alternative strategies for living with China.[10]

The changing strategy of the United States toward China from one of containment to one of conditional engagement has perplexed Taiwan the most, insofar as Taiwan has economically benefited from China's growth, but has also been politically threatened by it.[11] In the face of changing U.S.–China relations, President Lee took a more business-oriented approach to cross-strait economic exchanges in the beginning, which was geared toward gradual deregulation and taking mainland China as Taiwan's economic hinterland. Business circles and the planning technocrats in the government, who tended to see Taiwan's economic future as being dependent on close cooperation with the mainland, pressed for direct links and more rapid liberalization. However, as cross-strait political conflict began to surface after Lee's trip to Cornell in 1995, President Lee began to fear that economic overdependence on the mainland would enable Beijing to put political pressure on Taiwan, which was summed up in the political slogans "using people to pressure officials" and "using business to besiege politics."[12]

After the PRC's military drills against Taiwan in March 1996, President Lee was even more concerned about the PRC's strategy of encroachment by economic means. Right after the PRC's military drills, the president of Formosa Plastics, Wang Yung-ching, suddenly announced an unprecedented investment of $3 billion in a Fujian power plant, which angered President Lee, who began to reevaluate Taiwan's mainland policy. On September 14, Lee announced a new guideline called "go slow, be patient," and appealed for stricter regulation of Taiwan's mainland investment. About eight months later (on May 16, 1997), the Ministry of Economics further stipulated four limitations on investment:

1. any single investment to mainland China should be below $50 million;
2. investment in mainland China's infrastructure is prohibited;
3. investment in mainland China's high-tech industries should be more strictly regulated;
4. capital outflows of listed companies to mainland China should be more strictly regulated.

However, because Taiwan entered a period of economic liberalization at the same time, it was extremely difficult for the state to regulate capital flows in an age of global capital. As mentioned before, insofar as mainland China was the fastest growing market in the world, it would be against business interests to impose such antimarket measures. In the wake of such a policy change, Taiwan's businessmen became even more alienated from government, and, consequently, were also left alone to confront the PRC's sticks and carrots. Without cooperation from business circles, the Taiwan state's inability to regulate capital flows to mainland China was appalling, and apparent even in the government's statistics. Until 1997, for example, there were 11,000 Taiwanese firms investing $7 billion on mainland China by Taiwan's official data, but according to the PRC's statistics, there were 35,000 Taiwanese firms investing $16.6 billion on mainland China.[13] Even in a single year, 1996, the year that the new policy was announced, Taiwan's Ministry of Economics passed 383 items of mainland-bound investments worth about $1.2 billion, but according to the PRC's statistics, Taiwanese investments were as high as 3,200 items, totaling about $7.1 billion.[14] It was very clear that the Taiwan state was confronted with an unprecedented loss of power in regulating its economy.

In retrospect, President Lee's sudden shift toward cross-strait economic conservatism was not only tactically ineffective but also strategically unwise.[15] Lee's strategic reasoning was quite simplistic: To maintain Taiwan's security meant to keep autonomy from the PRC, namely, to avoid economic overdependence upon the PRC. But in view of the fact that cross-strait negotiation was inevitable and the PRC's growth of national strength was faster than Taiwan's, Taiwan would jeopardize its bargaining position if it maintained a "postpone and wait for changes" approach to cross-strait talks. In other words, it would be politically wiser for Taiwan to make earlier use of its still effective economic edge as a bargaining chip in exchange for political promises from the PRC, such as memberships in international organizations, confidence-building measures, peace agreements, and the like. However, despite President Lee's refusal to open three links and his turn to stricter regulations on mainland-bound investments, he never viewed these unilateral bans as Taiwan's bargaining chips for cross-strait negotiation, and he preferred to postpone cross-strait talks for as long as possible.

As mainland China caught up with the global economy, however,

Taiwan's earlier economic advantages vis-à-vis the PRC were no longer sustainable. For example, during the early 1980s, mainland China was still severely short of capital, while Taiwan was in a good position to offer joint development for political gains. By the end of the 1980s, Taiwan's investment on mainland China still constituted about 20 percent of the PRC's total foreign direct investment (FDI). It would be advantageous for Taiwan to make use of financial capital as bargaining chips for political benefits in return. In fact, even before Lee's proposal of the two-state theory in July 1999, the PRC still hoped to deal with Taiwan on three-links issues, which they thought to be highly critical regarding cross-strait integration. But Lee's continuing reluctance regarding cross-strait negotiation, his growing commitment to the sovereignty promotion campaign, and his shift toward economic conservatism all led to the neglect of Taiwan's economic bargaining chips.

Unfortunately, Lee's unwillingness to make timely use of these economic chips did not prevent the PRC from obtaining them elsewhere. Beginning in 1994, for example, the PRC jumped to the position of second largest receiver of FDI in the world behind only the United States. Taiwan's share of investment on mainland China was reduced to a mere 9.5 percent by the end of the 1990s, which was not as significant as it had been earlier. Moreover, as Taipei and Beijing were about to enter the World Trade Organization (WTO) in 2000 or 2001, Beijing began to perceive the three links as inevitable, and stopped advocating them as incentive for a cross-strait bargain.[16] Even Lee's most cherished "go-slow" policies were destined to change after Taiwan joined the WTO.

In short, Lee's insistence on stricter regulation was tactically ineffective because it was inconsistent with Taiwan's economic liberalization. Lee's reluctance to use Taiwan's economic edges as bargaining tools was strategically unwise in that it was a waste of Taiwan's very scarce political resources. Instead, Lee's growing interest in the sovereignty struggle with the PRC has alerted the PRC to political issues, leaving less room for political maneuver. Lee's actions ultimately led to escalation of the conflict and a political showdown across the strait, thus trapping Taiwan into a political predicament where the ROC's sovereignty was the only and last bargaining chip with the PRC. In sum, Lee's lack of strategic insight and shortage of tactical delicacy led to serious inconsistencies and jeopardized Taiwan's security beyond his anticipations.

Brinkmanship Without Solutions

Kissinger put it well: "The test of statesmanship is the adequacy of its evaluation before the event."[17] Unfortunately, President Lee did not pass this test and his evaluation of cross-strait development was full of wishful thinking.

In international politics, a small state is not qualified for high-risk games unless its people are well prepared to fight or sacrifice (as in Israel) or its leadership is both cunning and recalcitrant (as in North Korea). But the Taiwanese are not like the Israelis, just as President Lee is no Kim Il Sung. A small state without strong people and shrewd leadership can survive internationally only by bandwagoning with big powers and making enemies into friends (as in the case of Finland with the former Soviet Union).

As Herman Kahn noted, the escalation of conflict is a process whereby measures that individually appear logical and reasonable generate a momentum of their own.[18] The possibility of escalation is often associated with the politics of brinkmanship. Escalation is a "competition in resolve" or "competition in risk taking," and resolve is often measured by a willingness to pay costs in pursuit of certain objectives.[19]

In cross-strait interactions, however, the escalation of conflict occurred without a concomitant growth of people's resolve on Taiwan to protect their future. Lee's resort to the politics of brinkmanship without first equipping the Taiwanese people with national will was both dangerous and irresponsible. Moreover, Lee also opened a Pandora's box that has unleashed Taiwan's quasi-nationalist political forces on a collision course with Taiwan's increasing economic integration with mainland China. He left his people mired in a national identity struggle, unleashed a mass populism that is unfavorable for stimulating a rational debate over Taiwan's future, and failed to offer any workable solution to pacify cross-strait tensions, even less to untangle the cross-strait deadlock.

Notes

1. For a historical overview of cross-strait relations, see Zhang Zanhe, *History of Cross-Strait Relations* (Taipei: Buddha University, 1996).

2. Steven M. Goldstein, "Terms of Engagement: Taiwan's Mainland Policy," in *Engaging China: The Management of an Emerging Power*, ed. Alastair Iain Johnston and Robert Ross (London and New York: Routledge, 1999), pp. 79–80.

3. Ralph Clough, *Cooperation or Conflict in the Taiwan Strait* (Lanham, MD: Rowman and Littlefield, 1999), p. 34.

4. As to the cross-strait debates over sovereignty issues, it is very useful to consult Shao Zonghai, *Cross-Strait Relations: Cross-Strait Consensus and Dissensus* (Taipei: Wunan, 1998).

5. Andrew Nathan, "What's Wrong with American Taiwan Policy," *Washington Quarterly* 23, no. 2 (Spring 2000): 96–97.

6. While scholars from the PRC and the United States pointed out this irony, the ROC government was reluctant to admit it. See a sample of cross-fire debate from three sides in Gerrit W. Gong, ed., *Taiwan Strait Dilemmas: China-Taiwan-U.S. Policies in the New Century* (Washington, DC: CSIS, 2000).

7. See, for example, New Party, ed., *Ten Years Under Lee Teng-hui's Rule* (Taipei: Fengyun Forum, 1999).

8. See John W. Garver, *Face-off: China, the United States and Taiwan's Democratization* (Seattle: University of Washington Press, 1997); James Lilley and Chuck Downs, eds., *Crisis in the Taiwan Strait* (Washington, DC: National Defense University Press, 1997).

9. See Wu Yu-shan, *Balancing or Bandwagoning: A New Interrpretation of Cross-Strait Relations* (in Chinese) (Taipei: Chengzung, 1997). For an English version, see Wu Yu-shan, "Theorizing on the Political Economy of Cross-Strait Relations: An Analogy with Russia and Its Neighbors," *Issues and Studies* 31, no. 9 (September 1995): 1–18.

10. Ezra Vogel, ed., *Living with China* (New York: American Assembly, 1997).

11. See James Shinn, ed., *Weaving the Net: Conditional Engagement with China* (New York: Council on Foreign Relations, 1996).

12. Mainland Affairs Council, *Beyond the Historical Gap: Retrospect and Prospect of Ten Years' Cross-Strait Exchanges* (Taipei: Executive Yuan, Republic of China, 1997).

13. Zheng Yusuo, "The Role of Hong Kong in Cross-Strait Relations," in *The Return of HK and the Prospect of Cross-Strait Relations*, ed. Wang Jiaying and Zheng Chiyan (Hong Kong: Research Center on Cross-Strait Relations, 1999), pp. 19–30.

14. Leng Tse-kang, "Dynamics of Taiwan-Mainland China Economic Relations," *Asian Survey* 33, no. 5 (May 1998): 494–509.

15. Julian Kuo, "The Go-Slow Policy is Ineffective and Unwise," *China Times* (Taiwan), February 6, 1998. See also Yun-han Chu, "The Political Economy of Taiwan's Mainland Policy," *Journal of Contemporary China* 6, no. 15 (July 1997): 229–58.

16. Julian Kuo, "Political Logic of Cross-Strait Three Links," *Soochow Journal of Political Science*, no. 10 (September 1999): 65–96.

17. Henry Kissinger, *The Necessity for Choice* (New York: Harper and Row, 1960), p. 3.

18. Herman Kahn, "Escalation as a Strategy," in *Problems of National Strategy*, ed. Henry Kissinger (New York: Praeger), p. 17.

19. Ibid., p. 32.

11

Reunification Strategy

Beijing Versus Lee Teng-hui

Suisheng Zhao

The victory of Chen Shui-bian as Democratic Progressive Party (DPP) candidate in the presidential election of March 18, 2000, overturned fifty-five years of Kuomintang (KMT) rule on the island of Taiwan. It was the first peaceful and democratic transition of state power from one political party to another in modern Chinese history. While the election of Chen Shui-bian as Taiwan's president represented a monumental development of democratic politics in Taiwan, it also raised fears of a war across the Taiwan Strait, as it introduced unprecedented challenges and a new element of uncertainty into the fragile relationship between Beijing and Taipei.

Although Beijing reacted cautiously after the election, it was certainly deeply embarrassed by Chen's victory. Defying angry rhetoric from Beijing that threatened war if Chen was elected, the election outcome declared the failure of Beijing's strategy of national reunification, which has been a mixture of military coercion and peaceful inducement, known in China as a *liangshou chelue* (two hands or two-pronged strategy). Coercive strategy relies primarily upon the use or the threat of the use of force. It could be military actions aiming at the conquest of Taiwan or military brinkmanship using force in an exemplary and demonstrative manner. In contrast, peaceful inducement appeals to cross-strait political negotiations and economic and cultural exchanges to bind

---

An earlier version of this chapter previously appeared as an article published in *Problems of Post-Communism* 48, no. 2 (March–April 2001).

Taiwan's hands in seeking independence and to build goodwill and momentum for eventual reunification. Military coercion and peaceful inducement are two sides of the same coin and coercive logic is embedded in a peaceful offense.

Using this two-pronged strategy, Beijing wanted to force Taipei to sit at the negotiation table and come up with an eventual reunification resolution. However, this strategy has failed to reach its objective because Lee Teng-hui skillfully maneuvered Taiwan's domestic politics and international opportunities and successfully resisted Beijing's attempts. Lee's maneuver opened the way for Shui-bian Chen to win the 2000 presidential election. Since inauguration, Chen has not given ground to Beijing on the issue of sovereignty although he has held out an olive branch by offering to sit down and talk. This chapter examines the evolution of Beijing's two-pronged strategy and its failure in response to Lee's successful maneuver to change Taiwan's political landscape and disentangle the island from its previous legal and ideological connections with the mainland. The chapter concludes with an analysis of the impact of Lee's legacy on the across-strait relationship in the post–Lee Teng-hui era.

Beijing's Peaceful Offense and Its Failure

For Beijing, the Taiwan issue was a result of the civil war between the Chinese Communist Party (CCP) and the KMT, which was defeated and fled to the island in 1949. After conquering most of the mainland and Hainan Island off the South China coast in April 1950, the People's Liberation Army (PLA) was prepared to take back Taiwan soon afterward. However, the outbreak of the Korean War on June 23, 1950, and President Harry Truman's consequent order to the U.S. Seventh Fleet to patrol the Taiwan Strait forced the PLA to call off the attempt.[1]

Beijing never stopped threatening to "liberate" Taiwan by force. But, in a practical way, it turned to a new strategy of peaceful reunification, starting with a "Message" to the Taiwan people from the Standing Committee of the National People's Congress (NPC) on January 1, 1979. The new policy was fully elaborated in the nine-point proposal for peaceful reunification by Ye Jianying, the vice chairman of the NPC Standing Committee, on September 30, 1981. Ye suggested talks between the CCP and the KMT, and specifically proposed *santong* (three links, i.e., commercial, postal, and travel) and *siliu* (four exchanges, i.e., academic, cultural, economic, and sports) as the first step to "gradually eliminate antagonism between the two sides and increase mutual understanding."[2] Later, Deng Xiaoping proposed a formula of "one country, two systems" as a viable method of reunification. Beijing's peaceful offense reached a new stage when Jiang Zemin, the general secretary of the CCP and the president of the PRC, made an eight-point proposal on January 30, 1995. He suggested that the two sides across the Taiwan Strait start negotiations "on officially ending the state of hostility between the two sides and accomplishing peaceful reunification step by step."[3]

Beijing's adoption of the peaceful unification strategy was a calculated policy shift taking into consideration the change in both domestic and international situations. Domestically, it coincided with the beginning of China's economic reform, which needed a peaceful international environment to pursue its modernization drive. By suggesting the "three links" and "four exchanges" across the Taiwan Strait, Beijing wanted to establish a new image of peace and confidence to attract investment from Western countries as well as from Taiwanese entrepreneurs. In addition, the remaining first-generation leaders in Beijing were eager to resolve the Taiwan issue before the first generation on both sides died out altogether. They worried that, after the old generation leaders in Taiwan passed away, future political development in Taiwan might become more complicated. Despite the civil war, the CCP's veteran leaders felt more comfortable in dealing with the old KMT leaders because of their personal contacts in the past and also their shared sense of a common national identity. They were not familiar with Taipei's younger, foreign-trained leaders and worried that they would not politically identify with the Chinese nation. Deng Xiaoping expressed this feeling when he said:

> It is better for both the mainland and Taiwan to establish contacts and realize the goal of the country's reunification when the senior leaders of the CCP and KMT in Taiwan are still alive. The problems concerning the Taiwan issue can be resolved easier when people who know the history of both the CCP and KMT are alive. If the issue is further postponed, there are many questions the younger generation of the two parties do not understand.[4]

Due to this feeling of urgency, Deng listed reunification as one of the three great tasks that the CCP wanted to accomplish in the 1980s.[5]

The anxiousness of Beijing's first-generation leaders turned into a peaceful offense in 1979 also because they perceived the opportunities brought about by the change in Beijing's international environment. Two important international events that reversed Beijing and Taipei's international status were crucial. The first event is Beijing's taking over Taipei's seat in the United Nations General Assembly and Security Council in 1971. The second event is the switching of U.S. diplomatic recognition from Taipei to Beijing in 1979. These changes isolated Taiwan in the international arena and deprived it of its major supporters. More important, they altered Beijing's perception of international relations from the inevitability of world war to "peace and development" as the main world trend. Beijing felt that the island would no longer be a major threat to the mainland. As a result, Beijing became more confident in its ability to resolve the Taiwan issue on its own terms, and wanted to create a friendly and peaceful environment for early reunification.

Peaceful offense promotes economic and cultural exchanges and negotiations across the Taiwan Strait. It also advocates that socialism on the mainland and capitalism on Taiwan coexist with each other for a long time. According to Deng's design, Taiwan may enjoy a high degree of autonomy, including administrative power, legislative power, independent judiciary power, the power to keep its own troops, and certain powers of foreign affairs, such as signing commercial and cultural agreements with foreign countries. But "only the PRC represents China in the international arena."[6]

It is undeniable that the peaceful offense brought about some desirable changes in cross-strait relations. The most significant change was the rapid increase in economic interactions despite the occurrence of some political turbulence, for example, the Tiananmen massacre of 1989 and the Democratic Progressive Party's inclusion of an independence clause in its party platform in 1991.[7] When Taiwan first opened indirect trade in 1987, Taiwan's total trade value with the mainland was $1.7 billion. It grew about ten times, exceeding $20 billion in 1995, while Taiwan's total trade with other countries and areas grew only 138.9 percent in the same period. Despite intensified political tensions during the Taiwan Strait crisis, a March 1996 report of Taiwan's Board of Foreign Trade still predicted about 20 percent annual growth in cross-strait trade in 1996, of up to $25.7 billion.[8] This growth was particularly spectacular after 1989 although the West as well as the Taiwan government officially condemned the Tiananmen Incident. In contrast to some predictions at that time, the crackdown on the democracy movement did not cut, but rather accelerated the development of the mainland's economic links with Taiwan.[9] Exploiting Western countries' economic sanctions against mainland China, Taiwanese businessmen moved effectively to fill the vacuum. Cross-strait trade increased 28.02 percent in 1989, driven by the large-scale relocation of Taiwan investment into the mainland. Total trade value across the strait reached $5 billion in 1990 and $11 billion in 1993. It exceeded $20 billion in 1995, comprising a significant portion of the total trade of both sides. In 1995, Taiwan became the second largest supplier (after Japan) to the mainland and its seventh largest export market. Taiwan also ranked as the second largest investor in China only next to Hong Kong-Macao.

Another visible change was the beginning of functional contacts between semi-official institutions across the strait. In particular, semi-official agencies were established on both sides to begin functional consultations in 1992: the Association for Relations across the Taiwan Strait (ARATS) on the Beijing side and the Strait Exchange Foundation (SEF) on the Taiwan side. Wang Daohan and Koo Chen-fu, the chairmen of the two institutions, met in Singapore for the first time in 1993 and the second Wang–Koo talk was scheduled to take place in Taipei in 1995.

In spite of this progress, Beijing's peaceful offense never brought it closer to its major objective of inducing the Taiwan government to the negotiation table and moving the national reunification process forward. Facing Beijing's vigorous peaceful offense, the Taiwan government was quite effective in holding to the *sanbu* (three no's, i.e., no contact, no negotiation, no compromise) policy and successfully resisted pressures from the private sector to start *santong* or to lift the ban on direct trade and direct air and sea links with the mainland. Cross-strait contacts were strictly confined at the nonofficial and nonpolitical level. Taipei characterized the contacts between the SEF and ARATS as practical consultation (*shiwu xing xieshang*) instead of political negotiation (*zhengzhi tanpan*) and indicated that consultation (*xieshang*) is different from negotiation (*tanpan*).[10] As a result, intensified economic exchanges did not come up with any real breakthrough in the goal of reunification. The political relationship between the two governments remained officially nonexistent and hostile. To make things worse, in spite of the development of economic interdependence, the Taiwan independence movement gained momentum during this period.

The failure of Beijing's peaceful offense was related largely to the unexpected change in the game of the contest across the Taiwan Strait after Lee Teng-hui came to power in Taiwan in 1998. The Taiwan government under Chiang Kai-shek and his son, Chiang Ching-kuo, held the "one-China principle" by insisting upon itself as the sole legitimate government of China, including both the mainland and Taiwan, and called the Beijing government communist bandits (*gongfei*). Because Chinese on both sides of the straits agreed that there was only one China, the game of the contest across the Taiwan Strait was to compete for the legitimate representative position of China. Taiwan independence was not an issue in the contest for both the Taipei and Beijing governments at the time because Taiwan independence activities and even speeches to advocate independence were illegal in Taiwan. However, the game was changed gradually from the competition over the sole legitimate representative of China to a new issue of whether and how Taiwan should gain independent political status after Lee Teng-hui came to power. This change in the game coincided with the progress of political liberalization and democratization presided over by Lee Teng-hui.

After nearly four decades of authoritarian rule by the KMT, democratic forces began to gain ground in Taiwan during the final years of Chiang Ching-kuo's presidency in the mid-1980s. Political space for electoral competition gradually opened up, the degree of political contest intensified, and the scope of political discourse in the public domain widened. Various authoritarian legal constructs, particularly, the thirty-eight-year-old decree of martial law and the prohibition of new political parties and new newspapers, were dismantled, and rules for democratic politics were gradually established. One of the most important political consequences of democratization in Taiwan was the legitimization of the Taiwan independence movement. Notably, the DPP was established on September 28, 1986, and openly called for Taiwan independence. During the transitional years from Chiang to Lee, Taiwan independence activists were allowed to return to Taiwan from abroad to conduct open activities. Taiwan independence speeches and deeds were declared within the limits of free speech. Taiwan independence organizations competed freely in the political system and were provided with a potential opportunity for holding office. The DPP pushed for a national referendum to determine Taiwan's political status.

In the early years after Lee took office, he adopted a two-pronged approach in handling the island's politics. On the one hand, he tried to placate the traditional forces within his party by presiding over the formulation of the "National Unification Guidelines," and announced the three stages of communication and cooperation with the mainland. As revealed later, Lee even sent his personal aides, Su Chi-cheng and Cheng Su-ming, to hold a series of secret talks with mainland authorities in several locations of Hong Kong and Guangdong in the early 1990s.[11] On the one hand, as the first native Taiwanese president, he tried to win the support of the DPP and the centrifugal force by painstakingly pushing talks on reunification indefinitely and pursuing his political ideal of establishing Taiwan's sovereign space in the world. At the beginning of the 1990s, Lee's attitude toward Taiwan independence changed from making one concession after another to providing assistance and support.

For awhile, however, Beijing's leaders could not tell whether Lee belonged to the reunification faction or the independence faction because Lee attempted to win support from both factions. During the late 1980s and early 1990s, Beijing had some hopes in Lee, believing that only a handful of people, led by the DPP, demanded independence and that Lee was better than the DPP. Because Lee was not involved in China's civil war and had no personal association with the CCP, his historical burden may have been less. For this reason, he could play a role and make contributions to solving the Taiwan issue.

However, Beijing was wrong about Lee. Pursuing a two-pronged strategy, Lee gradually changed the contest across the Taiwan Strait into a realm that Beijing did not anticipate. Persisting on three prerequisites with regard to cross-strait relations—the mainland makes a commitment to refrain from the use of force, recognizes Taiwan's status as a political entity on an equal footing, and allows Taiwan space in international activities—Lee carefully but effectively disentangled the previous connections between the mainland and Taiwan. Eventually, Lee revealed his real intention as a supporter of the Taiwan independence movement with an approach that was more gradual, subtler, and quieter than that of the DPP who advocated Taiwan independence by calling for changing the national flag and setting up a Republic of Taiwan.

Lee's interview with Japanese writer Ryotaro Shiba in March 1994 was the first major wake-up call to Beijing in understanding Lee's real mindset. In this meeting, Lee talked about "the sorrow of being a Taiwanese," and told the interviewer that "the KMT is an alien regime." Lee compared himself to Moses, saying that he would lead his followers to escape from Egypt, cross the Red Sea, and build another country in another place. Beijing realized that "the analogy undoubtedly was Lee's self-analysis of his political direction."[12]

Before and after his meeting with Ryotaro Shiba, Lee pursued a new policy of pragmatic diplomacy, striving to expand Taiwan's international living space and to participate in international organizations. This new policy aimed at advancing Taiwan's substantive relations (*shizhi guanxi*) with countries that had cut off official ties with Taipei by keeping semi-official or unofficial relations. This new approach, known as flexible diplomacy (*tanxing waijiao*) in the early 1990s, abandoned Taiwan's insistence on being the only legitimate Chinese government in the international arena. When Saudi Arabia established diplomatic relations with Beijing in 1990, Taiwan for the first time decided not to terminate its official relationship with this country. It was Riyadh, under pressure from Beijing, that broke with Taipei. This new policy was elaborated in Taipei's first foreign affairs report in January 1993, which called for an expansion of international links without regard for the reactions of mainland China. In addition, Taipei's White Paper on Cross-Strait Relations of July 1994 stated that Taipei would "no longer compete with Beijing for the right to represent China in the international arena."[13]

Flexible diplomacy utilized Taiwan's greatest asset—its political democratization and economic prosperity—and it paid off particularly well. For a long time, Taiwan's authoritarian system held little appeal for the American public and proved a constant source of embarrassment to Washington. Taiwan's democratization helped to remove the political sore spot and facilitated a favorable reorientation of Washington's Taiwan policy. The Bush administration approved the sale of F-16 fighter aircraft to Taiwan in 1992. The Clinton Administration modestly upgraded the status of Taiwan's diplomatic representation in the United States after completing its Taiwan policy review in September 1994. In spite of the repeated promise of the U.S. State Department to Beijing that it would not grant a visa to President Lee Teng-hui, following an intensive lobby effort in Washington, Lee received a visa to visit his alma mater, Cornell University, in the United States in May 1995. While this decision was the result of a messy process of bureaucratic maneuvers, it not only broke Washington's promise to Beijing but also openly changed the policy that forbids Taiwan leaders to visit the United States, which had been successively upheld by past administrations over nearly seventeen years. In the U.S. visit, Lee was to play the role of Taiwan's president and propagate the existence of the Republic of China on Taiwan. In his speech at Cornell, Lee chanted the slogan "challenging the impossible," and stressed that "Taiwan is a country with independent sovereignty."[14]

To a great extent due to Lee's success in changing the nature of the contest across the Taiwan Strait from the issue of who should represent China to the issue of Taiwan's status, support for independence increased steadily in Taiwan's polls, although support for the status quo continued to be the majority. According to the surveys conducted by the Center for Election Research at National Taiwan University, despite the progress in cross-strait economic integration, the share of respondents who support independence increased from 12.4 percent in January–February 1994, to 13.8 percent in January–February 1995, and to 15.3 percent in January 1996. Surveys carried out by Gallup, Inc. (Taiwan) and the Public Opinion Survey Foundation (Taipei) indicated that support for independence, opposition to Beijing's "one country, two systems" policy, and resistance to reunification rhetoric were all increasing even more dramatically. In surveys conducted between 1989 and May 1994, the proportion of respondents who "strongly agree" or "agree" that Taiwan should be independent rose from 8.2 percent (December 1989) to 12 percent (December 1990), 12.7 percent (June 1991), 15.1 percent (October 1992), 23.7 percent (May 1993), and 27 percent (April 1994). In May 1994, after the Thousand Island Lake incident, support for independence increased again to 27.3 percent.[15]

In spite of these changes, Beijing still had high expectations for the success of the peaceful reunification strategy. In particular, Beijing had strong hopes that economic interaction would be a means of developing political relations and pushing for political negotiations. For this political purpose, the State Council of China promulgated a special decree in 1988 to encourage Taiwan investment in China, including many tax shelters and other preferential treatment for Taiwanese investment.[16] Beijing even tolerated a huge trade deficit with Taiwan: around $14.8 billion in 1995. After the first high-level meeting of the Wang–Koo talks in Singapore in 1993, a logical development, from Beijing's view, should be an across-strait summit. It was this logic that led President Jiang Zemin to make the eight-point proposal for high-level negotiations to end the hostility across the strait on January 30, 1995. The eight-point proposal was Jiang's first major policy initiative on Taiwan affairs, and he believed it would produce a breakthrough in cross-strait relations. As

Beijing's *Xinhua* commentary said, the eight-point proposal "opened up a new chapter in the development of relations between the two sides of the strait."[17]

However, Jiang's initiative was met with Lee Teng-hui's six-point response that required the mainland to acknowledge "the reality of divided rule between Taiwan and the mainland" and demanded that Beijing give up resorting to force against Taiwan as a prerequisite for talks between the two sides. Beijing was further disappointed when SEF Chairman Koo Chen-fu said that the topics planned for discussion at the second Wang–Koo meeting would not include preparatory negotiations for the ending of bilateral hostilities. Beijing was shocked when it learned that President Lee Teng-hui was granted a visa for the historical visit to the United States in May 1995. Embarrassingly, Beijing's leaders received relevant forecasts only two days before the U.S. Department of State officially announced Lee's visit. These developments were certainly beyond Beijing's expectations and clearly showed the failure of Beijing's peaceful reunification strategy.

Beijing's Strategy of Military Coercion and Its Failure

The failure of the peaceful offense forced Beijing to rethink its Taiwan policy. The result was a turn to a coercive strategy. Two months after Lee's visit to the United States, Beijing launched a series of military exercises aimed at Taiwan. In the wake of the military exercises, Beijing's Taiwan Affairs Office and the ARATS unilaterally declared, on June 16, that the second Wang–Koo meeting would be indefinitely postponed. On July 21 to 26, 1995, the PLA launched a series of surface-to-surface ballistic missile tests in the East China Sea, just 150 kilometers off the tip of northern Taiwan. On August 15 to 25, 1995, the PLA held a second series of military exercises, including guided missile, cannon and other military tests in the sea 136 kilometers north of Taiwan. In November, PLA marines and tanks made a beachhead landing exercise from amphibious landing craft, backed by jet fighters and naval vessels. On March 18 to 25, 1996, the PLA conducted a fourth wave of joint ground, naval, and air military exercises. Three missiles were launched on target areas just twenty nautical miles from Keelung, Taiwan's second busiest seaport, and just offshore from the harbor of Kaohsiung, Taiwan's largest port and the third largest container port in the world. In the announcement on the military exercises, Beijing's *Xinhua* (New China News) agency stated that "to strive to end the disunity of the country and nation by peaceful means in no way means allowing the process of peaceful reunification to be delayed indefinitely. If some people were to dare separate Taiwan from Chinese territory, the Chinese people would defend the country's sovereignty and territorial integrity with blood and lives."[18]

The military exercises marked a strategic shift in the emphasis of Beijing's policy from striving for a peaceful reunification to suppressing the Taiwan independence movement by the threat of force. This strategic shift was expressed in the following three aspects. The first was to move from nonintervention in Taiwan's international politics to *ganyu Taizheng* (intervening in Taiwan's internal politics), including efforts to influence Taiwan's presidential election outcomes. The second was to move from long-term waiting to *xianqi tongyi* (setting a deadline for reunification), which includes finding a timetable for the final reunification. And the third was to move from an emphasis on peaceful reunification to an emphasis on *wuli baotai* (taking Taiwan by force).[19]

Beijing's strategy shift largely resulted from Beijing's feeling of betrayal by Lee Teng-hui's "obstinacy and deceit." This feeling was revealed clearly in the fact that, while preparing the military actions of the summer of 1995, Beijing organized a large-scale media campaign of more than 400 articles attacking Lee Teng-hui personally.[20]

Jiang Zemin and other leaders in Beijing must have felt deeply disappointed because their policy did not effectively stop Lee's moving Taiwan politically further away from the mainland. Jiang had loyally implemented the peaceful reunification policy, which was formulated by the first generation of CCP leaders, and also took his own initiatives in proposing negotiations on equal footing to end hostility in 1995. But Lee Teng-hui's negative response to his eight-point proposal and particularly Lee's unexpected success in obtaining a visa to visit the United States deeply embarrassed Jiang Zemin and his foreign minister, Qian Qichen. Their policy toward Taiwan was under heavy criticism. They were seen as too innocent, in being unable to understand Lee thoroughly and believing the U.S. pledge too easily. Jiang's position suddenly changed from being the core of the leadership to being the focus of pressure from all sides because all Chinese leaders are nationalists with a strong belief in their definition of national sovereignty and territorial integrity. Although some leaders, such as Wang Daohan in Shanghai, may be more creative in their ways of dealing with the Taiwan issue, it was hard for any leaders of the top echelon to tolerate Lee's U.S. visit, which was seen as a prelude to the "Exodus" and the move of China's so-called family affairs into the international arena. Beijing was convinced that Lee's trip aimed at taking advantage of "the mind-set of some people in the U.S. who do not want to see a unified, powerful China, but are in a hurry to play the Taiwan card."[21] Beijing's leaders were afraid that Lee would brazenly campaign for Taiwan independence after becoming the first directly elected president in Taiwan in March 1996, and that the mainland should thus make preparations for this possibility.[22]

Caught between his efforts to use peaceful inducement and the need to flex military muscles, Jiang had to shift to the side of using military force in defending national sovereignty and territorial integrity. This tough position in response to Lee's perceived betrayal was supported by almost all of China's powerful military leaders, ideologues, and bureaucrats. The PLA had vested interests in flexing military muscles in order to get more budgetary allocations, particularly after it adopted a new grand strategy of "fighting modern warfare under high-tech conditions" beginning in 1992. To support this new strategy, the annual growth in the military budget was in double digits in the 1990s. Flexing military muscles in the Taiwan Strait would give the PLA an opportunity to demonstrate its accomplishment and to justify its demand for an increased military budget.[23] The ideologues might capitalize on the Taiwan Strait crisis to construct a state-centric nationalism as a new ideological base of legitimacy for the post-Tiananmen communist leadership. Safeguarding national sovereignty and territorial integrity was a central theme of this nationalist endeavor and the Taiwan issue was a convenient cause to arouse the nation's patriotism.[24] For bureaucrats, preparation for a military action served to enhance central authority over political and economic affairs. The Taiwan issue thus became a centripetal force binding political forces together and mobilizing popular support for the leadership. Under these circumstances, a consensus on turning to military coercion was formed in Beijing's leadership following Lee Teng-hui's visit to the United States in May 1995.

Adopting the strategy of military coercion did not necessarily mean that Beijing really wanted to fight a war with Taiwan at the moment. Beijing was reluctant to enter a war with Taiwan at the time for at least two reasons. First, the war contravened China's long-term and fundamental goals of economic modernization. Second, the PLA was not yet ready to win the war decisively. In this case, military exercises in 1995–96 were part of coercive military brinkmanship. In the fashion of coercive diplomacy, military force was used in an exemplary manner "to demonstrate resolution and willingness to escalate to high levels of military action if necessary."[25] The military exercise was an instrument for the political purpose of urging Taipei to halt what Beijing perceived as independent tendencies and warning the United States to stop what Beijing perceived as intervention in Chinese internal affairs. Military brinkmanship aimed at exploiting the fear of war in Taiwan in order to avoid war with Taiwan. The logic, as You Ji explains, is that: "(1) China would have to wage a war against Taiwan if the latter declares independence; so (2) military threats would reduce the likelihood of a declaration of independence; and so (3) military threats would make a war less likely."[26] In Beijing's view, due to the vulnerability of Taiwan's export-oriented economy, even a low-intensity armed conflict would do tremendous damage to Taiwan's economy. Most Taiwan people would be too vulnerable to stand up to a prolonged period of psychological terror and economic privation, and, therefore, would have to come to terms with peaceful reunification if Beijing demonstrated its willingness to use force. Beijing believed that "stability, relaxation, and improving cross-strait relations are the mainstream of Taiwan's popular will."[27] The military brinkmanship thus involved both war games and war avoidance.

The war, therefore, did not break out. Beijing declared its successful conclusion of military exercises with the demonstrated devastating consequence of independence to Taiwan following Lee Teng-hui's reelection as Taiwan's president in March 1996. Beijing noted that, intimidated by the military exercise, investors sold shares in panic and rushed to buy gold, which is customary in times of instability, and the index of the Taiwan stock market plunged to its lowest level. Taiwan's central bank had to dip into its $89 billion in reserves to bolster the local currency. Although Lee Teng-hui won a landslide victory with 54 percent of the vote, *Xinhua* noticed that the anti-independence candidates won more votes than the pro-independence DPP candidate (24.88 percent vs. 21.13 percent). According to Beijing, military exercises had a direct effect on the independence movement, which had a 41 percent support vote in a 1993 poll. *Xinhua* stated this effect in its announcement to conclude the military exercises:

> Beijing's opposition to separatism and "Taiwan independence" has dealt a heavy blow to the "Taiwan independence" and separatist forces. The facts show that the broad masses of the people in Taiwan demand stability

and development of the relations across the Taiwan Strait and cast aside "Taiwan independence."[28]

However, this was only wishful thinking because Beijing's military strategy was not as successful as it had declared and the Taiwan independence movement was not halted by Beijing's military threat. As a matter of fact, the DPP gained more popularity after the presidential election by changing their goal from an "independent Taiwan" to "Taiwan first" in an effort to address voter fears over Beijing's threat to invade Taiwan should independence be declared. Opinion polls held in late 1997 showed that for the first time in fifteen years, the proportion of Taiwanese who opted for independence (25 percent) exceeded that of those opting for unification (23 percent).[29] This shift in public opinion explained the landslide victory of the DPP in the November 29, 1997, county magistrate and city mayoral elections. This victory opened up the possibility that the DPP would replace the KMT as Taiwan's ruling party. Beijing was caught by surprise and was very concerned about this election outcome. Beijing preferred to deal with the KMT, which still clung to "one China" (despite its different interpretation of one China), rather than with the DPP, which had a party constitution that openly called for Taiwan independence. It was reported that before the November 1997 elections, Beijing's think tanks had concluded that the DPP would not win. But the election results showed otherwise. Jiang was reportedly very angry at that time because relevant data about the DPP was unavailable for twenty-four hours.

In spite of the significant change in Taiwan's political landscape, Beijing's leaders could not come up with any effective means short of war to deal with the situation after the failure of military brinkmanship in 1995–96. Therefore, Beijing had to return to an appeal for peaceful reunification and called for resumption of the Wang–Koo meetings. In his political report to the Fifteenth CCP National Congress in September 1997, Jiang Zemin emphatically reaffirmed his eight-point proposal for peaceful negotiations.[30] On September 29, 1997, immediately after the Party Congress, Beijing's vice premier and foreign minister, Qian Qichen, suggested to Taiwan that the two sides start cross-strait consultations on procedural arrangements for bilateral political talks.[31] After several months of maneuvering across the strait, Jan Jyh-horng (Chan Chih-hung), SEF deputy secretary-general, and his entourage, visited Beijing on April 22–24, 1998. Finally the second Wang–Koo meeting took place in Shanghai in October 1998. Koo then met with President Jiang Zemin in Beijing at the end of his first mainland trip. Following Koo's visit, in response, Wang was scheduled to visit Taipei in the fall of 1999.

While Beijing was preparing for Wang Daohan's first Taiwan trip, it was caught by surprise once again when Lee Teng-hui redefined "cross-straits relations as state-to-state relations or at least as a special state-to-state relationship rather than an internal relationship between a legitimate government and a renegade group" in his interview with a German reporter on July 9, 1999.[32] For Beijing, this so-called two-state theory (*liangguo lun*) was as troublesome as, if not more troublesome than, Lee's visit to the United States because the "two-state theory" constituted a major policy change in Taiwan's official position on cross-strait relations. A *Renmin ribao* observer stated that Lee's two-state theory "is an out-and-out negation of the one-China principle." According to this observer, "one of Lee Teng-hui's motives in proposing the two-state theory before the general elections is to deliberately continue the Taiwan independence political design to the post–Lee Teng-hui era, creating a fait accompli of separation so that the Taiwan authorities may not exceed this boundary in the future."[33]

As a result, Beijing postponed Wang Daohan's scheduled Taiwan visit indefinitely. Shadowed by this new tension, Beijing required other nations to clear aid offers with it before sending them into Taiwan after the devastating earthquake, which struck the island on September 21, 1999, killing well over 2,000 and injuring thousands more as well as leaving vast numbers homeless. This requirement, coming from a Red Cross official in Beijing, angered the people of Taiwan and seriously damaged Beijing's image in the international community. Although President Jiang Zemin expressed his "agony" at the suffering of the Taiwanese people and offered both condolences and aid to those living on the island,[34] the Taipei government turned down offers of some forms of assistance and charged that the mainland actually hurt efforts to get help to stricken areas of the island. Taipei's foreign minister, Jason Hu, stated that Beijing's "words and deeds violate international humanitarian principles" and that its actions "will be condemned and regarded with shame and regret by members of the international community."[35] Some observers had expressed hope that the disaster could at least help to heal the deepening animosity between the mainland and Taiwan. However, this hope was not realized and an opportunity to build some badly needed goodwill was missed because of Beijing's lack of sensitivity in handling the earthquake in Taiwan and Taipei's harsh criticism of Beijing's animosity.

The continued failure of peaceful gestures forced Beijing to return to the strategy of military threats, with the immediate goal of influencing Taiwan's March 2000 presidential election. The top priority was to prevent DPP candidate Chen Shui-bian from being elected as the president. Beijing released a white paper on February 21, about a month before Taiwan's presidential election. The white paper stated that China would use "drastic measures, including military force to safeguard China's sovereignty and territorial integrity" if Taiwan indefinitely refused "peaceful reunification through negotiations."[36] Before this white paper was published, China had threatened military action only if Taiwan declared independence or in the event of foreign invasion of the island. Chinese leaders had previously threatened invasion if Taiwan developed nuclear weapons or if unrest broke out on the island. The white paper added a new circumstance in which China would take Taiwan by force. The blunt warning showed Beijing's increasing frustration with the failure of the national reunification strategy and impatience after the return of Hong Kong and Macau to China. In his National People's Congress news conference on March 15, just three days prior to the election, Chinese Premier Zhu Rongji made a further threat to Taiwan people, stating that Taiwan people were worried that a "Taiwan independence forces' victory will spark a cross-strait war and hamper cross-strait peace. We believe that these worries are a logical inevitability and concern all the Taiwan people's personal destinies." He even tried to influence the election outcome by warning that, "at present, Taiwan people are facing an urgent historic moment. They have to decide what path to follow. They absolutely should not act impulsively. Otherwise, it will be too late for regrets."[37]

This coercive strategy once again failed. Most Taiwan people and all three major candidates rejected Beijing's threat. Beijing's most unacceptable candidate, Chen Shui-bian, was elected as the president on March 18. Beijing's threat in fact backfired as it infuriated many Taiwanese, especially Lee Teng-hui's supporters, and provoked the Taiwan people's antipathy toward Beijing. Although Beijing hoped to see KMT candidate Lien Chan win the election, Lien's relatively weak response to Beijing's threat and his use of Beijing's action to threaten Taiwan's voters into not supporting Chen frustrated Lee Teng-hui's supporters. As a result, many of Lee Teng-hui's supporters began to shift their support from Lien to Chen. This became an important factor in giving Chen the small margin of votes necessary to finally win the election.

Conclusion: Shadow of the Lee Teng-hui Era on Cross-Strait Relations

During the twelve years of the Lee Teng-hui era (1988–2000), Beijing became more defensive and reactive and less proactive, running to deal with one crisis after another across the Taiwan Strait. Although Beijing placed priorities intermittently on military coercion and peaceful offense in its national reunification strategy, both methods failed to stop Taiwan from going further away from reunification with the mainland.

From this perspective, Beijing's strategy of national reunification failed in the Lee Teng-hui era. While the election of Chen Shui-bian as Taiwan's president marked the end of the Lee Teng-hui era, it may not end its nightmare in dealing with the Taiwan issue. The most important legacy of the Lee Teng-hui era to the cross-strait relationship is the deep distrust and suspicion of Beijing's leaders over the intentions of Taiwan's leaders because Beijing's leaders believed that their failure was due to the betrayal of Lee Teng-hui in the past decade.

It was reported that, at the emergency Politburo meeting to discuss the Taiwan situation after Chen's election victory on the evening of March 18, "the atmosphere was very heavy and hinged with a sense of failure."[38] Although the Taiwan presidential election result was made available around 6:00 P.M. on March 18, Beijing's CCTV and other domestic media kept this quiet in their evening news, awaiting directives from the emergency Politburo meeting on how to handle the unexpected result. After the last round of harsh words of threat by Zhu Rongji three days before the votes, it was not entirely impossible that Beijing would make some emotional announcement or even decide to take irrational actions.

Finally, five hours after the election result was announced, the Taiwan Affairs Office in Beijing made the first official response, stating that Beijing would never allow independence for Taiwan but was willing to wait and see the words and deeds of new President-elect Chen Shui-bian. This statement firmly reiterated Beijing's "one-China" principle while left room for further maneuvering. On the one hand, the statement said, "the election of a new leader in Taiwan cannot change the fact that Taiwan is part of Chinese territory. The one-China principle is the prerequisite for peaceful reunification. Taiwan independence in whatever form will never be allowed. There is only one China, and Taiwan is an inseparable part of Chinese territory." On the other hand, the statement said, "we should listen to what the new leader in Taiwan says and watch what he does. We will observe where he (Chen) will lead cross-strait relations. We are willing to exchange views on cross-strait relations and peaceful reunification with all parties, organizations, and personages in Taiwan who favor the one-China principle." To repeat its long-standing position, the statement appealed to "Taiwan compatriots to combine their efforts with ours to safeguard the sovereignty and territorial integrity of the motherland, protect the fundamental interests of the Chinese nation, and realize the complete reunification of the motherland."[39]

The two-pronged vague wording of the statement showed that Beijing was not ready to carry out its harsh threat of war and wanted to open the door for possible reconciliation with Chen Shui-ban. It was reported that Jiang Zemin proposed a sixteen characters' guideline in response to the victory of Chen in the election, careful observation, patient waiting, no haste, and maintaining heavy pressure (*rezhen guancha, naixin dengdai, buji buchao, baochi gaoya*).[40] Since the election, Beijing's strategy has been one of sustained intensifying military pressure, combined with a political, economic, and diplomatic offense, to deter Chen and his government and to keep the situation from deteriorating. While Beijing has kept up the pressure, it has been waiting for Chen's words and deeds of concession to Beijing's demands in order to avoid actual fighting, to keep the danger and huge cost of real military conflict within limits.

However, the dilemma for Beijing lies in how to avoid a war while, at the same time, withholding Taiwan's independence. These two objectives had proved contradictory to each other in the Lee Teng-hui years. It can only become more difficult for Beijing's leaders to reconcile them after the remarkable institutionalization of democracy and the dismantling of the KMT's single-party state in Taiwan, manifested in the defeat of the KMT by the indigenous opposition, the DPP. As a *New York Times* editorial suggested, Chen Shui-ban's victory posed two serious challenges to Beijing's regime.

> First, it makes highly unlikely a reunification agreement cut by governments over the heads of their people (as occurred in Hong Kong and Macau, where Beijing negotiated with colonial authorities and the locals had no voice in their destiny). Second, it makes clear to the Chinese people that there are alternatives to the corrupt pseudo-communist system on the

mainland, whose legitimacy rests on continuous economic growth and, increasingly, on nationalist fervor.[41]

Facing this prospect, Beijing has almost exhausted its strategic options and is left with very little room to maneuver. Peaceful inducement did not work, nor did military brinkmanship in the Lee Teng-hui era. Lee had successfully downplayed the danger of a cross-strait war by taking all possible measures, including stock stabilization funds, to keep the Taiwan people from panicking and helping them gradually to get accustomed to the threat of war after being repeatedly subjected to such threats.

If Beijing cannot come up with a strategic solution that will be not only effective but would also be more positive than negative, it may be left no option other than to go beyond military brinkmanship, through means such as the blockade of Taiwan by air or submarine, missile strikes, the mining of harbors, and the seizure of offshore islands. Beijing has made it clear that "the day when Taiwan declares independence will be the day war begins."[42] It is true that the economic, military, and diplomatic costs would be very high and the final victory would be uncertain. It is also true that most of mainland Chinese might not actively and indefinitely support a military action having enormous costs and an uncertain outcome. But Beijing may find that a real military strike would ultimately be the necessary means should the situation require it to force Taiwan to accede to its demand of national reunification. This is not only because Beijing has reiterated that, in order to safeguard national unity and territorial integrity, it will not give up the use of force, but also because the rise of Chinese nationalism in recent years has tied the hands of Chinese leaders and may force them to take extreme actions. The patriotic education sponsored by the communist state in the 1990s emphasized China's territorial integrity and national reunification, and the high tide of protest that broke out over the accidental U.S. bombing of the Chinese Embassy in Yugoslavia was an expression of this patriotic sentiment.

It is true that Beijing would have to consider the cost of military action. But the question could become that what would be the strategic options left? In other words, of Beijing's very few and unfavorable strategic options, which one would be relatively more pro than con? While the criteria for weighing the pros and cons are obviously very complex, interviewing Chinese scholars and strategists, this author has often been reminded of popular Chinese sayings such as long-term pain is worse than short-term pain (*changtong buru duandong*) (meaning that it would be better to resolve the issue of Taiwan earlier rather later), and *liude qingshan zai, bupa meichai shao* (as long as the green mountains are there, one need not worry about firewood). It is certainly not groundless for Beijing to fear that the indefinite delay of reunification negotiations may lead to the permanent secession of Taiwan from the mainland. This cost, for many leaders in Beijing, would be much higher than the cost of a war.

Coming to the realization of this danger, President Chen Shui-bian has taken a pragmatic approach by vowing no declaration of independence if Beijing does not make plans to invade the island. In a seemingly more conciliatory posture than Lee Teng-hui, Chen said, "I will not incorporate the two-state theory (proposed by Lee) into the constitution while I am in office. Also I will not hold a referendum to choose between unification and independence, nor will I move to change the name of Taiwan." Chen further proposed to engage Beijing "in three areas: direct exchanges, a peace agreement, and the development of mutual trust." On the issue of independence, he said that his Democratic Progressive Party advocated only a referendum, the basic right of citizens, but said there was no urgency to hold it yet. Chen also urged the resumption of talks and negotiations with Beijing.[43] In his inauguration speech on May 20, 2000, Chen pledged that as long as the Beijing regime has no intention to use military force against Taiwan, during his term in office, he would not declare independence, change the national title, push for the inclusion of the so-called state-to-state description in the Constitution, or promote a referendum to change the status quo in regard to the question of independence or unification. Furthermore, there would be no question of abolishing the National Unification Guidelines and the National Unification Council.

In response to Chen's conciliatory posture, Beijing suspended its war of words for a while after the election. But it has certainly not softened its position on the one-China principle. It has insisted that, at the minimum, Chen has to accept the one-China principle for Beijing to deal with Chen's government. Following Chen's inauguration speech, Beijing accused the new Taiwanese president of lacking sincerity in his speech because he did not embrace China's cherished "one-China" principle, while at the same time offering him a compromise on the conditions for dialogue. Shortly after Chen's inauguration speech, Beijing issued a statement, dismissing Chen's offer about the possibility of a "future one

China" and demanding that he embrace the "one-China" principle. However, an hour and twenty minutes later, a second statement was issued stating that Beijing was prepared to hold a dialogue if Taiwan accepted that it could not negotiate as a sovereign state and if Taipei embraced a compromise reached in 1992 on the issue of "one China" for a dialogue, where both sides agreed to accept the principle, but not to define its exact meaning. According to the second statement, Beijing said it wanted to authorize the Association for Relations Across the Taiwan Strait to hold a dialogue with Taipei. Further, it said that the dialogue could be held on the condition that Taipei drop Lee Teng-hui's call for talks to be conducted on a "state-to-state" basis.[44]

However, polls in Taiwan before and after the election have indicated that Taiwan's people are not enthusiastic about Beijing's "one-China principle" in which only the mainland is a sovereign state, nor do they accept the "one-China, two systems" policy by which Beijing exerts control over Hong Kong and Macau. In this case, although Chen said the issue of "one China" could be a "topic for discussion, but not a precondition or set outcome of any discussion," as a DPP president, he could not be expected to accept such a principle.[45] Despite intensified pressures from the mainland, Chen has shown no signs of being rattled. His strategy has been to hold out an olive branch by offering to sit down and talk, but without giving ground on the issue of Taiwan's sovereignty or Taiwan as an independent state.

Thus, the relationship between President Chen Shui-bian and Beijing has come to a deadlock. This is a very dangerous situation. As a legacy left from the Lee Teng-hui era, Beijing can no longer trust Chen's words and it is doubtful that Beijing will wait as long to see Chen's deeds as they did for Lee. The current deadlock on the one-China principle between Taipei and Beijing has to be unlocked soon. In this case, the legacy of Lee Teng-hui will certainly loom large in the coming interactions between President Chen and Beijing. It is not certain whether this is fortunate or unfortunate for Chen and his DPP government. One thing is sure: If no solution is found within a reasonable time frame, the real danger of war across the Taiwan Strait can only increase over time.

Notes

1. Zhang Tongxing and He Zhongshan, eds., *Yiguo liangzhi yu haixia liangan guanxi* (One country two systems and the relations across the Taiwan Strait) (Beijing: Zhongguo renmin daxue chubanshe, 1998), pp. 66–67.

2. *Beijing Review* 24, no. 40 (October 5, 1981): 11.

3. *Remin ribao* (People's daily), January 31, 1995, p. 1.

4. *Beijing Review* 33, no. 48 (November 26–December 2, 1990): 17.

5. Deng Xiaoping, "The Present Situation and the Tasks Before Us," in *Selected Works of Deng Xiaoping (1975–1982)* (Beijing: Foreign Languages Press, 1984), p. 225.

6. White paper, "The Taiwan Questions and Reunification of China," *China Daily*, September 1, 1993, pp. 4–5.

7. For one study of the management of these two events, see Suisheng Zhao, "The Management of Rival Relations Across the Taiwan Strait," *Issues and Studies* 29, no. 4 (April 1993): 72–94.

8. Kelly Her, "Mainland Trade Tops $20 Billion," *Free China Journal* (March 15, 1996): 3.

9. A book published in 1990 on "Greater China" asserted that "The shift to a conservative regime in Beijing in mid-1989 killed all hope for the best, leaving fear and depression in an expectation of the worst. Fear was the dominant reaction in Hong Kong, depression in Taiwan." Penelope Hartland-Thunberg, *China, Hong Kong, Taiwan and the World Trading System* (New York: Macmillan, 1990), p. 98.

10. *Zhongguo shibao* (China times), April 14, 1995, p. 2.

11. "Lee Aides Admits Secret Mainland Contacts," Taiwan Headlines (www.taiwanheadlines.gov.tw), July 20, 2000.

12. *Xinhua*, June 11, 1995.

13. Kay Moller, "A New Role for the ROC on Taiwan in the Post-Cold War Era," *Issues and Studies* 31, no. 2 (February 1995): 84–85.

14. He Chong, "Lee Teng-hui Unmasks His False Pursuit of Reunification," *Renmin ribao* (overseas edition), June 21, 1995, p. 5.

15. "The Trend Toward Taiwan Independence Is Stable," *Zhongguo shibao*, June 3, 1994, p. 4.

16. For a text of the decree, see *Renmin ribao*, July 7, 1988, p. 1.

17. *Xinhua* editorial, "Lee Ruins Cross-Straits Talks," *China Daily*, August 2, 1995, p. 4.

18. Beijing *Xinhua* news agency (electronic version), July 27, 1995.

19. Ren Huiwen, *Zhongnanhai quanli jiaoban liemu* (Inside stories of China's power succession) (Hong Kong: Taipingyang shiji chubanshe, 1988), pp. 297–98.

20. *China News Analysis* (Hong Kong), September 15, 1995, p. 1.

21. Ren Huiwen, "Beijing Reassesses the U.S. and Lee Teng-hui," *Hsin pao* (Hong Kong economic journal), July 16, 1995, p. 23.

22. As one American analyst observed during the crisis, "I am convinced, based on talks with mainland officials, that Beijing three months ago believed that Mr. Lee would openly challenge the 'one China' principle—if only by declaring independence then, by pushing for and accepting an official 'state visit' to the United States or committing some other act that would be interpreted by Beijing as a de facto statement of independence," Ralph A. Cossa, "China's Missile Exercises Are Likely to Backfire," *International Herald Tribune,* March 9–10, 1996.

23. You Ji, "Changing Leadership Consensus: The Domestic Context of War Games," in *Across the Taiwan Strait: Mainland China, Taiwan, and the 1995–1996 Crisis*, ed. Suisheng Zhao (New York: Routledge, 1999), p. 88.

24. For the role of the Chinese communist state in promoting nationalism in the

1990s, see Suisheng Zhao, "A State-Led Nationalism: The Patriotic Education Campaign in Post-Tiananmen China," *Communist and Post-Communist Studies* 31, no. 3 (1998): 287–302; and Allen Whiting, "Chinese Nationalism and Foreign Policy after Deng," *China Quarterly*, no. 142 (1995): 295–316.

25. Alexander George, "Introduction: The Limits of Coercive Diplomacy," in *The Limits of Coercive Diplomacy*, ed. Alexander L. George and William E. Simons (Boulder, CO.: Westview Press, 1994), p. 2.

26. You Ji, "Making Sense of War Games in the Taiwan Strait," *Journal of Contemporary China* 6, no. 15: 300.

27. *Wen wei po*, March 29, 1996, p. A2; FBIS-CHI-96–068, April 8, 1996, p. 45.

28. *Renmin ribao*, March 24, 1996, p. 1.

29. *Straits Times* (Singapore), March 10, 1998, p. 47.

30. For the text of Jiang's political report, see *Renmin ribao*, September 22, 1997.

31. *Xinhua*, September 30, 1997.

32. "President Lee Teng-hui Interviewed by *Deutsche Welle*," in *Taipei Speaks Up* (Taipei: Mainland Affairs Council of the Executive Yuan, Republic of China, August 1999), pp. 1–2.

33. *Renmin ribao*, August 10, 1999, p. 1.

34. *Xinhua* (September 22) quoted Jiang as saying, "Compatriots of the two sides are as closely linked as flesh and blood. The catastrophe and agony of our Taiwan compatriots influences the hearts of all Chinese."

35. Phil Stephens and Yin De-an, "Taipei Turns Down Mainland's Offer of Rescue Workers," *China News Digest*, September 24, 1999 (electronic edition).

36. Taiwan Affairs Office and Information Office of the State Council, "The One-China Principle and the Taiwan Issue," in *Renmin ribao*, February 21, 2000, p. 1.

37. CCTV transcript of Zhu Rongji's comments on Taiwan during his National People's Congress press conference on March 15, 2000.

38. Wang Manla, "Jiang Zemin tichu shiliuzi fangzheng" (Jiang Zemin proposed the sixteen characters' principle), Duowei News Agency (Chinesenewsnet.com), April 5, 2000.

39. "The Statement from the Taiwan Affairs Office of the CCP Central Committee and the Taiwan Affairs Office of the State Council," *Xinhua*, March 18, 2000.

40. Wang, "Jiang Zemin tichu shiliuzi fangzheng."

41. Eliot A. Cohen, "The Election of Chen Shui-bian as President," *New York Times*, March 20, 2000 (electronic edition).

42. Liu Ji, "Making the Right Choice in Twenty-First Century Sino-American Relations," *Journal of Contemporary China* 7, no. 17 (March 1998): 99.

44. Xu Ming Yang and Wu Yiyi, "No Taiwan Independence if No Mainland Invasion," *China News Digest*, March 26, 2000 (electronic edition).

44. Ray Zhang and Yin De An, "Beijing Sends Mixed Responses to Chen's Inauguration Speech," *China News Digest*, May 21, 2000.

45. Taiwan Headline News (www.taiwanheadlines.gov.tw), April 10, 2000.

12

National Defense and the Changing Security Environment

Wen-cheng Lin and Cheng-yi Lin

Lee Teng-hui assumed the presidency of the Republic of China (ROC) and became commander-in-chief of the armed forces after the sudden death of President Chiang Ching-kuo on January 13, 1988. During Lee's twelve-year presidency, the international situation, Taiwan's domestic politics, and relations across the Taiwan Strait have all undergone tremendous changes. Some of these changes have been conducive to the island's security, while others may have endangered its survival as a sovereign state.

President Lee, the first native Taiwanese to reach the highest position in the ROC government, had no ties with the military, which was still controlled by mainlanders, when he assumed office.[1] Although some observers began to call Lee a military strongman by the mid-1990s,[2] he hardly qualified for that title. He was never powerful enough to dominate the military. Michael D. Swaine concludes, after conducting intensive interviews with senior Taiwan civilian and military leaders that "Lee Teng-hui apparently does not play a very active role in either oversight or the specific contents of Taiwan's defense policy or force structure."[3] However, President Lee still left a clear footprint on Taiwan's national defense during his twelve-year presidency, a period during which Taiwan's military faced tremendous challenges from both society and the People's Liberation Army (PLA).

The development of Taiwan's security environment, President Lee's relationship with the military, and Taiwan's domestic political changes affected Taiwan's national defense policy during this period. In his years as ROC commander-in-chief, Lee tried to streamline the military and to promote Taiwan's national security in the face of an increasing threat from the People's Republic of China (PRC). But his legacy is a mixed one. The PRC's threat to Taiwan is increasing, while there is doubt about whether Taiwan's military can fight for the island's survival. This chapter studies President Lee's legacy to national defense, beginning with a review of the changes in Taiwan's security environment.

Changes in Taiwan's Security Environment

The end of the cold war and the outbreak of the Tiananmen Square massacre in 1989 provided Taiwan with an improved international security environment. On the one hand, the end of the cold war and the collapse of the Soviet Union and the communist regimes of Eastern Europe in the early 1990s downgraded Beijing's strategic value to the United States and its Western allies. On the other hand, Beijing's bloody crackdown of the democratic movement on June 4, 1989, convinced Washington that the PRC would never change its hard authoritarianism. The disillusioned United States and its Western friends imposed economic sanctions on the PRC. The ROC predicted in the early 1990s that Washington–Beijing relations in the foreseeable future were unlikely to be as close as they had been.[4] Meanwhile, Taiwan, which caught the third wave of democratization in the late 1980s, won more support and sympathy from the international community. Washington reviewed its Taiwan policy in 1994, upgrading its relations with the island. In addition, since the end of the cold war, the arms sale industry has become a buyer's market. Taiwan, which had made efforts to procure a new generation of jet fighters for more than two decades, was finally able to buy 60 Mirage 2000–5s from France and 150 F-16 fighters from the United States in 1992. The international environment was, in general, favorable to the ROC in the early 1990s.

Cross-strait relations have also undergone dramatic change. The ROC became a full-fledged democracy in the 1990s and gained enough confidence to relax restrictions on cross-strait exchanges. On November 2, 1987, the ROC government lifted the ban on visits to the Chinese mainland. Since then, economic and people-to-people exchanges across the Taiwan Strait have quickly grown. The indirect two-way trade between Taiwan and the PRC increased from a trivial US$78 million in 1979 to more than US$31.2 billion by 2000, and Taiwan's businesses had invested more than US$47.8 billion in the Chinese mainland by the end of

2000.[5] In addition, Taiwan's people have made more than 17 million trips to the Chinese mainland in the past twelve years.[6]

On May 1, 1991, the ROC government announced the termination of the Period of Mobilization for Suppressing the Communist Rebellion, recognized the PRC regime as an unfriendly political entity effectively governing the Chinese mainland, and renounced the use of force as a means for settling cross-strait disputes.[7] This policy change by Taipei paved the way for a more straightforward relationship with its nemesis. Chairman Koo Chen-fu of the Strait Exchange Foundation (SEF), which is a semi-official agency created in February 1991 by the ROC government to tackle cross-strait affairs, accepted Beijing's invitation to go to Singapore in late April 1993 to hold the first meeting with his counterpart Wang Daohan of the Association for Relations Across the Taiwan Strait (ARATS), which had been created by the PRC in late 1991. Four agreements were signed during the talks to establish regular communication channels between the two organizations and to start talks that would be "nongovernmental, administrative, economic, and functional in nature" to deal with problems arising from cross-strait exchanges.[8] Rapprochement between Taipei and Beijing created a sense of euphoria across the strait. Many scholars no longer listed the Taiwan Strait as a flashpoint for war.

However, the PRC has refused to renounce the use of force as an option to take over the island. On the contrary, according to ROC government statistics, the PRC leadership threatened to use force against Taiwan on at least sixty occasions between November 1987 and July 1994, which was the period during which tensions in the Taiwan Strait were at their lowest level.[9] Cross-strait tensions resurged after President Lee Teng-hui paid a "private" visit to the United States in June 1995, and reached a peak in March 1996, when the PLA fired four M-9 missiles into waters about thirty to fifty kilometers off the north and south coasts of Taiwan. The purpose of this missile "test" was to intimidate Taiwan's voters into not supporting President Lee Teng-hui for reelection in the island's first direct popular presidential election. But some analysts have described the PLA's move as a rehearsal of a contingency plan to invade Taiwan.[10] As a result of the test, the international community rediscovered the dangerous situation in the Taiwan Strait. For instance, in a special report on January 1, 1996, Japan's *Sankei shinbum* listed the Taiwan Strait as the most dangerous area in the world that might trigger a war.[11] Both the *Far Eastern Economic Review* and the *New York Times* also carried reports in early 1996, claiming that Beijing had prepared to attack Taiwan.[12] The international environment seemed to turn against Taiwan in the second half of the 1990s. Washington and other Western powers seemed to be willing to please the PRC at the expense of Taiwan. President Clinton orally announced the "three-no's" policy in Shanghai on June 30, 1998, retreating further from Washington's position on the issue of Taiwan sovereignty.[13] Taipei realized that Washington–Beijing relations had significantly improved in 1998.[14]

As cross-strait relations deteriorated in the second half of the 1990s, Beijing gradually recovered from its diplomatic isolation. Washington, which softened its position on the PRC after 1992, increased high-level exchanges and confidence-building measures with Beijing after the 1996 Taiwan Strait crisis. The United States, which would like to avoid being dragged into a war between Taiwan and the PRC, has pressed Taipei to compromise with Beijing. East Asian countries, which live under the shadow of the China threat, are willing to accommodate Beijing on the Taiwan issue.

Cross-strait relations were finally put back on track when the SEF and the ARATS resumed their dialogue in 1998. Koo Chen-fu led a delegation to visit mainland China and held meetings with President Jiang Zemin, Wang Daohan, and Vice Premier Qian Qichen. Wang Daohan planned to pay a return visit to Taiwan in October 1999. However, this thaw in cross-strait tensions was cut short after President Lee, who was alarmed by Clinton's announcement of the "three no's policy" and Beijing's aggressive actions in 1998 to undermine the ROC's status as a sovereign state,[15] redefined the Taiwan–China relationship as "a state-to-state relationship, or at least a special state-to-state relationship" during an interview with a German radio station on July 9, 1999.[16] Beijing again suspended cross-strait dialogue, indefinitely postponed Wang's trip to Taiwan, and threatened to use force against Taiwan. In fact, a series of military exercises were conducted in the months after President Lee's remarks. Beijing has further intensified its threat to the island since Taiwan's people elected Chen Shui-bian, a pro-independence politician, to the presidency on March 18, 2000.

On February 21, 2000, Beijing issued a new white paper entitled "The One-China Principle and the Taiwan Issue," which escalates its threat against Taiwan. The paper officially sets three conditions for the use of force against Taiwan: (1) if a grave turn of events occurs leading to the separation of Taiwan from China in any name; (2) if Taiwan is invaded and occupied by foreign countries; and (3) if the Taiwan authorities refuse, *sine die* (i.e., indefinitely), the peaceful settlement of cross-strait re-unification through negotiations.[17] Those three conditions are not new, for they have long been raised one way or the other by the Beijing leadership. But it is the first time that Beijing has written down the third condition in a formal official document. In addition, the ROC government believes that Beijing might use force on Taiwan under three other conditions: (1) if domestic chaos erupts on the island; (2) if Taiwan's armed forces are found to be relatively weaker than those of the PRC in the Taiwan Strait; and (3) if Taiwan develops its own nuclear weapons.[18]

According to many experts, there are several options that Beijing may apply when it decides to use force against Taiwan.[19] An amphibious invasion of Taiwan is at one extreme of the spectrum, while a sabotage of Taiwan's society by a fifth column is at the other extreme. Beijing's other options include attacking Taiwan with missiles, conducting a naval blockade of Taiwan, shelling or invading the offshore islands controlled by the ROC, conducting military exercises near Taiwan, and conducting an information warfare to harass Taiwan's financial or communication system. Among the options, a naval blockade is regarded by many military experts as the most likely approach for Beijing to take.[20] Indeed, the PRC leadership has implied on several occasions that they might conduct a naval blockade of the island.[21] Recently, a PRC military expert claimed that Taiwan's economy could hardly withstand a naval blockade or other sorts of military harassment from the PLA.[22]

The missile threat from the PRC is another great concern for Taiwan. The missile exercises carried out by Beijing in March 1996 exposed the fact that Taiwan is vulnerable to missile attacks from the PRC. Admiral Dennis Blair, commander of U.S. forces in the Pacific, stated before Congress that "China has deployed 200 ballistic missiles against Taiwan."[23] The United States estimates that the number of PLA short-range ballistic missiles targeting Taiwan may reach 650 by 2005.[24] Beijing might use a missile threat to force Taiwan to enter political talks for unification or to launch a missile counter-force strike at about 200 targets, including harbors, airports, and various military facilities on the island, to pave the way for an amphibious invasion.[25]

President Lee's National Security Strategy

In the face of the enormous threat from the PRC, President Lee constructed a delicate national security strategy that was a composition of diplomatic, economic, and China policies, as well as strategies for domestic development and national defense. His goal was to maintain Taiwan's continuous survival as a prosperous and independent sovereign state.

As far as the China policy was concerned, Taiwan under President Lee's rule was interested in continuing the cross-strait talks, but it adopted a two-stage strategy for the talks. It did not exclude political issues from the talks, but it argued that talks should focus on technical and administrative issues at the first stage in order to increase mutual trust and to provide a basis for political talks at the second stage. In addition, Taipei firmly rejected Beijing's one-China principle and argued that Beijing should not ask Taiwan to accept any preconditions before entering talks. Taipei continued to test Beijing's limits on the island's sovereignty issue by bidding for membership in the United Nations and other intergovernmental organizations. It gradually moved from transparency to ambiguity on the one-China principle. Although President Lee redefined cross-strait relations as a "special state-to-state relationship" in July 1999, which was regarded by many observers as provocative, it was his strategy to test Beijing's limits. He had no intention of coming to a showdown with Beijing and was willing to compromise when Beijing's reaction was radical.

President Lee was also an advocate of confidence-building measures (CBMs) in the Taiwan Strait. In May 1990, President Lee called on Beijing's leaders to roll back the PLA's deployment to 300 kilometers from Fujian Province, facing Kinmen (Quemoy) and Matsu.[26] He encouraged Track II exchanges between scholars from both sides to discuss security and political issues. However, given the increased power projection capability of modern weaponry, there would be little point in establishing a buffer zone without a nonaggression agreement and a credible security guarantee by an impartial third party such as the United States. Even though Beijing adopted a militant strategy toward Taiwan, President Lee, in February 1996, said he would pursue a peace accord with China, and this should have priority over the opening of direct links of postal services, transportation, and trade in the Taiwan Strait.[27]

President Lee was also willing to embark on a journey of peace to China and to meet with the top Chinese leadership. He suggested that President Clinton tell Jiang Zemin during their summit meeting in 1998 to "invite President Lee to Beijing."[28] In addition to communications measures proposed by Taipei, President Lee also indicated the necessity of setting up "some mechanism to inform each other before any misunderstanding could develop" in the military area.[29] For President Lee, CBMs in the Taiwan Strait could not be implemented from a strictly military perspective, and any measures capable of reducing tensions between Taiwan and China were worth consideration by Taipei and Beijing. Therefore, in April 1999, President Lee suggested consideration of "establishing a mechanism for cross-Strait peace and stability," by implying that the CBMs practiced in Europe could be applied to ensure security in the Taiwan Strait.[30]

Economically, Taipei has tried to reduce its economic dependence on the Chinese mainland. Taiwan's exports to the Chinese mainland accounted for more than 18 percent of the island's total exports in 1999, far greater than the 10 percent mark that ROC leaders traditionally view as dangerous.[31] Taiwan's increasing dependence on the mainland market might give Beijing leverage to bring Taiwan to its knees, making Taiwan vulnerable to Beijing's threat to disrupt cross-strait trade. Therefore, President Lee urged the people in Taiwan to be cautious and patient in cross-strait exchanges, and his policy of go slow, be patient (*jieji yongren*) was adopted in 1996 out of this concern. The policy prohibits any single investment in mainland China of over US$50 million and bars certain industries (such as high tech) from investing altogether. Meanwhile, as mentioned above, the ROC government has encouraged its businesses to invest in Southeast Asia or in other countries that have diplomatic relations with Taiwan, in order to reduce Taiwan's dependence on the Chinese mainland.

Diplomatically, President Lee injected new thinking into Taiwan's foreign policy. Under the new strategy of pragmatism, Taiwan no longer asks its friends to sever or downgrade relations with Beijing as a precondition for establishing diplomatic relations with Taiwan. Taipei is willing to accept dual recognition because diplomatic recognition can strengthen Taiwan's status as a sovereign state. The strategy of pragmatism, therefore, downgrades the role of ideology in Taiwan's foreign policy. In addition, Taipei has been very active in seeking membership in intergovernmental organizations over the past decade. For instance, Taiwan has made bids for a seat in the United Nations since 1993, and has sought to be an observer to the World Health Organization. Moreover, Taipei has tried to establish more diplomatic relations and upgrade substantive relations with countries that do not recognize Taiwan.

Taiwan has made great efforts to win support from the United States, which is the most important country for the island's security. It has continued its lobbying of the U.S. Congress and would like to establish high-level regular communication with the executive branch. Taipei believes that the United States and Taiwan share a common concern with the PRC's military buildup and expansion of influence in the region. It would like to join the theater missile defense (TMD) system, which would help Taiwan establish close security ties with both the United States and Japan.

President Lee also believed that the security of Taiwan should be put in the context of a regional security structure, led by the United States and Japan. In August 1991, President Lee first raised a proposal to establish a regional security arrangement in the Asia Pacific. In September 1992, he told a U.S. delegation about his idea of an Asian collective security system. His proposal included the setting up of a collective security fund to which all the countries involved would contribute, arms reduction in the region, and joint exploration of natural resources to avoid possible conflicts over territorial disputes.[32] Ironically, even though Taiwan was one of the first countries to call for a new regional security arrangement, it has been excluded from participating in the later established ASEAN Regional Forum (ARF). Taiwan is not a member of the Council for Security Cooperation in the Asia Pacific (CSCAP), and its scholars attend various working group meetings as "other participants," sitting side by side with experts from other organizations. In order to promote mutual understanding between Taiwan and other Asian countries when it is excluded from the ARF and is not allowed to fully participate in the CSCAP, Taipei has actively engaged in bilateral second-track dialogues with other Asian countries. For instance, Taipei would like to promote security cooperation with Japan and ASEAN countries to cope with the common threat from Beijing, and would like to conduct dialogues with the United States to win support from the latter.

To President Lee, the strengthening of U.S.–Japan security ties was "aimed at safeguarding peace and stability of the Asia-Pacific region." He also indicated that Taiwan is willing to raise funds to support U.S. troops stationed in the Asia-Pacific.[33] President Lee once mentioned that if the United States and Japan can prevent China "from continuing to expand its military might in the South China Sea, there should not be any major problem."[34] He was particularly grateful for President Clinton's decision to dispatch two aircraft carrier battle groups to the region near Taiwan in March 1996. According to President Lee,

"[I]f the United States had stood idly by while the mainland authorities conducted military exercises and missile tests in a brazen attempt at intimidation, its allies and friends would have lost faith in the U.S. commitment."[35]

President Lee called upon leaders in the Asia-Pacific to replace military confrontation with economic cooperation through "joint ventures to develop natural resources." For him, the best approach to ease tensions in the South China Sea is to put aside territorial disputes and "to settle the disputes through dialogue, and to curtail military deployment."[36] In particular, President Lee proposed that a multilateral South China Sea Development Company with funds of US$10 billion be established and that the profits from its activities be used for infrastructure development in ASEAN countries.[37] In February 2000, the actual control of the Pratas (Tungsha) and Itu Aba (Taiping) islands was shifted from Taiwan's Ministry of National Defense to the jurisdiction of its Coast Guard Administration. Taipei also reduced the number of marines stationed on these two islands, but added some Coast Guard personnel to deal with fishery disputes on the high seas. Taiwan has long undertaken to exercise self-restraint in the conduct of its activities in disputed areas and not to take any action that might affect stability in the region. As one of the earliest claimants in the South China Sea, Taiwan also urges other countries to reduce their troops stationed in the South China Sea and refrain from new occupation of presently unoccupied islands.

Domestically, President Lee accelerated political reforms in order to make the Republic of China a full-fledged democracy. He believed that democracy was the most powerful weapon both to win international support for Taiwan and to deflect pressure from Beijing for unification. The first step toward democracy was to build a multiparty political system. In January 1989, the Law on Civic Organizations was passed to legitimize the formation of new political parties. The second step was to return to the rule of the constitution. The third step was to amend the constitution, which was enacted in 1936, in order to reflect Taiwan's political realities. Ten constitutional articles were either amended or added in 1991, providing the legal basis for the comprehensive elections of the three central representative bodies. All the senior parliamentarians, who were elected on the Chinese mainland in 1947 or 1948 and never reelected since then, were retired in December 1991. All of the seats in the National Assembly and the Legislative Yuan were opened for public competition in 1991 and 1992, respectively.

More important, a new article, stipulating that "the president and vice president shall be directly elected by the entire populace of the free area of the Republic of China," was added to the constitution in July 1994. This completed the first phase of constitutional reform. The milestone in Taiwan's democratization was the presidential election held on March 23, 1996. The election was the first time in Chinese history that the highest position in the government was directly elected by the people. The Republic of China on Taiwan became a new sovereign state that was based on the idea of popular sovereignty.

President Lee's National Defense Strategy

As mentioned above, Taipei has tried to expand its diplomatic ties, to establish a quasi-alliance relationship with Washington, to cooperate with Japan and ASEAN countries on security issues, and to carefully manage its relations with Beijing in order to increase Taiwan's security. But the backbone of Taiwan's security is its national defense.

One author has compared the relationship between Taiwan and China to that of David and Goliath.[38] Indeed, Taiwan is engaging in an asymmetrical campaign against a giant. The PRC is 60 times bigger in population, 260 times in land size, and 10 times in number of military personnel than Taiwan. It would be an enormous challenge for Taiwan to survive a military attack from the PRC.

As commander-in-chief for twelve years, President Lee tried to reform the military and to teach soldiers and Taiwan's people new ideas of national defense. First of all, Taiwan's defense strategy shifted from offensive to defensive operations. President Lee declared a total defense strategy for Taiwan in July 1996. The Chinese missile test in March 1996 convinced him of the necessity to build up the consciousness of total defense. If national defense could garner support, attention, and participation from all walks of life, he reasoned, then the PRC would face a formidable counterattack to any military coercion against the island.[39] In this total defense strategy, Taiwan must not overlook the dimensions of civil, social, economic, and psychological defense. For President Lee, "[c]ooperation between the military and civilian sectors will increase public awareness and support of national defense and bring about national defense development, thereby assuring national security."[40] President Lee believed that psychological defense is the bedrock of a total defense strategy and he combined the concept of "Gemeinschaft"(common community) with the consciousness of new Taiwanese to foster the consensus that joys and sorrows are to be shared and problems jointly tackled on the island of Taiwan.[41] The new Taiwanese include people in Taiwan who are willing to fight for the prosperity and survival of the Republic of China on Taiwan, regardless of their arrival time or provincial and linguistic backgrounds. By promoting those values, President Lee hoped to strengthen the military's will to fight for Taiwan's survival in case of a cross-strait war.

Second, the guidelines for Taiwan's armed forces focused on maintaining effective deterrence and strong defense. Taiwan's military buildup is based on the following three principles: (1) to maintain air and naval superiority over the Taiwan Strait; (2) to counterblockade; and (3) to engage fighting off the coast.[42] Taiwan has been implementing an "elite troop plan" since 1993. The armed forces will be restructured, command levels streamlined, and logistic systems renovated.[43] Chief of the general staff General Lo Pen-li revealed in an interview that after the Ten-year Troop Reduction Project is completed in 2003, the size of Taiwan's armed forces will be cut to less than 400,000.[44] In fact, the number of Taiwan's soldiers was only 376,000 in 1999.[45]

Third, overwhelmed quantitatively by the PRC, Taipei has made efforts to maintain its military supremacy by acquiring more advanced weapons and improving the quality of human resources. It has actively built up a second-generation armed forces by acquiring advanced weapons from abroad, in particular from the United States and France.[46] Taiwan has been one of the leading arms importers in the past decade. Naval and air forces buildups, which have been priorities, took a lion's share of the ROC defense budget for acquiring weapons.[47] The plan to build up second generation naval and air forces is basically completed. Under the plan, twenty-two new missile frigates, twelve 580-ton patrol boats, about ten to fourteen 1000–1500 ton corvettes, fifty fast missile boats, and 340 new jet fighters have joined these two services (see Table 12.1). Other major weapons procurements include 300 M-60A3 main battle tanks, 1,299 Stinger surface-to-air missiles, four E-2T early warning aircraft, and twelve C-130 transport aircraft.[48]

To Taiwan's regret, it has failed to acquire more submarines. The PRC's fleet of about forty-seven to ninety-seven submarines has always been of concern to Taiwan.[49] As mentioned above, a naval blockade is the most likely approach for Beijing to use force against Taiwan. Taiwan is an island state and could easily be blockaded by the PRC, which

Table 12.1

The Republic of China's Second-Generation Navy and Air Force Buildup Plan

Name of the Program	Context
Guanghua I (Glorious China I)	Seven U.S. Perry-class missile frigates
Guanghua II	Six LaFayette-class missile frigates
Guanghua III	Twelve Jin Chiang-class 580-ton patrol guided missile combatants
Guanghua IV, V, and VI	Ten to fourteen 1500–2000 ton corvettes, fifty fast attack missile boats (150–250 ton)
Others	Nine Knox-class frigates
Feilong (Flying Dragon)	Sixty Mirage 2000–5s jet fighters
Feng-huang (Phoenix)	150 F-16 A/B jet fighters
Xiangying (Soaring Eagle)	130 IDF jet fighters

Source: Ziyou shibao (Liberty times), July 6, 1996, p. 4; U.S. Department of Defense, "Report to Congress Pursuant to the FY99 Appropriations Bill," *DefenseLINK*, March 4, 1999, p. 8.

"has deployed more than a hundred old and new submarines in the East China Sea."[50] Taiwan has made it a priority to strengthen its antisubmarine warfare capability. Currently, it has four submarines (two Zwaardvis class and two obsolete U.S. Guppy class). Taipei, which hopes to increase its fleet to ten submarines, has approached Washington, Paris, Bonn, and Canberra to strike a deal. Those efforts failed to bear fruit in President Lee's era. In fact, President Lee doubted "the number of submarines Taiwan could purchase would be adequate to defend Taiwan on a submarine-to-submarine basis."[51]

Fourth, Taiwan has made efforts to develop its own defense industry. The Republic of China emphasizes two principles for acquiring arms: self-sufficiency in development and research and the diversification of arms supply sources.[52] It further suggests that the acquisition of arms carries with it a duty to help attain the ultimate goal of a self-reliant defense industry, and that Taiwan will follow the development of the international situation and make use of every channel to diversify its arms supply in order to expand the sources for acquiring major weapons systems and to reduce the reliance on any single region (country).[53]

From the 1950s through the 1970s, Taiwan regarded the United States as a secure source of arms. The ROC–U.S. Mutual Defense Treaty, which was signed in 1954, made Washington the protector of the island. However, the situation changed after Washington established diplomatic relations with the People's Republic of China (PRC) on January 1, 1979, leading to the termination of the ROC–U.S. Mutual Defense Treaty the following year. It was at that time that Taiwan seriously considered the urgency of developing its own defense industry.

The Chungshan Institute of Science and Technology, which was established in July 1969, is the most important institution in Taiwan for research, development, and design of defense technology. In the past two decades, Taiwan's efforts have had great success. Its defense industry is now able to produce a wide range of modern weapons, including artillery, tanks, helicopters, tactical missiles, and jet fighters. For instance, Taiwan has developed and built several types of tactical missiles: the Tianjian (Sky Sword) I and II AAMs, the Xiong Feng (Gallant Wind) I and II antiship missiles, the Tiangong (Sky Bow) I and II SAMs, the Qing Feng (Green Bee) antiship guided missile, and the Gong Feng 6A rocket. The China Shipbuilding Corporation in Kaohsiung is able to build fast attack missile craft. Under the Guanghua I (or Glorious China I) program, the first of eight domestically made Chenggong missile frigates (4,100 tons), which were modeled on the U.S. Perry-class guided missile frigate, entered service in May 1993. The Guanghua III program is another indigenous project aimed at building twelve 580-ton Jinqiang-class guided missile patrol combatants. By 2000, seven of twelve Jinqiang missile craft were in service.[54] Another significant achievement is the production of the Ching-kuo Indigenous Defense Fighter (IDF). After its requests to purchase new-generation jet fighters were repeatedly turned down by Washington in the 1970s and 1980s, the ROC Executive Yuan established a "Self-reliance Committee" in 1981 to begin the task of making its own fighter. The initial design for the IDF was completed in 1983 and the first prototype was produced in 1988. In 1994, the first indigenous fighter was delivered to the air force and a total of 130 IDFs had joined the service by 1999. It is said that the IDF is in many respects superior to the PRC's Jian-8II.[55] Taiwan is the only country in Asia other than Japan and the PRC that has designed and built its own modern fighter and missile systems.[56]

Fifth, President Lee tried to increase professionalism in the military. Professionalism has two meanings in Taiwan. One means to prevent the military from intervening in politics or being controlled by any political party; the other means to increase the military's capability for fighting high-tech warfare. Quite similar to China's PLA, the military in Taiwan has a strong tradition of loyalty to the previous ruling party, the Kuomintang (KMT). It is ideologically anti-Taiwan independence and in favor of the island's final unification with the Chinese mainland. All of the top brass are KMT members and the military has been ordered to intervene in elections to support KMT candidates in the past. President Lee's first step to nationalize the military was to reduce the power of General Hau Pei-tsun, who had been chief of the general staff, the most powerful position in Taiwan's military. In 1989, General Hau was transferred to the position of minister of defense—a more prestigious but less powerful position. In 1990, General Hau was designated as premier, but his influence in the military was further diluted and a civilian was assigned to be his successor as defense minister. President Lee chose another civilian as the defense minister when the cabinet was reshuffled in 1993.

In addition to politically socializing the military to support the new Taiwanese values, the Legislative Yuan passed a new National Defense Law in January 2000, prohibiting political parties from operating in the military and forbidding soldiers to be involved in politics. The new National Defense Law also combines the military administrative and military command systems into one. Previously, the Ministry of National Defense exercised only administrative authority. The minister of national defense must be a civilian, but it is quite common for the post to be held by a retired senior officer. As Michael Swaine points out, the Ministry of National Defense as an institution did not in fact "play the lead role in formatting and revising defense policy or in determining Taiwan's force structure."[57] The General Staff Headquarters controlled about 99 percent of the national defense budget and was in charge of formulating policies, procuring weapons and equipment, and supervising a wide range of military activities.[58] The chief of the general staff as the head of the military command system was the most powerful figure in the ROC military. However, the new National Defense Law designates the minister of national defense as responsible for both the military administration system and the military command system and reduces the power of the chief of the general staff. The president is now able to "exercise his authority as commander-in-chief of the military indirectly, via the minister of national defense."[59] Moreover, democratization has increased the power of the Legislative Yuan to supervise the military. The military, which has become more sensitive to public criticism, has paid more attention to improving its public image by conducting direct communication with communities neighboring military bases, releasing military news to the public, and increasing transparency in the policymaking process.

In addition to the increase of firepower in order to fight high-tech warfare, the ROC military has made efforts to recruit professional and skilled soldiers to join the armed forces. Currently, conscripted soldiers, who serve only two years, still make up the majority of the military. Most of the conscripted soldiers are low skilled and poorly trained and are unlikely to be familiar with the weapons systems within two years. The goal in the long run is to create a professional army that is completely composed of commissioned officers and soldiers.

An Evaluation of President Lee's Legacy

President Lee's legacy to Taiwan's national defense is mixed. President Lee's most remarkable reform is that he successfully pushed the military to increase its interaction with society. The military is no longer a closed community. On the contrary, it has begun to throb with the pulse of society and is sensitive to public opinion. Training has become more humanized; exchanges between military and civilian experts in security studies have increased rapidly in recent years; and the military has become more responsible to the legislature.

However, President Lee's most visible achievement is the buildup of a second-generation armed forces, making Taiwan a respectable military power in East Asia (see Table 12.2). Taiwan's navy has blue-water capability and its air force is one of the best in the region.[60] Taiwan continues to enjoy an edge in its military competition with the PRC in the Taiwan Strait area.

Unfortunately, military buildup has not increased Taiwan's security. Although many experts have challenged the theme of a "China threat," some even using the term "obsolete" or "paper tiger" to describe the PLA,[61] there is a consensus that Beijing has rapidly built up its military muscle in the past decade and has the potential to become a real tiger in the future. In recent years, the PRC has acquired a great number of advanced weapon systems from Russia and Israel.[62] Many experts have estimated that Taiwan's armed forces, which are overwhelmed quantitatively by the PLA, will be surpassed qualitatively by their rivals in a decade, unless Taiwan can further streamline its defense industry or acquire more sophisticated weapons from foreign suppliers.[63]

Table 12.2

Development of Taiwan's Armed Forces

Year	1987	1999
Total armed forces	270,000	240,000
Army	Regular: 424,000 Para-military: 25,000 Reserves: 1,457,500 Major weapon systems: Tanks: 309 M-48A3/-A5 325 M-24; 795 M-41/Type64 SAM: 5 battalions (2 with Nike Hercules; 3 with HAWK)	Regular: 376,000 Para-military: 26,650 Reserves: 1,657,500 Major weapon systems: Tanks: 100 M-48A5; 450 M-48H; 169 M-60A3; 230 M-24; 675 M-41/Type64 SAM: 40 Nike Hercules; 100 HAWK; Tiangong (Sky Bow); 30 Avenger; 2 Chaparral; and 6 Patriot
Navy	77,000 (including 39,000 marines) Major weapon systems: Submarines: 4 Destroyers: 26 (14 U.S. Gearing; 8 U.S. Summer; 4 U.S. Fletcher) Frigates: 9 (3 Lawrence and 6 Crosley) Corvettes: 4 (1 domestic and 3 Auk)	68,000 (including 30,000 marines) Major weapon systems: Submarines: 4 Destroyers: 16 (11 U.S. Gearing; 2 U.S. Summer; 3 U.S. Fletcher) Frigates: 21 (7 Chenggong; 6 LaFayette; and 8 Knox)
Air Force	77,000 Major weapon systems: Combat aircraft: 562 (including 225 F-5E; 30 F-5F; 42 F-100A/D; 80 F-104G; 15 F-104A; 8 RF-104G) AAM: Sidewinder; Shafrir ASM: Bullpup; AGM-65A Maverick	68,000 Major weapon systems: Combat aircraft: 598 (including 200 F-5; 130 IDF; 150 F-16A/B; 60 Mirage 2000–5; 22 AT-3; 4 E-2T) AAM:AIM-4D Falcon; AIM-9J/P Sidewinder; Shafrir; Sky Sword I and II; MATRA Mica; MATRA R550 Magic 2 ASM:AGM-65A Maverick

Sources:: The Military Balance 1987/1988, pp. 172–73 and The Military Balance 1999/2000, pp. 205–6.

However, President Lee should not be blamed for the changing military balance in the Taiwan Strait in favor of the PRC, because Beijing's military buildup was beyond his control. He had been fully aware of this development and expressed concern that the military balance in the Taiwan Strait might shift to the PRC's favor by 2005.[64] In particular, President Lee had worried about the PRC's missile threat, and indicated an interest in joining the TMD system established by Washington and Tokyo in Northeast Asia, because such a system "not only meets the needs of the current situation, but also is in line with the long-term interests of the country."[65]

It is believed that President Lee seldom "intervene[d] directly in budget and [arms] procurement decisions."[66] However, he did indicate that it is imperative for Taiwan to acquire two specific weapons systems, i.e, submarines and TMD. In April 2001, the Bush administration agreed to provide Taiwan with four Kidd-class destroyers, eight diesel-powered submarines, and twelve P-3C Orion antisubmarine surveillance planes. The submarine item was a major breakthrough in that Taiwan had long attempted to acquire them but had failed for two decades. However, the United States has cautiously declined to provide Taiwan with four Aegis-class destroyers, which it deemed to be a TMD system. Even though one expert has argued that "Lee has long pressed for such a system despite the fact that significant elements of the ROC military are not enthusiastic about it [TMD]," a majority of people on the island (77 percent) support the option.[67] Judged from Taipei's official position on the TMD issue, President Lee was inclined to reconsider the TMD option if the PRC decided not to deploy missiles targeting Taiwan.[68] President Chen Shui-bian does not deviate from this posture. In this regard, Taipei actually took a defensive posture in considering the purchase of the PAC-3s and Aegis-class destroyers, but it was disappointed to see the Clinton administration's decision to block the sale of this TMD system.[69]

Facing the PRC's missile threat, Taiwan's legislators and members of the National Assembly have advised the government to reconsider a nuclear option for Taiwan's ultimate defense. President Lee Teng-hui first responded that Taipei "should restudy the question from a long-term point of view," but later he clarified that Taiwan would not pursue a nuclear option.[70] President Lee also maintained a low profile when Vice President Lien Chan raised the option of a medium-range surface-to-surface missile to acquire a credible deterrence for Taiwan. Nevertheless, a few security experts in Taiwan have argued that under the

Chinese military threat and the U.S. policy of strategic ambiguity, Taiwan should reconsider the desirability of going nuclear or acquiring medium-range surface-to-surface missiles.[71]

In addition, despite the fact that Taiwan's defense industry has made significant achievements in recent years, it still lags behind world standards. In fact, foreign technology, especially U.S. technology, has been critical to those sophisticated weapons systems made in Taiwan. For instance, the Sky Bow SAM, Xiong Feng antiship missile, and the Chenggong-class frigate, all rely on foreign technology or subsystems.[72] The IDFs were developed with the help of General Dynamics (airframe), Garret (engine), and Westinghouse (radar systems). As David Shambaugh suggests, with military technology rapidly innovating, "Taiwan's dependency on foreign supplies will only increase over time."[73]

President Lee's efforts to professionalize the military nevertheless left much to be desired. First of all, in a democratic society, victory in elections is the only way for the KMT to remain in power. Therefore, President Lee, who was chairman of the KMT from 1988 to March 2000, did not really keep the military out of politics. On the contrary, he continued to mobilize the military to support the candidates of his party in elections.

Second, the military's morale is not high because it is ideologically divided. It is agreed that Taiwan's people have reached some consensus on cross-strait relations. For instance, an overwhelming majority of Taiwan's people, regardless of their ethnic background, agree that priority should be given to Taiwan's security and to the welfare of the 23 million people of Taiwan when dealing with the PRC. They reject Beijing's "one country, two systems" formula for unification and believe that Taiwan's people have the final say on any agreement reached between the two sides of the Taiwan Strait. Nevertheless, Taiwan is still a divided society with regard to the issue of independence versus unification. The military, which has been educated to fight for the cause of unification, is especially hostile to Taiwan independence. President Lee did not complete the task of changing the culture of anti-Taiwan independence in the military. Some of the soldiers, in particular those of mainlander ethnic backgrounds, might refuse to fight if they believe that their government is pursuing the cause of independence.

Third, Lee's idea to appoint a civilian as defense minister proved to be a failure. Taiwan's military is still a very conservative and hierarchical organization. A civilian, who has no military connections, is unlikely to perform well as defense minister. After the failed experiment of assigning Chen Lu-an and Sun Chen as civilian defense ministers from 1990 to 1994, President Lee was forced to search for his defense minister among the generals. However, he did reduce the military's political influence and encourage the military to listen to the public. More important, drawing a lesson from the 2000 presidential election in which the ruling KMT tried to mobilize the military to support its candidate against Chen Shui-bian and James Soong, the military has decided not to intervene in any election in the future.

Finally, President Lee did not succeed in creating a favorable environment for recruiting talent to the military. The social status of the military is still not high and brain drain is a serious problem. The lack of enough capable soldiers to operate the advanced weapons systems is a serious problem for Taiwan.

Conclusion

A page closed in Taiwan's history as President Lee completed his term on May 20, 2000. Having served as commander-in-chief for twelve years, President Lee has left his footprint on Taiwan's military. But his legacy to national defense is mixed. On the one hand, President Lee tried every approach to increase his country's security. His most visible achievement was to modernize Taiwan's military both by acquiring advanced weapons and by restructuring its organization. Equally significant, he laid the foundation to professionalize and nationalize the military, and he increased legislative supervision of the military. In addition, he began the task of bringing the military under civilian control. On the other hand, President Lee did not succeed in polishing the military's image and upgrading its social status. The military still has problems recruiting enough talent to handle sophisticated weapon systems. It is still a question whether the military can fight as a whole against the PLA, because its morale is not high and it is ideologically divided.

President Lee's era was a transitional period during which the state transformed itself from authoritarianism to democracy. The military during this period had to adjust itself from a KMT army to a national army. It still has a long way to go to change the military's deep-rooted conservative culture. It will not be easy for President Chen Shui-bian to finish his predecessor's incomplete task. First of all, it is more difficult for President Chen, who is pro-independence and whose party has only a few supporters among military officers, to establish mutual trust with the military. Second, Beijing, which is growing impatient with following a peaceful approach to unification, will increase military pressure on Taiwan. Third, Taiwan's options for increasing its national security will remain limited due to its diplomatic isolation. The international community is unlikely to become friendly to Taiwan if the PRC can maintain its economic growth. Under such circumstances, President Chen will try to stabilize the military in order to win its support, instead of carrying out major reforms to risk alienating the military. Therefore, one should not expect radical changes in the military in the near future.

Notes

1. The mainlanders, who came to Taiwan from China after 1945, and their children, account for about 13.6 percent of the island's 23 million people.

2. See, for example, Tien-bien Lou, *Military Strongman Lee Teng-hui* (Taipei: Formosa, 1995).

3. Michael D. Swaine, *Taiwan's National Security, Defense Policy, and Weapons Procurement Processes* (Santa Monica, CA: RAND Corporation, 1999), p. xi.

4. *1992 National Defense Report, Republic of China* (Taipei: Li Ming Cultural Enterprise, 1992), p. 46.

5. Mainland Affairs Council, *Cross-Strait Economic Statistics Monthly*, (Taipei: Executive Yuan, April 2001): 22–26.

6. Ibid., 35.

7. *Republic of China Yearbook 1994*, p. 159.

8. According to one of the agreements, SEF–ARATS talks would be held every three months at the deputy secretary-general level, every six months in general at the vice-chairman level, and at the chairman level according to need and based on mutual agreement.

9. Mainland Affairs Council, *White Paper on Cross-Strait Relations* (Taipei: Executive Yuan, July 1994), pp. 176–202.

10. Quoted in Eric A. McVadon, "PRC Exercises, Doctrine and Tactics Toward Taiwan: The Naval Dimension," paper prepared for the Conference on the People's Liberation Army, co-sponsored by AEI and T.M.I. Asia, Coolfont, West Virginia, September 6–8, 1996, p. 1.

11. *Sankei shinbum*, January 1, 1996. Quoted in *Ziyou shibao* (Liberty times), January 2, 1996, p. 3.

12. *Far Eastern Economic Review*, February 8, 1996, p. 20; and *New York Times*, January 24, 1996, p. 3.

13. President Clinton stated: "I had a chance to reiterate our Taiwan policy, which is that we don't support independence for Taiwan, or two Chinas, or one Taiwan, one China. And we don't believe Taiwan should be a member in any organization for which statehood is a requirement." Quoted in the *Wall Street Journal*, July 1, 1998.

14. *1998 National Defense Report*, Republic of China (Taipei: Li Ming Cultural Enterprise, 1998).

15. For example, the PRC President Jiang Zemin visited Russia and Japan in November 1998 and asked these two countries to follow Washington's lead and announce the "three-no's" policy.

16. *Zhongguo shibao* (China times), July 10, 1999, p. 1.

17. "The One-China Principle and the Taiwan Issue," a white paper released by the Taiwan Affairs Office and the Information Office of the State Council, People's Republic of China.

18. Ministry of Defense, *1993–94 National Defense Report*, Republic of China (Taipei: Li Ming Cultural Enterprise, 1994), p. 62.

19. David Shambaugh, "Taiwan's Security: Maintaining Deterrence amid Political Accountability," *China Quarterly*, no. 148 (December 1996): 1284–318; Chong-Pin Lin, "The Role of the People's Liberation Army in the Process of Reunification: Exploring the Possibilities," in *China's Military: The PLA in 1992/1993*, ed. Richard Yang (Taipei: Chinese Council of Advanced Policy Studies, 1993), pp. 161–79; and Felix K. Chang, "Conventional War across the Taiwan Strait," *Orbis* 40, no. 4 (Fall 1996): 577–607.

20. See, for example, David G. Muller, Jr., "A Chinese Blockade of Taiwan," *U.S. Naval Institute Proceedings* 110, no. 9 (September 1984): 53.

21. For instance, Deng Xiaoping mentioned to Japan's Komeito Party leader, Yoshikatsu Takeiri, in October 1984 that Beijing did have the capability to blockade Taiwan (*New York Times*, October 12, 1984), p. A8.

22. Chang Chao-chung, "Dasui Denghui de sange meng" (Break Lee Teng-hui's three dreams), *Wen wei po* (Hong Kong), August 21, 1998, A6.

23. Quoted in *Asiaweek*, June 2, 2000, p. 28.

24. Cited in a memo entitled "Taipei on TMD" released by the Mainland Affairs Council, Executive Yuan, Republic of China, in March 1999.

25. *Wen wei po* (Hong Kong), August 13, 1999, A1.

26. *Lianhe bao* (United daily news), May 23, 1990, p. 2.

27. Virginia Sheng, "Lee Says March 23 Victor Must Pursue a Peace Pact," *Free China Journal*, March 1, 1996, p. 2; *President Lee Teng-hui's Selected Addresses and Messages, 1996* (Taipei: Government Information Office, 1997), p. 23.

28. "Full Text of President Lee Teng-hui's Inaugural Speech," *CNA*, May 19, 1996; *Time*, June 22, 1998, p. 28.

29. "The Reality Is a Divided China," *Time*, June 22, 1998, p. 27.

30. "Lee Seeks Beijing Dialogue, Exchange of Visits by Leaders," *China Post*, April 9, 1999, p. 1.

31. Mainland Affairs Council, *Cross-Strait Economic Statistics Monthly*, no. 83 (Taipei: Executive Yuan, July 1999): 26.

32. Lee Teng-hui, *Creating the Future: Towards a New Era for the Chinese People* (Taipei: Government Information Office, 1993), p. 157.

33. Lee Teng-hui, *Listen to the Voice of the People* (Taipei: Cheng Chung Books, 1998), p. 78; *President Lee Teng-hui's Selected Addresses and Messages, 1998* (Taipei: Government Information Office, 1999), p. 98.

34. Lee Teng-hui, "Asia-Pacific and America," *Sino-American Relations* (Taipei) 19, no. 3 (Autumn 1993): 12.

35. *President Lee Teng-hui's Selected Addresses and Messages, 1997* (Taipei: Government Information Office, 1998), p. 73.

36. Ibid., p. 112.

37. "$S14b Firm Proposed," *Straits Times*, August 23, 1995, p. 17.

38. Anthony Apaeth, "Playing with Fire," *Time*, July 26, 1999, quoted in cgi.pathfinder.com/time/asia/magazine/1999/990726/taiwan1.html.

39. *Qingnian ribao* (Youth daily), July 10, 1996, p. 1.

40. *President Lee Teng-hui's Selected Addresses and Messages, 1997*, p. 98.

41. Lee, *Creating the Future*, p. 117.

42. Ministry of Defense, *1996 ROC National Defense Report* (Taipei: Li-ming Cultural Enterprises, 1996) p. 62.

43. *Republic of China Yearbook 1994*, p. 159.

44. *Yuanjian* (Global view), March 5, 1997, pp. 52–53.

45. International Institute for Strategic Studies, *The Military Balance 1999/2000* (New York: Oxford University Press, annual), p. 205.

46. Taiwan imported more than US$22 billion in weapons from 1988 to 1998. See *The Military Balance 1996/1997*, p. 280, and *The Military Balance 1999/2000*, p. 283.

47. In fiscal year 1996, a total of NT$58.75 billion was allocated to purchase major weapon systems. It was divided into four parts: NT$21.65 billion (36.85 percent) to purchase aircraft; NT$26.29 billion (49.86 percent) to purchase naval vessels; NT$3.5 billion (5.96 percent) for antilanding weapon systems; and NT$7.31 billion (12.44 percent) for missiles and air defense weapon systems. In addition, a special budget of several billion New Taiwan dollars was appropriated each year from 1993 to 2001 to pay for the order of 150 F-16A/B and Mirage 2000–5s. In 1996, the budget for those jet fighters was more than NT$61 billion. In fiscal year 1997, the budget for the acquisition of major weapon systems was NT$60.5 billion. This included NT$24.8 billion (41 percent) to purchase naval vessels and NT$17.39 billion (28.7 percent) to buy aircraft. An additional NT$58.2 billion was given to the purchase of American and French jet fighters, *Ziyou shibao* (Liberty times), March 13, 1996, p. 3.

48. *The Military Balance 1999/2000*, pp. 178–79.

49. According to Admiral Eric A. McVadon, the PRC has five Han-class nuclear submarines (plus a Xia SSBN), four Kilo-class, one Song-class, twelve Ming-class, and thirty to seventy Romeo-class (number in reserve is uncertain) diesel attack submarines. See McVadon, "PRC Exercises, Doctrine and Tactics Toward Taiwan," Table B.

50. In the mid-1990s, the PLA Navy had more than one hundred submarines. However, most of the ROMEO-class and WHISKEY-class submarines were in reserve. The number of submarines in service was reduced to seventy-one in 2000. See *Military Technology*, January 1995, p. 271; and *The Military Balance*, 1999/2000, p. 187.

51. "President Lee's Interview with German Radio," cited in <www.taiwaninformation.org/view/world/lee070999.html>.

52. Ibid., p. 87.

53. Ibid., pp. 89–90.

54. *Ziyou shibao* (Liberty times), May 25, 1996, p. 4; U.S. Department of Defense, "Report to Congress Pursuant to the FY99 Appropriations Bill," *DefenseLINK*, March 4, 1999, p. 8; *The Military Balance, 1999/2000*, p. 206.

55. Shambaugh, "Taiwan's Security," p. 1303.

56. Gary Klintworth, "Island State Modernises Defence Force," A-PDR 1997 Annual Reference Edition, p. 30.

57. Swaine, *Taiwan's National Security*, pp. 36–37.

58. Ibid., pp. 39–40; and *Lianhe bao* (Taipei), January 7, 2000, p. 15.

59. Swaine, *Taiwan's National Security*, p. 38.

60. Gary Klintworth, "Developments in Taiwan's Maritime Security," *Issues and Studies* 30, no. 1 (January 1994): 65–82.

61. See, for instance, John Zeng, "China: A Status Quo Power with an Obsolete Air Force," A-PDR 1996 Annual Reference Edition, p. 5; and James L. George, "China: Paper or Potential Tiger?" *Naval Forces* 17, no. 2 (February 1996): 91–96.

62. In particular, the Russians are willing to sell anything to the PRC except nuclear weapons. See Alexander Sergounin, "Sino-Russian Military-Technical Co-operation: Incentives, Major Programs, Security Implications," paper prepared for the International Forum on Peace and Security in the Taiwan Strait, co-sponsored by the Twenty-first Century Foundation and the American Enterprise Institute, Taipei, July 26–28, 1999, pp. 8–9.

63. For instance, David Shambaugh suggests that Taiwan's loss of its military advantage is only a matter of time. See David Shambaugh, "A Matter of Time: Taiwan's Eroding Military Advantage," *Washington Quarterly* 23, no. 2 (Spring 2000): 119–33.

64. *Zhongyang ribao* (Central daily news), July 23, 1997, p. 2.

65. *Lianhe bao*, March 2, 1999, p. 1; Myra Lu, "Perry Visit Prompts Talk of TMD and 'Track Two,'" *Free China Journal*, March 12, 1999, p. 1; Michael Laris, "Taiwan Seeks Place Under Missile Shield," *Washington Post*, August 19, 1999, p. A15.

66. Swaine, *Taiwan's National Security*, p. 34.

67. *Lianhe bao*, April 10, 1999, p. 13; Swaine, *Taiwan's National Security*, p. 35.

68. Cited in <www.mac.gov.tw/mlpolicy/880310/tmdc.htm>.

69. "Arming Taiwan," *Washington Post*, April 19, 2000, p. A26.

70. *Ziyou shibao* (Liberty times), July 29, 1995, p. 3; "Military Promises Not to Use Uranium for Nuclear Weapons," *China Post*, August 18, 1996, p. 11.

71. Kevin Murphy, "Taiwan Dusts off Nuclear Threat in its Dispute with Beijing," *International Herald Tribune*, July 29–30, 1995, p. 1; Tim Zimmerman and Susan V. Lawrence, "Will Taiwan Succumb to the Nuclear Temptation?" *U.S. News and World Report*, February 12, 1996, p. 44; Andrew Mack, "Nuclear Arms Are Not the Solution for Taiwan," *International Herald Tribune*, January 30, 1996, p. 8; Gerald Segal, "Taiwan's Nuclear Card," *Asian Wall Street Journal*, August 4, 1998, p. 10.

72. Richard A. Bitzinger and Bates Gill, *Gearing up for High-tech Warfare? Chinese and Taiwanese Defense Modernization and Implications for Military Confrontation Across the Taiwan Strait, 1995–2005* (Washington, DC: Center for Strategic and Budgetary Assessments, 1996), pp. 36–42.

72. Shambaugh, "Taiwan's Security," p. 1303.

—— 13 ——

Taiwan's Challenge to U.S. Foreign Policy

Bruce J. Dickson

American policy toward Taiwan is inevitably linked to China. Since the Nixon presidency, successive administrations have struggled to find the proper balance between their desire to build a stronger relationship with China and the political and moral imperative to maintain informal ties with Taiwan and to provide for its security. For its part, the People's Republic of China (PRC) has said from the beginning that the Taiwan issue is the central issue in U.S.–China relations. This was true during the ambassadorial talks of the 1950s and during normalization talks in the 1970s, and it remains true today. Congressional critics of the administration's China policy repeatedly seek to enhance and clarify the U.S. commitment to Taiwan. Their support for Taiwan is strongly influenced by their disdain for the PRC. This was particularly apparent during the Clinton administration, but has been true for every president going back to Nixon, and is likely regardless of which party is in the White House. Conversely, many mainstream China specialists in the United States see Taiwan primarily as an irritant in U.S.–China relations, and would like to limit the U.S. commitment to Taiwan in order to promote better relations with the PRC.

During Lee Teng-hui's administration, the link between policies toward China and Taiwan grew more complicated. Lee initiated a series of changes in Taiwan's foreign relations to try to break out of the isolation imposed by China's insistence that other countries abide by its "one-China" policy in their dealings with Taiwan. Lee and many others in Taiwan grew frustrated by this marginal international status and lack of participation in many key international organizations. Lee took a number of steps in the early 1990s that seemed very pragmatic, but by the end of his administration his actions and statements were seen by many as provocative and even reckless. In 1991, he announced the end of the period of communist insurrection and redefined the Republic of China's claim of sovereignty to only the territories it currently occupies: Taiwan and the islands off the coast of Fujian. Throughout the 1990s, he and other government leaders embarked on "flexible diplomacy" with ostensibly private trips to Southeast Asia, Europe, and elsewhere. The culmination of these foreign trips was Lee's visit to Cornell in 1995, which led to a crisis in U.S.–China relations that ended with missile tests off the northern and southern tips of Taiwan and the dispatch of two U.S. aircraft carrier groups to the Taiwan Strait. Beginning in the mid-1990s, Lee began describing Taiwan as an independent, sovereign state. Finally, he made explicit his view of cross-strait relations in 1999 with his "special state-to-state relations" announcement. Throughout his tenure as president, Lee increasingly challenged the notion that Taiwan was inseparably part of China. His efforts to create more international space had the unintended consequence of increasing the immediate threat from China. It also strained ties with the Clinton administration in Washington, which felt Lee and other Taiwan leaders had needlessly provoked the 1995–96 crisis in the interest of domestic political gain and lobbied Congress to force the administration's hand in granting Lee a visa.

These changes in Taiwan's international relations were matched by equally dramatic changes in its domestic politics. The democratization of the political system begun under Chiang Ching-kuo was carried further by Lee. New elections were held for the National Assembly, Legislative Yuan, governor of Taiwan, mayors of Taipei and Kaohsiung, and eventually, president. The result of this institutionalization of democracy was the dramatic victory of Chen Shui-bian and the historic first peaceful transfer of power from one party to another. This democratization was accompanied by the further Taiwanization (also begun under Chiang Ching-kuo) of the KMT, government, and military. The popular foreign image of Taiwan as being dominated by mainland émigrés who fled to Taiwan after the Chinese civil war became untenable. Although further progress is needed to eliminate corruption from the political process and to improve the party system, Taiwan's democratization is a rare example of a peaceful and gradual transformation in the "third wave" of democracy.[1]

U.S. policy toward Taiwan has not kept pace with these sweeping changes. Most government officials and policy analysts believe that the existing "one-China" policy has maintained peace and stability in the Taiwan Strait and allowed Taiwan to enjoy increasingly high levels of prosperity and democracy. Taiwan, and Lee personally, are often blamed for trying to upset this familiar and successful arrangement. From the U.S. government's perspective, the benefits of acknowledging Taiwan's economic and political progress with a fundamental change in policy are outweighed by the likely repercussions in U.S.–China relations. Despite the prominence of Taiwan in policy debates, most people in the United States, Taiwan, and China are unsatisfied with American policy toward Taiwan. Why has this been such a contentious issue?

Lee Teng-hui's Legacy to U.S.–Taiwan Relations

Since 1979, when the United States established diplomatic relations with China, relations between the United States and Taiwan have been unofficial, with little direct contact between the leaders of the two governments. Nevertheless, Lee Teng-hui had a major impact on the dynamics of the relationship and the style in which they were conducted. During his tenure as president, he developed a reputation for repeatedly pushing the envelope, attempting to create more international space for Taiwan while China was simultaneously trying to isolate it. A key element of his strategy to avoid being boxed in by Beijing's efforts—to add dynamism to the status quo—was maintaining strong support in the United States. Although Taiwan's leaders and diplomats had limited direct contact with their counterparts in the U.S. government, there were no restrictions on interactions with members of Congress. Consequently, Lee perfected the art of playing Congress off against the White House, State Department, and the rest of the executive branch. This was a rational tactic: As noted above, Taiwan has always enjoyed more support in the Congress than in the White House. Lee used this tactic so often, and so effectively, that, by the end of his tenure, many veteran State Department officials had grown resentful of his interventions in American politics and his knack for disrupting U.S.–China relations. Lee's wedge tactics had short-term benefits; for example, it was Congressional pressure that compelled the Clinton administration to approve Lee's request for a visa to visit Cornell University in 1995. But his tactics also did long-term damage to his and Taiwan's credibility and reputation for reliability. As will be described below, one of Chen Shuibian's challenges has been to repair relations with the executive branch,

strained by years of Lee Teng-hui's initiatives and surprise announce-
ments, while still maintaining Congressional support.

Lee's legacy to U.S.–Taiwan relations was shaped in large part by
three episodes: his airport stop in Hawaii in 1994; his visit to Cornell in
1995 and its aftermath; and his "special state-to-state relations" announcement in 1999. The first two episodes were good examples of his ability
to drive a wedge between the Clinton administration and Congress, creating resentment all around. The third episode was not so clear-cut. While
some in Congress applauded his effort to explode the "one-China" myth,
other supporters of Taiwan were less enthusiastic, concerned that Lee's
last major diplomatic initiative was fraught with risk and had little immediate benefits.

After the United States switched its diplomatic relations from Taipei
to Beijing, Taiwan's leaders had more limited access to American officials and even to U.S. territory. The latter restriction was the cause of
the first episode that shaped Lee's legacy to U.S.–Taiwan relations. In
the spring of 1994, Lee asked permission to spend one night in Hawaii
to rest and refuel his plane before continuing on to an official visit to
Central America and Africa. The State Department was reluctant to approve this unprecedented request. It was wary of allowing Lee to be
even an overnight guest in the United States, fearing that this might
convey a degree of officiality in the relationship. The Clinton administration was also embroiled in the issue of linking the renewal of China's
"most favored nation" (MFN) status with its human rights record, and,
therefore, unwilling to add another contentious issue to an already difficult agenda. The result was a standoff. Washington would not allow him
to leave the airport, but did permit him to rest in a transit lounge in
Wickham Air Force Base. But Lee felt this was inadequate and insulting
and refused to leave his plane.

This first episode produced hard feelings across the board. Lee felt
that he had been denied the dignity he and his country were due. State
Department officials felt that Lee had intentionally timed his request to
complicate their negotiations with China and Congress regarding MFN
linkage, and had embarrassed them with his grandstanding by refusing
to leave the plane at all. This solidified his reputation as a troublemaker,
a label that he and his supporters angrily rejected. Many in Congress felt
that the State Department once again showed poor judgment and improper priorities by denying Taiwan's president a simple favor. The resentment in Congress toward the State Department was compounded as

the tale was twisted in the retelling: It became accepted truth that the State Department had denied Lee permission to deplane at all.[2]

This embarrassing episode led directly to the next year's flap over granting Lee a visa to visit his alma mater, Cornell University. The State Department initially denied Lee's request, arguing such a trip was unprecedented and would damage U.S.–China relations. This refusal mobilized Taiwan's lobbying machine and its supporters in Congress. The House passed a unanimous resolution in favor of Lee's visit, and the Senate passed a similar resolution by 97 to 1 vote. Faced with such strong support in Congress, and without a compelling reason why it should deny a visa to the president of a democratizing country with a long history of friendly relations with the United States, President Clinton directed the State Department to overturn its previous decision and issue a visa to Lee. His visit to Cornell led to a prolonged crisis in U.S.–China relations, including the potential of military conflict, as described in the chapters by Julian Kuo and by Suisheng Zhao.[3] It also solidified the view of many that Lee was willing to sacrifice the long-term interests of the United States for his own short-term political needs, in this case the presidential election of 1996. Lee showed himself willing and able to enlist Congress in his efforts to promote his interests, and by extension Taiwan's visibility, even when those efforts led to dangerous consequences for both the United States and Taiwan. While he was championed by many on Capitol Hill, he was not trusted by many others elsewhere in the government.

These first two episodes shared some common features, such as Lee's efforts to visit the United States, the State Department's reluctance to allow him to do so, and Congressional criticism of the State Department's obstruction. While the third episode did not directly involve the United States, it nevertheless led to concerted diplomacy and damage control. Lee's announcement to a German interviewer that Taiwan's relations with China should be conducted on a state-to-state, or at least a "special state-to-state" basis (i.e., as separate by equal governments) challenged the commitment to "one China" that underlay cross-strait relations and U.S. relations with both China and Taiwan. Although some in Washington complained that Lee had not consulted with the United States before dropping this bombshell, the subsequent reaction showed why he did not bother to do so. Washington would not have approved or supported the statement, regardless of whether it had received advance notice. Moreover, Lee did not even consult with his own officials in charge of mainland policy, as noted in the chapter by Julian Kuo. The immediate result was a recommitment by the Clinton administration to the traditional "one-China" policy, and the dispatch of separate diplomatic teams to Beijing and Taipei to deliver that message face to face. The longer-term result was a reminder that Taiwan would not always defer to American interests on the subject of its international status. While the long history of relations between Washington and Taipei shows that they have rarely seen eye to eye, Lee proved himself to be a master of political manipulation, driving a wedge between the branches of government in Washington in pursuit of his agenda. He was unwilling to accept the State Department's authority over diplomatic affairs, and he found a willing partner in the Congress, which, under Republican control, was increasingly critical of the State Department's conduct on a variety of issues, including relations with China and Taiwan.

These three episodes contributed to Lee's reputation and ultimately his legacy to U.S.–Taiwan relations. Although he denied being a trouble-maker, and defended his actions as simply reactions to decisions made in Beijing and Washington, he nonetheless created new problems for the Clinton administration, in its dealings with both China and Congress. The request for a transit stopover came in the midst of the debate over linking China's MFN status with its human rights record. The "special state-to-state" relations announcement came shortly after the United States bombed the Chinese embassy in Belgrade. While there may never have been a good time, at least from the U.S. point of view, to make such a surprise announcement, it revealed Lee's knack for selecting particularly sensitive times to throw a wrench into the works. Lee was committed to creating greater international space and recognition for Taiwan and to pursuing his own political interests, which often seemed one and the same. His short-term gains, however, had long-term costs that were inherited by the Chen administration.

The Dilemma of U.S. Policy Toward Taiwan

Recent tensions in the Taiwan Strait, beginning with the 1996 missile crisis and continuing with Beijing's threatening rhetoric during Taiwan's 2000 presidential campaign and ongoing military modernization, have revealed the difficulty of managing a situation where the common understandings that previously bound the United States, China, and Taiwan to the myth of "one China" have broken down. In the process, these tensions have also revealed the dilemma inherent in U.S. policy toward Taiwan. On the one hand, a key goal of American foreign policy has been to promote free markets and democracy. In this regard, Taiwan is a model of both rapid economic growth, with an increasing role played by the private sector, and a peaceful transition to democracy. Taiwan's citizens today enjoy high standards of living, a lively media, good opportunities for education, travel, and work, and the ability to pass judgment on all their leaders through direct elections. Such an impressive record would normally call for strong U.S. support and increased international visibility.

But on the other hand, another key American goal has been to ensure its national security by preserving peace and stability. Since at least the early 1970s, successive U.S. administrations have seen a cooperative relationship with China as the means to protect American security interests, particularly in the Asia-Pacific region but to some degree more globally as well. This has led administrations of both parties to pursue a close working relationship with China, even though Congress and the American public have often been skeptical of the merits of the U.S.–China relationship. Most China specialists in the policy and scholarly worlds view Taiwan as an irritant in U.S.–China relations, not as a political actor deserving priority for its own sake. Although the United States continued to sell arms to Taiwan and allowed occasional meetings between government officials (which are always met with stern objections by China), during Lee's tenure as president, U.S. policy generally supported Beijing's view of the cross-strait relationship and accepted Beijing's position on Taiwan's international status.

The modern goal of promoting markets and democracy need not conflict with the traditional goal of protecting national security. Indeed, Taiwan is often offered as proof that a peaceful and gradual transition to democracy is possible in a traditionally Confucian society such as China's, and that such a transition would be in American and regional security interests. But that is a long-term process, and the outcome of China's political evolution remains to be seen. In the present context of U.S. relations with China and Taiwan, however, these competing goals appear mutually exclusive. American policymakers and scholarly analysts are caught in a trap: They can either emphasize prosperity and democracy by siding with Taiwan but in the process angering China, or they can promote national security through closer ties with China but in the process not be able to develop closer relations with an increasingly prosperous and democratic Taiwan. Up to now and for the foreseeable future, policymakers have sought to avoid making an ultimate decision on whether to emphasize democracy or national security interests. Instead, the United States preaches patience to both sides, hoping that someday, somehow an alternative might be found.

The key to this middle course consists of encouraging China and Taiwan to negotiate their differences. Although it has so far refused to mediate this dispute, the United States has actively promoted a dialogue between the two sides. For instance, during 1999 (following Lee's "special state-to-state relationship" pronouncement) and 2000 (following Chen's victory), the United States sent delegations simultaneously to Beijing and Taipei urging caution and reiterating the U.S. position that resolution of cross-strait relations be achieved through peaceful means. Previously, former cabinet members such as William Perry and Anthony Lake traveled between Beijing and Taipei, presumably carrying messages between the two sides or at least conveying the perspective of the other side to enhance mutual understanding. These efforts helped deflate tense moments, and reflected the U.S. insistence that it is neutral in the cross-strait relationship even though it is hardly a bystander.

The Domestic Political Conflict over Taiwan Policy

Devising an appropriate policy toward Taiwan is further complicated by the domestic political and partisan debates in the United States. The Taiwan issue has been a recurring topic for debate since the end of the Chinese civil war. The sterile "who lost China?" debate of the 1950s not only exaggerated the degree of American influence over the outcome of the CCP–KMT conflict, it also destroyed the careers of many innocent public servants and deprived the government of much-needed expertise. More recently, the debate that began in 1999 over the Taiwan Security Enhancement Act (TSEA) was shaped more by a desire to change Clinton's policy toward China than by a direct concern for Taiwan. The TSEA was designed not just to enhance Taiwan's security, but more generally to change the direction of U.S. policy toward China and East Asia. The bill authorized the United States to expand military coordination with Taiwan, including the creation of secure communication links, direct military-to-military contacts, and expanded training of Taiwanese military officers. It also required the administration to submit to Congress an annual report of Taiwan's defense needs and what the United

States was doing to meet those needs, thus giving Congress a more direct role in deciding what weapons the United States would sell Taiwan, as well as more general oversight of the security arrangement with Taiwan.

The origins of the TSEA go back to Clinton's "three-no's" declaration in Shanghai in July 1998. This unequivocal statement of support for Beijing's perspective on Taiwan's international status was not balanced with a call for peaceful resolution or placed in the broader context of U.S. relations with China and Taiwan. As such, it was widely interpreted as a definite tilt away from the neutral position to which the United States had previously adhered and to which Clinton subsequently tried to return.[4] The results of this perceived tilt toward Beijing's viewpoint was both Lee's "state-to-state relations" and the TSEA originally introduced in 1999 and passed by the House in January 2000. The bill was punitive in its intent, and ignored the views even of those in the Pentagon who were not strong advocates for the Clinton administration's tilt toward Beijing. Taiwan's legitimate security needs are not well served by this pursuit of domestic political gains. In any event, the key goal of the bill—a closer military relationship between the United States and Taiwan—was already taking place quietly, an outcome of the 1996 missile crisis.[5] The bill ultimately died in the Senate. With the Clinton administration's return to a more neutral position on the Taiwan issue, and a generous arms sales package in spring 2000, the goals of the TSEA were largely accomplished even without the passage of the bill. It was not reintroduced after George W. Bush became president.

A more dangerous element of this debate over U.S. policy toward China and Taiwan is that many of the most influential people in the anti-China chorus have little expertise or knowledge of China, they simply see it as a threat to the United States.[6] Republican leaders in Congress are remarkably ignorant of or indifferent to U.S. foreign policy commitments or diplomatic practices.[7] Soon after Lee Teng-hui's visit to Cornell in 1995, Newt Gingrich reacted to Chinese criticisms by recommending that the United States simply recognize Taiwan's independence and wait for China to get over it. After a few days, and presumably some discussions with Taiwan's representatives in the United States, who explained that they were not seeking international recognition for Taiwan's independence, he retracted the statement. In early 2000, Republican whip Tom DeLay advocated abandoning the "one-China" policy that had guided U.S. policy toward both China and Taiwan since the Nixon administration and even tried to physically intimidate Chinese ambassador Li Zhaoxing outside a television studio.[8] Without knowledge of the issues involved, their statements can be unhelpful at best and counter-productive at worst.

Being anti-China has been a popular position in American politics in recent years. It is virtually cost-free, and can offer a variety of benefits. China's policies regarding military modernization, human rights, international trade, and other issues have created a negative impression in American pubic opinion, which is something on which politicians can easily capitalize. Its often harsh rhetoric toward the United States and the international community more generally raises doubts regarding its willingness to cooperate on these types of issues. Defenders of a strong U.S.–China relationship have a difficult time offering new or satisfying arguments about how China can contribute to regional peace and prosperity or why China is a reliable diplomatic partner.

But the anti-China mood in American public opinion does not automatically translate into support for a strong commitment to Taiwan's defense. A poll released by the Luce Foundation in October 1999 showed that only one-quarter of Americans felt the United States should defend Taiwan against an attack from China.[9] This suggested that despite the historic ties between the United States and Taiwan, and despite the general public perception that China is emerging as a threat to American interests, there is little interest in having the United States go to war with China over Taiwan. But another study released about the same time showed that Americans were willing to defend Taiwan and to accept a large number of casualties if their leaders made a convincing case that it was in U.S. interests to defend Taiwan.[10] That is a powerful message. The United States is often portrayed as being unwilling to engage in military missions if there is a chance that U.S. soldiers will be killed, and, in fact, many in China's policy community have questioned American resolve on the Taiwan issue. But if, and only if, the president and other political leaders made the case that active defense of Taiwan is in American interests, there may be strong public support. At present, U.S. leaders are not able to make this case for fear of further arousing Chinese suspicions. In fact, the Taiwan issue has become so politicized that a reasoned debate on the degree of U.S. commitment to Taiwan's security —whether in terms of arms sales or the conditions under which the United States would or would not defend Taiwan—has been impossible.

The decision about whether or not to defend Taiwan will likely not turn merely on public opinion. The American public is rarely supportive of intervention in foreign conflicts, at least in the abstract, and it is up to political leaders to build and maintain popular support for such actions. Can the United States simply stand by if China attacks Taiwan (leaving aside the different scenarios about how this might come about)? Congressional sentiment has typically been strongly in favor of Taiwan. This was particularly true during the last terms of Lee's and Clinton's presidencies (i.e., the late 1990s) when cross-strait tensions were rising. President George W. Bush reinforced this commitment when he stated that the United States would do "whatever it takes" to help Taiwan defend itself. Even though his aides quickly clarified his remarks by saying they did not reflect a change in U.S. policy, his strong statement of support departed from the "strategic ambiguity" of the Clinton administration. U.S. defense of Taiwan would also reassure allies throughout Asia of the credibility of the American commitment to the peace and security of the Asia-Pacific region. But although they want to be reassured of the American commitment to their own defense, they also do not want the United States to take steps that would trigger a conflict with China. They prefer the current U.S. policy of urging caution and patience in both China and Taipei to avoid conflict.

How strong is Congressional commitment to Taiwan's defense? Despite the strong rhetoric in favor of Taiwan, Congressional support is primarily limited to selling Taiwan the weapons it needs for its self-defense, but does not include a more open-ended commitment.[11] The dispatch of two aircraft battle groups to the Taiwan Strait in the 1996 missile crisis and the potential for further escalation of conflict was very sobering to many congressmen. While most members of Congress may be opposed to, or at least wary of China, they do not want to be drawn into a military conflict with it either. Several congressmen were concerned that Clinton's strong statements regarding Taiwan's defense increased the chance of a U.S.–China conflict over Taiwan, and privately encouraged him to soften his tone. By providing Taiwan with the defensive capabilities needed to deter a Chinese attack, both the White House and the Congress hope to avoid the issue of deciding what the United States should do if in fact China decides to attack anyway. Increased arms sales to Taiwan are accepted as a reasonable way to provide for Taipei's self-defense capabilities without committing the United States to active defense of Taiwan.

This is a potentially dangerous strategy because the increased volume and technological sophistication of weapons sold to Taiwan during the 1990s had the exact opposite effect of what its supporters claimed to intend. Not only did China protest these arms sales as a violation of the 1982 Shanghai II communiqué, it also began an extensive arms buildup of its own along the coastal areas near Taiwan. This created a situation similar to the classic security dilemma:[12] Taiwan felt that China's explicit threats and the modernization of PLA capabilities, which became increasingly apparent after Lee's 1995 visit to Cornell, had reduced its security. It therefore sought to enhance its security relationship with the United States to counter the growing threat from the mainland. Proposed arms sales, discussions of including Taiwan in a proposed theater missile defense system, and the formerly proposed TSEA were designed to do just that. But if such proposals are actually implemented, Beijing is not likely to let it stop there. On the Taiwan issue, it typically overreacts to increased military sales (ask the French) or to perceptions that the United States has tilted toward Taiwan by breaking its commitments or departing from past practice (as the issuing of a visa to Lee Teng-hui in 1995 showed). Increasing the quantity and quality of U.S. weapons sales to Taiwan in such a public way plays into the hands of hardliners in Beijing, who would have an easier time arguing for increased budgets to develop and deploy more of the kinds of weapons that created feelings of insecurity in Taiwan in the first place. The end result is that Taiwan's security is further undermined rather than enhanced, the exact opposite of what the efforts were designed to achieve.

Supporters of increased arms sales include a wide mix of motives for what they want to achieve. Some see it as a realistic response to the changing balance of power in East Asia, and in the Taiwan Strait in particular. With China's ongoing military modernization program, Taiwan's qualitative advantages in weapons and technology are likely to dissipate. Selling increasingly sophisticated weapons may help to maintain a dynamic status quo.[13] At the other extreme, some see it as an opportunity to damage U.S.–China relations. They see China as a hostile country, a threat to American interests in the region, and a future threat to the United States itself. Creating a more confrontational relationship between the United States and China is part of their agenda, and support for Taiwan is a convenient symbol of their antipathy toward China. In between these two extremes is a desire to restore the balance in U.S. policy toward China and Taiwan.[14] Some non-Congressional supporters of the TSEA admitted they would be happy to abandon the bill if the Clinton administration would agree to some important changes in its policy. From this perspective, the TSEA was simply a tactical ploy to get the attention of the White House—and China as well—and steer them away from their current course. It was a risky ploy, however, and threatened to exacerbate the very problem it tried to solve.

Even as leaders change in both Washington and Taipei, the debate over the proper relationship between the United States and Taiwan will endure. What degree of commitment would deter an attack from China, rather than provoke one? What level of arms sales will ensure Taiwan's self-defense without escalating the tacit arms race between Taiwan and China and without further straining ties between the United States and China? What role, if any, should the United States play in cross-strait relations? These are fundamental questions that lack definitive answers. The arrival of Chen Shui-bian as the new president of Taiwan introduced a new uncertainty into this debate. How China will ultimately respond to Chen's presidency, and whether cross-strait relations will improve or further deteriorate, is still uncertain. How American politicians will react to the new political dynamics represented by Chen's administration is also uncertain.

U.S. Policy in the Chen Shui-bian Era

Prior to Chen's victory, many people in the United States were also concerned about the potential of a Chen administration and the prospects for the DPP as the ruling party in Taiwan. Chen and other DPP leaders recognized this concern and during the late 1990s made repeated visits to Washington, New York, and elsewhere to try to reassure their American audiences that they would be peacemakers, not troublemakers, if Chen won. Most people remained skeptical, recognizing that the DPP's platform remains committed to Taiwan's independence despite the softening of its current policy. Regardless of these concerns, however, Chen and the DPP were able to have talks with a wide variety of officials, Congressmen, and scholars to increase mutual understanding on important issues in the U.S.–Taiwan relationship and the dynamics of domestic politics in both the United States and Taiwan. Above all, Chen's statements and actions after he took office belied the popular misconceptions that the DPP is a one-dimensional party, committed to independence and little else. In fact, the independence clause in the DPP's political platform was put there as a compromise to gain support for more practical political reform proposals (see the chapter by

Shelley Rigger). The foreign media still tend to describe the DPP as pro-independence, but that is misleading. Many in the DPP are not committed to Taiwan's independence, and see unification as one—although not the only—option for Taiwan's future. However, disavowing the independence clause would alienate some of the DPP's core members and most dependable voters.

Chen's victory began a new era for U.S.–Taiwan relations. During the past 50 years, the U.S. government had grown accustomed to dealing with the KMT, with its familiar personalities, policies, and style of diplomacy. Chen inherited a difficult relationship with the United States. The executive branch was wary of Lee's tendency to play the White House and the State Department off against the Congress. Republican leaders in Congress were prepared to legislate U.S. policy toward Taiwan, but in ways that were not always in Taiwan's best interests. More important, Chen's victory added uncertainty to the depiction of Taiwan in U.S. policy debates. Just as China has preferred to view the Taiwan issue as an unresolved element in the civil war, the United States has tended to view Taiwan as a subsidiary of U.S.–China relations. Chen's election challenged several traditional U.S. perspectives regarding Taiwan.

First of all, a key pillar of U.S.–China relations, and of U.S. policy toward Taiwan, has been the "one-China" policy, which states "that all Chinese on either side of the Taiwan Strait maintain there is but one China and that Taiwan is a part of China." That may have been true when the "three communiqués" of 1972, 1978, and 1982 were signed, when Taiwan remained under martial law, and when it claimed to be the sole legitimate government of all of China, but what of today? Lee Teng-hui's actions and statements steadily undermined the validity of that statement, and Chen has refused to accept the "one-China" principle as a precondition for restarting talks with Beijing. Lee renounced the ROC's claim to sovereignty over mainland China in 1991, and both he and Chen have claimed Taiwan need not declare independence because it is already an independent, sovereign state. It is no longer clear how many in Taiwan remain committed to future unification with the mainland, or believe that Taiwan and the mainland are both part of "one China," or even how many still view themselves as "Chinese." Chen's vice president, Annette Lu, described Taiwan's relationship to China as that of "distant relatives and close neighbors," which captured a growing sentiment among Taiwanese. In hindsight, Lee Teng-hui's portrayal of cross-strait relations as state-to-state relations may have had unintended benefits, despite the immediate tensions it created with Beijing and Washington. It exposed the gap between rhetoric and reality that has prevented a consensus on Taiwan's international status. Chen's cross-strait policy seemed less of a departure from the status quo, and possibly even more conciliatory, in the wake of Lee's statement.

If Taiwan's leaders and citizens do not subscribe to the "one-China" principle, can U.S. policy continue to be based on it? If the goal of U.S. policy toward Taiwan is not to advocate an outcome—either unification, independence, or the indefinite perpetuation of the status quo—but simply to preserve peace in the Taiwan Strait, it may still be the best policy, even though it makes assumptions that no longer seem tenable.[15] Andrew Nathan argues that the "strategic ambiguity"[16] policy remains the best approach, despite the fact that both China and Taiwan are not satisfied with it (and that the United States denies this in fact is, or ever was, its policy): "a tilt against Beijing risks encouraging Taiwanese adventurism just as the tilt against Taipei encouraged Beijing to harden its line."[17] The problem with U.S. policy toward Taiwan, according to Nathan, is that Clinton deviated from the previous posture of "dual deterrence," that is, preventing destabilizing moves from either Beijing or Taipei, when he tried to improve relations with China during his second administration, highlighted by his enunciation of the "three-no's" policy during his visit to China in 1998. Deviating from the former neutral position intensified the problem, rather than improving it. The irony is that the usefulness of the "one-China" myth—in particular, making it clear to both Beijing and Taipei that the United States does not advocate Taiwan's independence and would not recognize a declaration of independence—may endure even as the reality behind the "one-China" principle erodes.

The second traditional U.S. perspective regarding Taiwan has been its proxy status for anti-China and anticommunist sentiment. Taiwan's main benefactors within Congress come from the extreme right wing of the Republican party, which has vehement anti-China feelings. However, Chen's policies on the environment, on social and gender equality, and on giving international institutions greater importance relative to traditional notions of sovereignty and territorial integrity do not fit the Republican agenda. In fact, they are more similar to the liberal Democratic perspective. Chen's election provided a good opportunity for Taiwan to reach out to a broader spectrum of politicians in the United States and to improve ties with the executive branch by abandoning Lee's tactic of driving a wedge between the administration and Congress. This helped to reduce the partisanship and the institutional divisions that permeate the discussion of Taiwan in Washington.

The Clinton administration quickly reached out to Chen. Because Chen and his campaign were primarily focused on domestic issues, he was not as deeply familiar with international affairs. The KMT reportedly did not immediately make available to Chen the files on cross-strait relations. Consequently, Raymond Burghardt, the head of the American Institute in Taiwan (and therefore de facto ambassador to Taiwan), had frequent meetings with Chen to brief him on a range of foreign policy and security matters. For example, prior to making public its decision on the latest request for arms sales to Taiwan in April 2000 (namely, agreeing to sell a package of radar and antimissile technologies but deferring a decision on the most sensitive request, the destroyers equipped with Aegis radar technology, until at least 2001), the Clinton administration briefed Chen on the decision and sought his support. Congressional leaders were critical of the arms sales decision and indicated they would try to push the TSEA through the Senate to ensure a higher level of arms sales. But Chen announced his support for the decision and its rationale, making it difficult for either Congress or Taiwan's military to push the matter. Chen and his top aides were also strongly in favor of granting China permanent normal trade relations status as part of its entry into the World Trade Organization. On these and other matters, Chen has shown that Taiwan can be a constructive element in U.S.–China relations, not simply an irritant.

An episode in 1999 toward the end of the Lee Teng-hui era indicated how Congressional efforts to portray China as a threat can complicate efforts by Taiwan's leaders to manage cross-strait relations and manage Taiwan's security. In response to an early draft of the TSEA, Defense Minister Tang Fei (who later briefly served as Chen's first prime minister) expressed some vague and mild reservations about its impact on Taiwan's security. Benjamin Gilman, a conservative Republican leader in the House of Representatives and one of the sponsors of the bill, was visiting Taipei at the time and publicly rebuked Tang for his lack of complete support. If a minister of defense cannot be heard on matters that affect his country's national security, it indicates that other motives are involved. Fearful of antagonizing their Congressional patrons, KMT, and even some DPP, leaders adopted the position of thanking Congress for its support without wanting to offer an opinion on pending legislation. This is too coy, especially on such a sensitive issue. The United States should not decide on issues concerning Taiwan's security without the active involvement of Taiwan's leaders and especially its president.

As the leader of a divided government, Chen's is not the only voice speaking on behalf of Taiwan. When he assumed office in May 2000, Chen's party did not control the Legislative Yuan. Opposition legislators repeatedly criticized his actions on foreign policy and cross-strait relations. After Tang Fei resigned as prime minister, Chen's influence over the military diminished, making it more likely that Taiwan's military will lobby in Washington for a larger arms sales package with or without Chen's consent. Groups such as the Formosan Association for Public Affairs also lobby actively in Washington, although their goals and strategy are not well coordinated with the government in Taipei. This splintering of Taiwan's international voice could easily complicate the efforts of Chen and of future presidents to provide a coherent message and may also frustrate U.S. efforts to discern Taiwan's interests.

Future Options

Key trends from the Lee Teng-hui era highlight the potential for renewed conflict in the Taiwan straits, with likely detrimental implications for China, Taiwan, and the United States. First, cross-strait relations became remilitarized, which is detrimental to a peaceful resolution of differences. Beginning in the 1980s, military tensions between China and Taiwan noticeably declined, allowing dramatic increases in trade, travel, cultural exchanges, and other types of interactions, and culminating in the creation of new political institutions in Beijing and Taipei to manage the relationship.[18] In recent years, and especially since 1995, the trend has shifted back toward confrontation, fueled by China's military modernization and Taiwan's efforts to improve its defensive capabilities.

Second, both China and Taiwan felt that time was no longer on their side; patience was lost to a desire to do something sooner rather than later. Not too long ago, both sides felt that they could afford to wait indefinitely for a final resolution of the Taiwan issue. By the end of the Lee era, China felt that Taiwan was rapidly moving toward greater independence and that only increased military pressure could prevent a formal declaration. Taiwan felt that this arms buildup directed against it reduced its security and therefore its room for flexibility in cross-strait dialogues. The time horizons of decision makers in Beijing and Taipei shrank, making them less willing to cooperate and compromise.

Third, both China and Taiwan felt that the United States favors the other. This remarkable paradox was complicated by the acrimonious bipartisan debate in the United States during the second Clinton administration. White House actions to restate and reinforce American commitments to Taiwan's security aroused suspicions in Beijing that the United States tacitly supported Taiwan's independence. Efforts to delineate the limitations to the American commitment to Taiwan, on the one hand, and to restore a better working relationship with China, on the other, inflamed Congressional critics of U.S.–China policy and created doubts in Taipei about the credibility of the American commitment. In this highly charged domestic and international environment, there seemed to be no stable equilibrium. Many people involved in this complicated set of relationships seemed intent on pulling the United States in one direction or the other, rather than finding common ground.

It is hard to imagine a scenario in which China would willingly accept an independent Taiwan. It is equally difficult to imagine a situation in which Taiwan would willingly agree to unification. There is little room for compromise, and, at this point, little to discuss. The situation is not like Northern Ireland or the Middle East, where warring sides grew weary of the protracted struggle and sought U.S. involvement to negotiate a compromise solution. (Even in those situations, however, peace settlements did not remain in place for long.) In cross-strait relations, there is no such mutual desire for compromise. The United States should not try to mediate between the two sides, which would only redirect their frustration toward the United States without moving them any closer to a harmony of views. It should also not try to propose a solution to the current stalemate, which should be the prerogative of China and Taiwan alone. It should simply be a cheerleader, encouraging a resumption of dialogue without playing favorites or getting directly involved in the process. Regular and simultaneous missions to Beijing and Taipei by current and former officials have been effective and should be continued.

But this does not mean that the United States should play no role at all. The United States has not done enough to encourage greater flexibility on Beijing's part. When President Clinton declared the "three-no's" in Shanghai in June 1998, he got little in return. China did not renounce its right to use force against Taiwan, did not allow Taiwan to contribute to the relief efforts during the Asian economic crisis or the reconstruction efforts in Kosovo, and did not stop protesting U.S. relations with Taiwan. Even though the United States has said clearly and consistently that it does not support Taiwan independence, China opposes every U.S. arms sale to Taiwan and every exchange between incumbent officials. Having declared repeatedly and consistently that it does not support Taiwan's independence, the United States should tell China to stop interpreting every interaction between the United States and Taiwan as tacit support for Taiwan's independence.

More important, the United States should continue to encourage Taiwan and China to resume their dialogue but should not compel Taiwan to enter talks on terms laid down by Beijing. Clinton's statement after Chen's election that a resolution of the Taiwan issue must be achieved by peaceful means and be acceptable to the people of Taiwan added a new twist to a familiar formula. This second condition takes into consideration the full implications of Taiwan's democratization on its foreign affairs and indicates more clearly than ever before that the United States will respect political sentiment on Taiwan on this important issue. It also implies that the United States will not pressure the government of Taiwan to accept a formula that is unacceptable to the people of Taiwan. The Bush administration is unlikely to waver from this position, and future administrations should also uphold it.

At the same time, Washington should continue to make clear the limits of support for Taiwan's ambitions, above all that it will not support a declaration of independence. However, the United States should increase the number and frequency of high-level exchanges with Taiwan, including cabinet officials on at least an annual basis. If these were more routine, Beijing would not be so agitated when they do occur. Washington should also support Taiwan's greater involvement in international affairs, and not allow Beijing to set the limits on American relations with Taiwan. China's behavior toward Taiwan in the World Trade Organization will be an important test case of Beijing's willingness to allow Taiwan to play a more active international role. The United States should be prepared to defend Taiwan's interests in the World Trade Organization if China tries to deny it the full rights and privileges and equal status that its membership should convey.

So far, the United States has shown little desire to encourage China's flexibility on relations with Taiwan. The U.S.–China agenda already has a host of contentious issues, including trade, human rights, espionage allegations, conflicting security interests in East Asia, and the ill will created by the U.S. bombing of the Chinese embassy in Belgrade and collision of Chinese and American planes in April 2001. With trust and good will at a low ebb, an American initiative to convince Beijing to be more flexible toward Taiwan would probably be doomed to failure. However, the United States should not use the Taiwan issue to rebuild that trust and good will. It should not offer reassurances beyond what it has previously pledged, nor provide new concessions to China, such as cancellation of arms sales to Taiwan or a halt to exchanges among government officials.

The challenge for the United States is not to resolve the often tense relationship between China and Taiwan, for there seems little room for compromise and therefore little opportunity for American mediation. Instead, the best we can hope for is that all three sides will be able to manage this delicate policy dilemma in order to prevent military conflict. In the long run, simply managing the relationship may not be enough. Neither China nor Taiwan will be happy if the current unsatisfactory status quo remains without progress toward a final resolution. But until conditions change to make China more accepting of the reality of Taiwan's independent status or make Taiwan more willing to consider unification, little progress will be possible. Only the people in China and Taiwan can make that determination, as unlikely as it seems at present. Until then, the ability of the United States to prevent war in the Taiwan Strait and to resist direct intervention in lesser conflicts will be tested repeatedly.

Lee Teng-hui's primary legacy to U.S.–Taiwan relations may prove to be his unwillingness to remain within the parameters that others set for him. He insisted that he was the president of an independent, sovereign country and deserved to be treated accordingly. In doing so, he upset the delicate diplomacy that has governed cross-strait relations and U.S. policy toward both China and Taiwan for decades. His policies, statements, and actions continually pushed the limits of what Beijing and Washington would tolerate. In many ways, his initiatives toward both Beijing and Washington were the outcome of the political changes occurring within Taiwan, and reflected a popular desire for Taiwan to enjoy greater international space. While Washington welcomed Taiwan's economic modernization and subsequent democratization, it was not prepared to alter its policies toward Taiwan in light of these remarkable changes. Lee's efforts were a continual reminder that the assumptions that underlay U.S. policy toward Taiwan had not kept pace with the changes within Taiwan. Although Lee demonstrated how untenable the myth of "one China" was, no alternative was found that was preferable and mutually acceptable. U.S. relations with Taiwan have always been intimately tied to U.S. relations with China, and that remained the case during the Lee era. Washington was not willing to further damage an already troubled relationship with Beijing in order to accommodate Lee's desire to modify the status quo. Lee will be remembered as a leader who was dedicated to raising Taiwan's international profile and strengthening ties with the United States, but whose tactics and timing were questionable, and even counterproductive. Although his goals will endure, the divisive manner in which he handled relations with Washington may not.

Notes

1. For a description of transformation and other modes of democratization, see Samuel P. Huntington, *The Third Wave: Democratization in the Late Twentieth Century* (Norman, OK: University of Oklahoma Press, 1991).

2. For more details of this episode, see David M. Lampton, *Same Bed Different Dreams: Managing U.S.-China Relations 1989–2000* (Berkeley: University of California Press), pp. 46–47.

3. See also Lampton, *Same Bed Different Dreams*, pp. 47–54.

4. Andrew J. Nathan, "What's Wrong with American Taiwan Policy," *Washington Quarterly* 23, no. 2 (Spring 2000): 93–106.

5. See Jim Mann, "U.S. Has Secretly Expanded Military Ties with Taiwan," *Los Angeles Times*, July 24, 1999.

6. Robert G. Kaiser and Steven Mufson, "'Blue Team' Draws a Hard Line on Beijing," *Washington Post*, February 22, 2000.

7. Robert Kaiser, "Foreign Disservice," *Washington Post*, April 16, 2000.

8. Kaiser, "Foreign Disservice," offers this story from Representative Tom DeLay (Republican of Texas), House majority whip: "When you come up against . . . dictators or communists or tyrants, whatever they may be, they only understand two things: power and resolve. . . . When you confront them, they back down. . . . I'll give you a little story. . . . I was on 'Meet the Press' . . . right after the bombing of the Chinese embassy in Kosovo [he meant Belgrade], and the [Chinese] ambassador [Li Zhaoxing] was on before me, and if you remember, he's kind of an obnoxious fellow and he's screaming and yelling about how bad the Americans were, and I had it up to about here. So he's coming off the stage and I'm going onto the stage and I intentionally walked up to him and blocked his way and stuck out my hand. And he was very happy to shake my hand. I grabbed the hand and squeezed it as hard as I could and pulled him—kind of a little jerk like this—and I said: 'Don't take the weakness of this American president as the weakness of the American people.' And he looked at me kind of funny, so I pulled him real close, nose to nose, and I repeated it, very slowly, and said, 'Do–not–take–the–weakness of this president as the weakness of the American people.' And he just turned and kind of walked off. His

legs almost fell out from under him. I guess he'd never been treated that way, or whatever. . . . Later . . . outside [the television studio] . . . I walked right out and stood beside him and didn't say a word, and he was ranting and raving about America, and then he turned and looked at me and just scooted off. And it shows you that if you stand up to a bully, then you control the bully. If you kowtow to the bully, the bully will run your life forever. And that's the way I see these people."

Ambassador Li later told his aides he had no idea who DeLay was.

9. "Poll Shows Lukewarm Support for U.S. Security Assistance to Taiwan," *Central Daily News*, October 19, 1999.

10. Peter D. Feaver and Christopher Gelpi, "How Many Deaths Are Acceptable? A Surprising Answer," *Washington Post*, November 7, 1999.

11. This reasoning is based on formal and informal remarks by a former U.S. ambassador to China and by Hill staffers.

12. This is similar to a security dilemma, but not fully equivalent to it. Taiwan does not pose a threat to China, so its arms buildup simply denies China's ability to impose its will on Taiwan. It reacts by further building up its weapons targeted against Taiwan, not to counter an increased threat but to try to regain the upper hand. The logic is slightly different, but the behavior is quite similar. I would like to thank Philip Yang for pointing out this distinction.

13. As many military experts have noted, simply selling Taiwan more and better weaponry is no panacea. Taiwan is already having difficulties integrating previous purchases into its force structure and may not be able to absorb and utilize more advanced technology.

14. Another motive for increased arms sales, rarely articulated in public but frequently heard in private meetings, is the strong desire to get new contracts for shipyards and other military contractors located in the states of powerful Congressional leaders.

15. Some observers have suggested that there is room for ambiguity in the U.S. "one-China" policy, and that the U.S. interpretation of it need not accept Beijing's interpretation. However, official statements, most notably Clinton's enunciation of the "three-no's" in Shanghai in 1998, leave little space for creative ambiguity on this issue.

16. The "strategic ambiguity" policy refers to the U.S. refusal to state clearly and openly what it would do in the event of an attack by China against Taiwan. On the one hand, it wants to deter military action by China that would jeopardize U.S. interests. On the other hand, it does not want to state unequivocally that it would defend Taiwan, lest it embolden Taiwan's leaders to be provocative, even to the point of declaring independence, confident of U.S. support if a conflict arose.

17. Nathan, "What's Wrong with American Taiwan Policy," p. 104. However, policymakers in Taiwan argue that it was the perceived tilt of U.S. policy against Taiwan, and, in particular, the pressure for Taiwan to accept some form of "interim agreements" as a prelude to eventual resolution, that led to Lee's "two-state theory," a point he acknowledges elsewhere in the article.

18. According to several top aides to Chiang Ching-kuo, the decline in the perceived threat from China in the mid-1980s also facilitated the democratic breakthrough of that period by creating a benign international environment. See Bruce J. Dickson, *Democratization in China and Taiwan: The Adaptability of Leninist Parties* (Oxford: Oxford University Press, 1997), pp. 211–12.

About the Editors
and Contributors

Chien-min Chao is a professor at the Sun Yat-sen Graduate Institute of Social Sciences and Humanities at National Chengchi University. He has been a visiting distinguished professor at George Washington University. His publications include *Taiwan and Mainland China: Relations and Foreign Competition* (1992), *Authoritarian Politics* (1994), *An Analysis to Contemporary Chinese Politics* (1997), and *Cross-strait Relations and Taiwan's Foreign Policies* (2000). He is also co-editor of the book *The ROC on the Threshold of the 21st Century: A Paradigm Reexamined* (1999).

Linda Chao is a novelist and short story writer as well as Research Fellow of the Hoover Institution, Stanford University. She is the co-author of *The First Chinese Democracy: Political Life in the Republic of China on Taiwan* (1998).

Shu-Heng Chen is a professor in the Department of Economics at the National Chengchi University. He now serves as the director of the AI-ECON Research Center, National Chengchi University, and is a member of the Editorial Board of the *Journal of Management and Economics*. Dr. Chen holds a masters degree in mathematics and a Ph.D. in Economics from the University of California at Los Angeles. He has many publications in international journals and special volumes. He is also editor of the book *Evolutionary Computation in Economics and Finance* (2002).

Tun-jen Cheng is a professor of government at the College of William and Mary, and the editor-in-chief of *American Asian Review*. He has written extensively on development and political change in East Asia.

Bruce J. Dickson is an associate professor of political science and international affairs at George Washington University. He is the author of *Democratization in China and Taiwan: The Adaptability of Leninist Parties* (1997) and co-editor of *Remaking the Chinese State: Strategies, Society, and Security* (2001), and has written other publications on political change in China and Taiwan. He is also associate editor of the journal *Problems of Post-Communism.*

John Fuh-sheng Hsieh is a professor of government and international studies and director of the Center for Asian Studies at the University of South Carolina. He has written extensively on constitutional choice, electoral systems, electoral behavior, political parties, democratization, and foreign policy.

Yung-ming Hsu is an assistant professor of political science at National Chung Cheng University. His research analyzes issues such as political learning, party realignment, and ethnic politics in Taiwan. He received his Ph.D. in political science from the University of Michigan in 1999.

Julian J. Kuo received his Ph.D. in political science from Yale University (1995). He is now an associate professor of political science at Soochow University. His research fields are comparative politics, party politics, and Chinese politics.

Tai-chun Kuo is an associate professor at the Institute of American Studies at Tamkang University in Tamsui, Taiwan, and currently a visiting scholar at the Hoover Institution at Stanford University. She is co-author of *Understanding Communist China: Communist China Studies in the United States and the Republic of China 1949–1978* (1986). She specializes in the political economy of Taiwan and China.

Cheng-yi Lin earned his Ph.D. in international relations from the University of Virginia (1987). He is now director and research fellow at the Institute of European and American Studies at the Academia Sinica. His research areas are international politics, Sino-American relations, and national security policy.

Wen-cheng Lin is an associate professor of negotiation and international security at the Institute of Mainland China Studies at National

Sun Yat-Sen University. He received his Ph.D. from the Fletcher School of Law and Diplomacy of Tufts University in 1993. He is the co-author of three books about China and Asia-Pacific security and the author of thirty articles, in both Chinese and English, on cross-strait relations, security studies, and China's foreign policy.

Ya-li Lu is a professor in the Department of Political Science at Chinese Cultural University in the Republic of China and a senior professor of political science at National Taiwan University. He has written extensively on Taiwan's democratization and development theories.

Peter R. Moody, Jr., received his Ph.D. from Yale University (1971) and is a professor of government and international studies at the University of Notre Dame. His interests include the study of Chinese politics, Taiwan politics, the comparative politics and international relations of East Asia, and Chinese political thought. His most recent book is *Tradition and Modernization in China and Japan* (1995). He is also the editor of *China Documents Annual*.

Ramon H. Myers is curator of the Hoover Institution East Asian Archives and Senior Fellow of the Hoover Institution, Stanford University. He is co-author of *The First Chinese Democracy: Political Life in the Republic of China on Taiwan* (1998). He specializes in the political economy of Taiwan and China.

Shelley Rigger is the author of two books on Taiwan politics, *Politics in Taiwan: Voting for Democracy* (1999) and *From Opposition to Power: Taiwan's Democratic Progressive Party* (2001). She is the Brown Associate Professor of Political Science at Davidson College.

Suisheng Zhao is an associate professor and executive director of the Center for China–U.S. Cooperation at the Graduate School of International Studies at the University of Denver. He was Campbell National Fellow for 1999–2000 at the Hoover Institution of Stanford University. His most recent books are *Across the Taiwan Strait: Mainland China, Taiwan and the 1995–96 Crisis* (1999), and *China and Democracy: Reconsidering the Prospect for a Democratic China* (2000).

Index